The **Politically Incorrect Guide**™ to

WESTERN
CIVILIZATION

The **Politically Incorrect Guide**™ to

WESTERN
CIVILIZATION

ANTHONY ESOLEN

Since 1947
REGNERY
PUBLISHING, INC.
An Eagle Publishing Company • Washington, DC

Cataloging-in-Publication data on file with the Library of Congress

ISBN 978-1-59698-059-4

Published in the United States by
Regnery Publishing, Inc.
One Massachusetts Avenue, NW
Washington, DC 20001

www.regnery.com

Manufactured in the United States of America
10 9 8 7 6 5 4 3 2 1

Books are available in quantity for promotional or premium use. Write to Director of Special Sales, Regnery Publishing, Inc., One Massachusetts Avenue NW, Washington, DC 20001, for information on discounts and terms or call (202) 216-0600.

For Brian Barbour, Mario DiNunzio, and all my elders
in the Western civilization program at Providence College

CONTENTS

Preface   xi

Chapter 1:   **Ancient Greece: Love of Wisdom and Beauty**   1
             Laws that cannot be amended
             Athens: Better than the rest
             Father, not mother
             The Greek Isles effect
             Tradition and the natural law
             Athenian relativists
             Beauty is not merely in the eye of the beholder
             The universal Good
             The State and the end of man

Chapter 2:   **Rome: An Empire of Tradition and Patriarchy**   39
             Respecting your elders
             Father knows best
             Tradition's wisdom vs. democracy's fickleness
             Peace through strength
             The real reason Rome fell

Chapter 3:   **Israel: How God Changed the World**   67
             A God above nature, not a nature god
             Not a political god, but the King of kings
             Knowing God yields science
             They that humble themselves shall be exalted
             A thousand years are as a day
             Jesus of Nazareth, King of the Jews
             The peace of God that passeth understanding

Chapter 4:   **The Early Church: Charity and Tolerance Are Born**   97
             How Christianity saved the West

Christianity brings equality and tolerance

The State, that pagan god

How Christians elevated culture

The truth about heretics

The Good News brings charity

Chapter 5: **The High Middle Ages: The Bright Ages**   131

Islam vs. civilization

Warmer is better—someone tell Al Gore

Ruggedly alive

The Bright Ages: Life in the cathedrals

Drama's rebirth: Another fruit of Christianity

PC myth: The Middle Ages were the Dark Ages

When love and nature were richer

PC trope: Dancing angels and pinheads

Before PC: When intellectual curiosity could thrive

Chapter 6: **The Renaissance: It's Not What You Think**   167

The PC myths about the Renaissance

Is there a nature in this man?

Honoring the past

Shakespeare on his knees

Where the Renaissance went wrong: Undermining
   authority

Chapter 7: **The Enlightenment: Liberty and Tyranny**   203

The will enslaved

"Enlightenment" yields tyranny

Écrasez l'infâme!

The Pilgrim Fathers

Conservative Founders?

America's forgotten models: Rome and Athens

Saving reason from itself

Rousseau and the State

Samuel Johnson

Chapter 8:   **The Nineteenth Century: Man Is a God; Man Is a Beast**   **243**

The Romantics' new religion: Nature

Worshipping man

What the Industrial Revolution wrought

Is there such a thing as bad art?

Nietzsche: The honest atheist

Conservative champions of human dignity

Chapter 9:   **The Twentieth Century: A Century of Blood**   **281**

Walter Mitty, rugged individual

The empire strikes back

The health of the State, the poverty of the soul

Art from the people; Art against the people

Science without knowledge

The Pill's bitter effects

History can restore us

Notes   **311**

Index   **329**

PREFACE

Christianity. Judaism.
Dead white males. Old-fashioned morality.
The traditional family. Tradition itself.

These are the *bêtes noires* of the elites. They are the pillars of political incorrectness. Together, they constitute that thing called Western civilization.

Political correctness, at its heart, is the effort to dissolve the foundation on which American and European culture has been built. It has been a demolition project: undermine Western civilization in whatever way possible, and build a brave new world from the rubble.

Multiculturalism has nothing to do with genuine love for natives of the Australian outback or the monks of Tibet. It is an effort to crowd out our own cultural traditions. Radical secularization—in the name of "separation of church and state"—aims to burn our religious roots. Public education, purveying convenient untruths about our past—the Middle Ages were miserable, the ancients were simpletons, the church is oppressive—has sought to rob us of our heritage. Misrepresentations of the Renaissance, the Enlightenment, and the last two hundred years serve to create an illusion of unvarying progress made possible by abandoning the old ways. And that is the central myth that justifies the continued discarding of our religious, intellectual, and moral traditions.

Once our culture is untethered from Athens, Rome, and Jerusalem—once we've forgotten about or dismissed Moses, Plato, and Jesus—then the PC platoons in academia, government, and the media hope to steer the ship of culture to new shores.

Because political correctness is a project of destruction, the message has not always been consistent. Either Shakespeare was a subversive, closeted homosexual, or he was an ignorant chauvinist. Either Jesus was a non-judgmental hippie, or he was a preacher of hate. But this much has been consistent: anything that reeks of the West is therefore politically incorrect and must be denigrated or condemned.

For those of us who love the West, it's a daunting battle. The other side has the mainstream media, the Ivy League, the political classes, and a lot more money. Thankfully, on our side, we've got thousands of years of history and some pretty big guns—with names like Aristotle, Augustine, Burke, and Eliot.

The bad ideas touted today as revolutionary and enlightened are hardly new; the West's great minds have battled relativism, atheism, materialism, and State-worship for millennia. The great ideas can hold their own against anything today's most renowned Women's Studies professor can devise.

Chapter One

ANCIENT GREECE: LOVE OF WISDOM AND BEAUTY

A blind old man, led by his daughter, has stopped to take his rest, perhaps his final rest, in the shade of a cool grotto. The water of a spring mutters nearby; the spice of grapevines and the olive is in the air. A chorus of local villagers sings of its holiness and beauty, where the

> ... golden crocus gleams
> Along Cephisus' slow meandering streams,
> Whose fountains never fail. (*Oedipus at Colonus*)

These villages had attempted, halfheartedly, to drive the poor man away. For that blind man has been cursed: he is Oedipus, the wretch who fulfilled a terrible oracle in attempting to evade it, fleeing what he believed was his native Corinth, lest he kill his father and marry his mother, and arriving at Thebes, whose king had recently been slain on the highway, and whose queen was ripe for marrying.

Oedipus is an emblem of the crushing malice of the gods. Call no man happy, says Sophocles, the poet who portrays this scene for us on stage, "until that day when he carries his happiness down to the grave in peace." When Oedipus, compelled by his quest to uncover the truth, finally learned of his unnatural parricide and unnatural plowing of the field that gave him birth, he put out his eyes in a rage of self-loathing. It

Guess What?

- ✦ Athens' culture was, simply, superior.

- ✦ Philosophy was born in a men's club.

- ✦ Moral relativism brought down Ancient Greece.

is years later now. Suffering has instructed him. He is still not gentle towards blind and foolish mankind. But he is humble, and he insists, calmly, upon his innocence. His reason has recovered. He accepts his suffering, and dimly understands—it is a wisp of a hope in the pagan twilight—that his suffering has a purpose, that the man accursed may be a blessing to others. So a later oracle has declared: the city that welcomes Oedipus will be blessed by the gods.

What does this mean? Why do I begin with this story?

In all of drama there has, I think, never been a moment as poignant as this. I don't mean within the play, but between the play and the audience. It is Athens, 402 BC. The playwright, the beloved Sophocles, has died. The people are watching a posthumous production, reverently put on by his son. They hear a wise man's last lyrical judgments, after ninety-two years, on life and death, good and evil, justice and mercy.

Maybe it was a good thing that the old poet had died. It spared him the sight of Athens' final agony. Athens, richest and most powerful of the Greek city states, had established herself as the head of an empire. Other states paid tribute to her for their common protection. Her might had threatened the security of her chief military rival, Sparta, and her trade on the seas, from Sicily all the way to south Russia on the Black Sea, threatened her chief naval rival, Corinth. It had come to war. The democratic leader of Athens, the general Pericles, had adopted a strategy of endurance. Athens could not muster an army half as large or as effective as the Spartan infantry; but Sparta, for her part, could not muster from her small population an army sufficient to bring the whole city under. So, while the Spartans razed the Athenian countryside, burning farms and villages, the people retreated inside the city walls, waiting, while their navy sailed forth to harass the ports near Sparta and her allies. Pericles, in other words, required his people to be patient, to see ahead, and to sacrifice.

He was probably the only man in Athens who could have succeeded at it, just as Washington was the only man in the colonies who could have held together the rag-end of the Continental Army at Valley Forge. But a plague arrived by rats aboard trading ships from the East. Many thousands of ill-housed people were crowded into Athens; and many thousands of them died, including Pericles himself. No more preaching of patience then. The demagogues prevailed—men who played to the passions of the mob. Athens, increasingly arrogant and unscrupulous, given to wild swings in strategy, was on her way to self-destruction. Finally in 405 BC, its sailors demoralized, possibly betrayed by their officers, the Athenian fleet, of all things, was surprised by the Spartans, and four thousand citizens aboard were put to death. In 404 the Athenians fell to the final Spartan siege, and they knew they must now suffer the cruelties they had caused others to suffer in the days when they were filled with insolence and pride:

> That night no one slept. They wept for the dead, but far more
> bitterly for themselves, when they reflected what things they
> had done to the people of Melos, when taken by siege, to the

Athens' Athletes

No citizen has any right to be an amateur in the matter of physical training: it is part of his profession as a citizen to keep himself in good condition, ready to serve his state at a moment's notice.

From **Xenophon**, *Memorabilia* (3.12)

That was before sports were turned into mass entertainment. The Greek citizen understood that he had better keep himself prepared for war—which meant hand-to-hand combat—at any time. It would have made as much sense to him to give voting rights to women as to throw armor on them to be mowed down on the battlefield.

people of Histiaea, and Skione and Torone and Aegina, and many more of the Hellenes. (Xenophon, *Hellenica* II. 2, 3)

Sophocles had died just before the end. He had been a fine lad back in the old time of Athenian glory—chosen to lead a band of boys to celebrate the great Athenian victory over the Persians at Salamis. All his life he had praised Athens, rejoicing in the freedom of mind that a democratic constitution can foster. Yet he also warned against believing that civic laws need pay no attention to laws that are older than the city, laws as old as man.

Laws that cannot be amended

Note that well: some laws are as old as man. Today, our elites and social planners will have none of it. In the infamous case *Planned Parenthood v. Casey*, Supreme Court Justice Anthony Kennedy, writing for the majority, declared that "at the heart of liberty is the right to define one's own concept of existence, of meaning, of the universe, and of the mystery of human life" (505, US, 851). Do not be seduced by such airy talk. When we detach ourselves from our heritage, our traditions, our most deeply held beliefs about the world and our place in it, we gain alienation, not freedom. It may be that *my concept of existence* includes redistribution of wealth, at gunpoint. The chaos that Kennedy's nonsense invites would be intolerable. So the State steps in—and what prevails is not the culture of a free people, living and celebrating and, yes, sometimes worshiping together, coming to compromises that will respect their way of life and the nature of man. What prevails are the whims of judges such as Anthony Kennedy. And we "progress," like lemmings.

Sophocles had warned against such separation of the laws we pass from the laws of our being. Now he bids farewell to his beloved Athens, and to the little rural Athenian village of Colonus where he was a boy. Colonus is where old Oedipus has arrived—Colonus, lovely as of old, not trampled and charred. And the Athens on stage will be blessed for welcoming Oedipus, not for gain, but for right. Those Athenians of old were pious, and knew the laws that our common suffering teaches. Says the governor Theseus to the blind man in the grotto:

> I do not forget my own upbringing in exile,
> Like yours, and how many times I battled, alone,
> With dangers to my life, in foreign lands.
> I could not turn from any fellow-man,
> Coming as you come, or deny him help.
> I know that I am man; in the day to come
> My portion will be as yours, no more, no less.

So the old Athens, now no more.

The new Athens, once brash, now humiliated, never again to rise to the same glory, was losing her moral bearings even before she swaggered into war with Sparta. "Man is the measure of all things," said the sophist Protagoras, preaching a moral relativism that democracies find hard to ignore.[1] It's easy to see why: it flatters the people and gives them leave to choose what laws they please, or what wars they please. Tradition helps to bind us to our duty, but relativism brushes duty aside with a lazy sweep of the hand. If I'm the one who chooses what is "good" and "bad," then I might as well call "good" the things I like—voting myself shares of other people's money, or shacking up with a whore from Crete—and call "bad" the things my enemy likes. The result is not tolerance but, again, alienation. But somebody has to prevail, unless we're going to suffer looting in the streets for fun and profit. The somebodies, in our day, are the policymaking elites. They will tell us that an unmarried woman with a child is as good as a family, or that a man attracted to other males should be a scoutmaster. Then if we try to tell them they are "wrong," they will hurl our relativism back in our teeth. "Wrong? There is no such thing as wrong," they smile. "And if there is, we'll be the first to let you know."

Athenian policy after the death of Pericles took Protagoras at his words. "Do not talk to us of justice," say the Athenian ambassadors to the rulers of the neutral island of Melos. "You will submit to us, or we will destroy you; justice is merely the will of the powerful." When the Melians declined, the Athenians slew the men and herded the women and children into slavery.[2] The audience remembers. They see an Athens on stage that calls them back to their better aspirations. And they see a Thebes, mercenary, unnatural Thebes, that reminds them of what they have become. And they weep.

It would be interesting to list the reasons why such a dramatic moment could not transpire in another fading democracy, ours. Surely one reason has to do with piety, that forgotten virtue. Those Athenians could still be

Nine Politically Incorrect Truths about Greek Homosexuality

1. It was a shame to be considered effeminate.
2. Effeminacy included the constant pursuit of sexual pleasure.
3. Grown men who had relations with one another were thought contemptible.
4. The phenomenon cannot be understood apart from those male blood-brotherhoods and friendships which in most cultures do not involve sexual intercourse.
5. Older men sought adolescent (and beardless) boys.
6. It was never accepted by members of every class.
7. It seems to have gone promiscuous after the demise of the free *polis*.
8. It spread venereal disease.
9. At its most spiritual, as in Plato, it directed men toward lives of virtue, of struggle in the battlefield or in the assembly. Athens was not San Francisco.

shamed for not revering the example of their forefathers at Salamis, then united with the Spartans against their common enemy the Persians. They could be shamed by the virtue of their legendary ruler, Theseus. They were still willing to hear hard truths about themselves.

But shame is not so powerful a weapon now. We live in an effeminate day. We slander our fathers, and hug ourselves for doing it. It costs us nothing but the chance to grow wise.

Then let us recall what the Greeks bequeathed to us, which we have squandered. We might discover the errors the Athenians made in the fifth century, those that brought sadness to the last days of Sophocles. I don't mean errors of political judgment, which in this world are inevitable, but intellectual errors, born of self-satisfaction and nursed by idleness and wealth.

Athens: Better than the rest

As I write, Buddhist monks are marching through the streets of Burma, denouncing the nation's military dictatorship and chanting, "Democracy, democracy!" How strange that is! Would Catholic priests, even in secular France, chant for rule by lamas? For better or for worse, when the world thinks of a just and rational system of government dedicated to liberty, it turns to the West. It turns not to ancient Peking or Persepolis, but to Athens. Even when our despots lie, they use the language of democracy. They lie in a vulgar Greek.

I'm no idolator of the vote. It's a tool, and needs to be judged as such, according to how well it secures justice, and encourages a people to live good lives. But our schools teach two contradictory things about our democratic culture, and, marvelous to behold, they get both wrong. First, they teach that the vote is not a tool but the very *object* of justice. Choice is everything, and it doesn't matter what you choose. Second, they teach that different cultures are all equal, even cultures that do not respect our idol of choice! But this happy lie is impossible to uphold when we look at the legacy Athens has left us in government, science, art, and philosophy. Where do people prosper, enjoy leisure, and reap the benefits of great inventions and discoveries? In lands where the heirs of Athens dwell.

Sure, the Greeks were far from perfect. They were sinners just as we. They employed plenty of slaves. The worst-treated of these were those prisoners of war sent down into the silver mines; in a couple of years the toxic fumes would kill them. Sparta survived and thrived by turning all of its free men of fighting age into professional soldiers, to ensure that the enslaved people of the surrounding countryside could not revolt. Greek aristocrats developed a cult of pederasty: if your son had curly hair and a nice physique, you had to watch out. Women did much of the work in and around the house, but were not consistently honored for it; the farmer-poet Hesiod calls them pests sent down by Zeus to punish mankind.[3]

Nor was Greek politics always a matter of rational argument in open debate. Athens had at times been seized by tyrants, usually supported by the middle class. Pisistratus once tried to win an election by dressing an unusually tall woman as the goddess Athena, and having her cry out from a racing chariot, "Athena for Pisistratus!"[4] That early piece of demagoguery didn't work, so he took power by a military coup. Then (for he was a benign man, otherwise) he bought the people's support by means of building projects and elaborate festivals. His sons who succeeded him never mastered that art. One was slain by a rival in a homosexual affair. The other was exiled, traveling to Persia to help the emperor Darius turn the Greek world into a tributary province.

So there was good reason why Plato labeled democracy as the most debased form of government.[5] It was democracy that brought Athens to humiliating defeat at the hands of Sparta. It was democracy that sentenced his teacher Socrates to death. It was democracy that handed power to the passions of a rabble. Imagine what Plato would say of our polls and focus groups.

Still, we owe those Greeks an incalculable debt. They gave us the defining epics of the West, Homer's *Iliad* and *Odyssey*. Out of an old religious festival to the wine god Dionysus they developed that heady form of art we call drama. They sculpted the human form with a beauty and scientific precision that would not be equaled until the Renaissance. They erected human-scale temples and courts of such incomparable beauty and convenience that even now, 2,500 years later, our homes and offices in the West echo their porticoes and pediments and colonnades. They learned all the mathematics the Babylonians had to teach, and incorporated it into a systematic geometry. Breaking free of the bonds of practical utility and bookkeeping, they invented the notion of *proof*, and added astonishing discoveries of their own, *without the assistance of numerals*. Archimedes estimated the number of grains of sand on earth, and in the midst of this *jeu d'esprit* came within a hair of inventing calculus.[6] When he wasn't playing with number theory, Archimedes was more practically employed: inventing fancy catapults, for instance, to defend his city, Syracuse, against Roman invaders.

The Greeks invented rational analysis of modes of government—what we call political science. Herodotus journeyed across Asia Minor and into Egypt to learn what he could about local life, and to pick up information from eyewitnesses of the Persian War. He is called the father of history, but he might as well be called the father of geography and the father of ethnography. The Greeks began man's quest to discover the unseen unity and order underlying the wild variety presented by physical nature. Democritus coined the term *atom*, meaning a particle that cannot be split.[7]

But when they turned their attention to man, and the good that man longs to possess, the Greeks burst into a flowering of creativity that puts our schools to shame. They invented philosophy and all its branches: linguistic, metaphysical, moral, political, and epistemological. Seldom has a poet written with more sensitivity to beauty than did the philosopher Plato, and among poets only Shakespeare and Dante can rival Sophocles for philosophical acuity. Only a philosopher at heart could have written *Oedipus at Colonus*, but only a philosophical people could have fully appreciated it.

The Greeks weren't naturally more intelligent than anybody else. Then why did these things happen *there*? The answers will entangle us in political *incorrectness* at every step.

Father, not mother

At the dawn of historical records, the people who lived in Greece, like other people near the Mediterranean Sea, worshipped fertility gods.[8] They sacrificed to Mother Earth, the womb and the tomb for us all, blindly ever-generating and ever-destroying nature. But around 1500 BC, nomads from the steppes of central Asia, the so-called Dorians, swept into Asia Minor and Greece. These Dorians spoke an Indo-European language, related to Germanic, Latin, Celtic, and Sanskrit. As they were not farmers, they did not adore the earth. Rather they worshipped the gods of the vast sky they saw all about them on the plains.

These sky gods were also, naturally enough, gods of light and the things we associate with light: freedom, beauty, laughter, and intelligence. Their chief god was Father Zeus (Germanic *Tiw*, as in "Tuesday," and Roman *Deus pater*, which became *Deuspiter* or *Jupiter*). He was endowed with the glory and cunning and might that make one *divus* (Lat.) or *dios* (Gk.). He was bathed in light.

Now an odd thing happened: Just as the invading Dorians did not wipe out the natives, so their religion did not wipe out the old fertility cults. It only suppressed them, and that made for a rich system of incompatible gods. The story is told in Hesiod's *Theogony* as a battle between the generations. The old gods ruled by brute force, or tried to: Ouranos, god of the heavens, hated the children of his wife Gaia, the earth, and stuffed them back into her belly. Then Gaia, showing the first glint of intelligence in the cosmos, gave her son Cronus an iron sickle and told him to wait in ambush the next time Ouranos made love to her. When night fell, Ouranos "covered" Gaia, but Cronus sliced off his father's testicles and cast them into the sea. No testicles, no throne.

Cronus then ruled by force. His trick was to swallow his children whole. But his wife Rhea, aided now by Ouranos and Gaia both, slipped him a rock in a blanket while spiriting her baby away to be raised in hiding. That baby's name was Zeus. He in turn overthrew his father, but—and here is the point—*by intelligent alliances*, and not by force alone. He gave powerful positions to some of the older gods. Hecate was made goddess of the underworld and patron of warriors. The Styx, dread river of the underworld, gained the honor of being invoked whenever the gods swore an oath. The horrible Titans of the hundred arms, Briareus, Cottus, and Gyes, were allowed to eat and drink with the young gods on Olympus. They proved indispensible when the other Titans tried to dethrone Zeus. It was no small advantage to have creatures who could hurl a hundred spears at once.

It's a strange concoction. The "old" gods, associated with earth and blood and lust and vengeance, still exist, and claim their due. *But they must be governed.* They submit to Zeus, the cunning and mighty. He is cunning, but he can be tricked; he is strong, but not strong enough to ignore the rest. It's a system that invites the mind to probe the riddles of human life. How can the passions be governed by reason? Should they always be? What is the relationship between authority and goodness? Can the old traditions be violated at will? Is there a law

Hippocrates Was Pro-life

"I swear by Apollo the healer . . .

"I will not give a fatal draught to anyone if I am asked, nor will I suggest any such thing. Neither will I give a woman means to procure an abortion.

"I will be chaste and religious in my life and in my practice."

From *the Hippocratic Oath*

to which even the gods must submit—a law which Ouranos and Cronus violated, and perhaps Zeus too? Is there such a thing as progress or moral evolution, and if so, where is it going? What remains changeless?

Man turned a corner in Greece, and this religion was partly responsible. The dramatist Aeschylus recounts it in mythic form.[9] Orestes learns that his father, King Agamemnon, has been butchered. Blood calls for blood; that is the ancient law of vengeance. But the murderer was his own mother, Clytemnestra. How can he kill the woman who bore him and suckled him? The mother's claim too is primal. What must he do? The traditions, by themselves, offer no escape. When he does kill Clytemnestra, he is pursued by the Furies, ancient and hideous goddesses of the underworld, who avenge those who violate the old taboos of blood. They are also the terrible gnawings of Orestes' awakening conscience. He cannot endure it; he flies to Athens to stand trial before the gods. There the young goddess of wisdom, Athena, will preside. It is the old against the new, the instinctual against the rational, the Furies against Apollo, Orestes' protector, with Aeschylus giving the Furies the better of the argument. The jurymen deadlock. Athena casts the deciding vote, for acquittal. Because she was born from the head of Zeus, she says, she always favors the father. Therefore she favors the rights of the city: the king's murderer must be punished.

We mark here a shift from the tribe to the *polis*—free men debating and determining what course to take. The biggest surprise is not how the jurymen vote (and, given the case, their vote is fair), but that there is a jury at all. They are none other than the free men of Athens. Men have the capacity—not the *right*, but the *capacity*, if they set their minds to it—to govern themselves. They can acknowledge the rights of tradition, of the unwritten laws, of mothering nature, and in so doing they can order their affairs rationally. If they have a king, he should be like Sophocles' Theseus: calm, patriotic, and wise in the glory and the frailty of man's soul. This self-government of a people is a gift from Zeus. It conforms them to that god enthroned upon Olympus whom they call "father of gods and men" not because of his reproductive habits (which are prodigious), but because of his political strategy and the power of his mind.

The Greek Isles Effect

The compromise on Olympus reflected the sorts of government the Greeks almost had to invent. Consider the terrain of the Greek lands. It is furrowed with rugged mountains and ravines. There are plenty of splendid harbors, but no long navigable rivers. The weather is excellent for farming, especially for cultivating the grape and the all-purpose olive, but it is hard to find enough flatland for raising huge stores of grain. The Greeks, then, could not be self-sufficient; they had to trade. Nor could any one city establish a vast empire covering the whole area. Before Alexander the Great and his armies, it was impossible.

So the Greeks built small outposts of highly advanced civilization: the *polis*, or city-state, from which we derive our word "political." These city-states studded the Greek peninsula, the Aegean, the Turkish shores, and, eventually, Sicily and southern Italy, with hundreds of self-governing communities. They were not all democratic. Most began as hereditary kingdoms or as aristocracies, governed by the influential men of the oldest and most established families. It was, if you will pardon an anachronism, a kind of federalism, guaranteeing plenty of freedom for the *polis*, and making each into a laboratory for statesmanship, the arts, poetry, philosophy, and almost any other creative endeavor you can name.

It's worthwhile to pause to appreciate this phenomenon, which I'd like to call the Greek Isles Effect. It isn't peculiar to Greece. We can find it among the Christian monasteries in the Middle Ages, the fledgling states in America, and the Italian republics of the Renaissance. We can find it, though disincarnate, on the Internet now. In all these cases there is some form of unity, more cultural than governmental, coinciding with great freedom to experiment.

Let's look at the unity first. Allowing for dialects, the Greeks were united by a single language. They were united by forms of worship; we see this at the Pan-Hellenic games, the most famous of which were in Olympia. They were united by their mythological and literary heritage. A Greek from Halicarnassus off the coast of Turkey would recall Achilles' dilemma in the *Iliad*, and would be able to discuss it with a fellow Greek born in Thebes on the mainland but now residing in Acragas, thousands of miles away in Sicily. Precisely because they valued that tradition, they could converse with one another. Unlike the students in our tradition-despising schools, they had something to look at in common. Ask a college senior to recite a short poem by that most American of poets, Robert Frost, and he will look at you blankly. Ask him to name a single general of the Revolutionary War *other than* Washington, and he will ask why you are troubling him with trivia. Even if he has learned to think, he has very little to think *about* or *with*. He is, intellectually, like a peasant without the wheel and the plow. The Greeks did not suffer that deprivation.

Did Plato Foresee Madonna?

The introduction of a new kind of music must be shunned as imperiling the whole state; since styles of music are never disturbed without affecting the most important political institutions.

From Plato's *Republic* (Book IV, 424c)

Hardly anything in Plato strikes us as sillier than his caution about music. The typical charge against the philosopher was that he distanced himself too coolly from the demands of the body, but here he acknowledges them frankly, while we are the ones who believe that the pounding, unorganized, relentless beats of hip-hop will have no effect on us at all.

The shared myths were the fertile soil wherein their imaginations took root.

But it did not take root in the same way in all places. Why should it have? We now preach a superficial diversity, but there's more variety in the polar ice cap than among the regimens of our public schools. The Greeks enjoyed real diversity. In a way, they had to. I've mentioned Greek unity; no less important was their separateness. They could feast one another, and they could fight one another. Since their cities were relatively small, they had to train their boys both for self-government and for war.

The Greeks found that infantry made up of the "hoplite" warriors, men disciplined to fight as a team, each shielding the man to his left, could withstand noblemen on horse or the slave armies of Persia. But citizens who fight demand a say in government. So the Greek boy, at the age of reason, was taken to the open-air *palaestra* to be educated to be a self-disciplined fighter and citizen. He would learn music, to train his soul— the songs, that is, of Homer and the poets; and he would train his body in strength and agility, by regular competition.[10]

The gymnasia (literally, "places to be nude in") were at the heart of Greek political and cultural life. They did not treat the boys as babies. Far from it. Consider what the boys must have overheard. Every adult man who could spare the time from his occupation was expected to keep his body fit at the gymnasion, in part because his city might need him in war, but also because it was the right and beautiful thing to do. There, as men always do when they are free, they engaged in ceaseless conversation about city life, money, sport, the gods, truth and illusion, good and evil. Philosophy was born in a men's club, in the sweat of a wrestling ring.

So then, each city developed its own ways, as each trained its own fighters. Some, like Sparta, had kings; and some kings were genuine rulers, while others were cultic figureheads. Some cities were governed by wealth. Some marched towards democracy, with Athens the most daring among them. By the middle of the fifth century BC, all Athenian offices but the few requiring special expertise (the generalship, for example) were filled by lottery. Every free man had an equal chance of sitting in the legislative council of five hundred, and almost everyone would, at some time in his life, serve the city in some important capacity. No election campaigns, then, and no empty promises. Better yet, no *sincere* campaign promises to reward the idle at the expense of the industrious, or the restless at the expense of the contented. So long as there were leaders who were intelligent and patriotic, who could resist equality's tendency to slouch towards mediocrity and envy, the system worked.

Each city was known for a skill or a virtue or a habit that set it apart from the rest. Mytilene had the best masons. Corinth made the finest pottery. Thebes enjoyed a fertile plain. People were proud of their homelands, in a way we find hard to understand, because we lack the vitality of their local civic life. It explains why Socrates, condemned to death unjustly for "corrupting the youth of Athens," would not try to escape. The law of the city, though unjustly applied, commanded his respect, even his love. So Socrates imagines the Laws of Athens speaking to him:

> Are you so wise as to have forgotten that compared with your mother and father and all the rest of your ancestors your country is something far more precious, more venerable, more sacred, and held in greater honor both among gods and among all reasonable men? Do you not realize that you are even more bound to respect and placate the anger of your country than your father's anger? (*Crito*, 51a-b)

The notes of that same love, fierce and noble, without self-pity or sentimentality, can be heard too in the epitaph to the Spartan three hundred who gave their lives blocking the pass against Persian invaders at Thermopylae: "Stranger, go tell at Sparta that we lie here in obedience to her command."[11]

The Greeks believed so strongly that the free *polis* provided man the best chance for enjoying the good life, that when their cities grew too crowded they sent people away to form new cities elsewhere. These would maintain commercial and military alliances with the mother city, but they were not colonies in our sense. They governed themselves. When Aristotle said, "Man is a political animal," he didn't mean "Man loves to meddle in the affairs of others," but "Man by his nature best thrives in a *polis*"—a small, self-governing city-state, whose citizens would know one another by sight or family or reputation, and would take an active and regular part in the city's direction.[12]

Anything else is "barbarian" and to be pitied. It could mean suffering rule by imperial bureaucrats sent from a capital far away, or immersion in a state so large that almost no one is intimately involved in governing. It could mean a life like that of the Cyclops in Homer's *Odyssey*:

> Nor do they meet in council, those Cyclops,
> Nor hand down laws; they live on mountaintops,
> In deep caves; each one rules his wife and children,
> And every family ignores its neighbors. (9.112–15)

All such conditions cramp the arena for intellectual and practical virtue. For all practical purposes and despite ceaseless electioneering, they also characterize life in the technocratic welfare states of contemporary America and most of Western Europe.

Tradition and the natural law

What happened, then? What brought the Athenians to mourn their lost integrity, as they sat silently under the sky and heard the songs of *Oedipus at Colonus* as of a voice from the dead? What happened to Athens has, in great measure, happened to the West all over again. Pride and stupidity explain much; rapacity explains more. But also deeply implicated

A Book You're Not Supposed to Read:

The Greeks by H. D. F. Kitto; New York: Penguin, 1950.

A splendid, genial book written before the culture wars were underway, by a man who loved Greek art and drama and poetry, and who will give you a most friendly and sensible introduction to them. Criticism nowadays will not condescend to clarity or charity—or common sense.

in the Athenian fall were a few destructive ideas: there is no such thing as what is objectively good or bad. The "wisdom" of the past is mere social convention. It grows obsolete with the setting sun. It marks no hard-won victory for a people, demanding reverence. It should be left to the dustheap.

Do these ideas not sound familiar? Can an American read three pages of a newspaper or listen to a political pundit or a schoolteacher for five minutes without encountering them?

I define modern man partly by his scorn for tradition. He cannot see it as the distilled experience of his ancestors, the result of generations of men and women coming to terms with the laws that govern our existence. Yet the sense that traditions are *holy* provided those energetic Greeks with a constant source of moral and religious issues to ponder. They were restless intellectually and politically; yet their sense of the beauty of the cosmos and the deep order of all things gave them salutary boundaries. Such piety, even when not well thought out, helped to protect them from the nonsense that "right" is whatever a majority may wish it to be. It may be seen in Plato's *Euthyphro*, a savage satire against the self-serving, "intellectual" wordplay of a young man about to testify in court against his own father—and who is proud to do it. Culturally, our schools turn out Euthyphros all the time. If in little else, they succeed in that.

That piety reminds men of the natural law they must obey, lest they destroy themselves. Nor does it matter that the law may be hard to apply to the particular case. The tragedians Aeschylus, Sophocles, and Euripides enmesh their characters in terrible quandaries. Should you keep your promise to your comrades in arms and cajole the poor Philoctetes to rejoin the Trojan War, even if it means deceiving the man once again—since it was you, Odysseus, who had marooned him on an uninhabited island nine years before? Should you, Prometheus, submit to the overbearing power of Zeus, and let him know of the prophesied threat to his throne? Should you, Eteocles, pay heed to the wailing women of your city and *not* confront your brother with the sword, though he is leading a force of seven armies against your seven gates? Should you, Theseus, slay your son Hippolytus when your wife, Phaedra, claims that he has ravished her? The answer is never easy. And it is never, "act according to your opinion."

Athenian relativists

The idea that good and evil are "socially constructed," mere conventions, is not new to us. For it's not only truth that is timeless; the more obvious falsehoods are, too. This one emerged from the hotbed of fifth-century Athens. It is, in part, the work of the Sophists, the first professional educators in the West. The Sophists, up for private hire, trained young men in rhetoric, to hold their own in the debates at the Assembly. Soon they acquired the reputation of tonic salesmen. In *The Clouds*, Aristophanes casts Socrates, of all people, as a Sophist who makes money by teaching various forms of slick impiety.

His students laugh at the inconsistencies in the stories of the gods. They learn how to argue, to satisfy their greed or their lust, that good is bad and bad is good. Socrates, descending from the clouds, has replaced the gods, substituting verbal trickery for virtue. That's unfair to Socrates, who was no Sophist. But in that new and utilitarian education, we abandon truth for the willingness to score points; and that, finally, subjects the mind to both worldliness and impracticality. It's a foul combination. We are worldly because we scorn the truth in favor of what will turn heads in some political arena. We are impractical because the truth is the truth—whether we like it or not.

Marx reduced the spirit of man to material desires, and believed that central planning could deliver goods more efficiently than could a free market. He was wrong on both counts. Our feminizing schools reduce male and female to a few minor details of plumbing, and then preach that pills and white balloons will provide a remedy for human lust. Wrong—and soul-destroying—on both counts.

But in Athens, as now, there was a market for the sophistical wares. Man *needs* wisdom, but what he needs and what he buys are two different things. Wisdom may cry at the gates, but man is too busy at the mall to hear. He likes to hear Protagoras say that man is the measure of all things, and concludes that the good or the evil or the existence or nonexistence of a thing depends upon how he chooses to consider it. "Justice is the will of the stronger," says Thrasymachus, lampooned in Plato's *Republic*.[13] The historian Thucydides suggests that Athens gleefully accepted that "wisdom," and tried to use it, as I have mentioned, to bludgeon the island of Melos.

Thucydides wrote after Athens' great defeat. He loathed such opportunism and relativism. In fact, every one of the great playwrights and thinkers of ancient Greece believed in objective moral truth. They did not believe it was easy to grasp. It must be sought, struggled for, and granted new life from age to age. But it exists, and is universal. When the old and feeble Priam, king of Troy, appears in the tent of his enemy Achilles to plead for his son Hector's body, the great warrior is astonished. There is nothing impressive about an old man on his knees, but to Achilles at that moment Priam looks like a god. He reminds him of another old man, his father Peleus, far across the Aegean, whom he has not seen in ten years, and whom he knows he will not see again. "Honor then the gods, Achilles," cries Priam,

> . . . and take pity upon me
> remembering your father, yet I am still more pitiful;

I have gone through what no other mortal on earth has gone
through;
I put my lips to the hands of the man who has killed my children. (*Iliad*, 24.503–506)

Give me back my son, he cries. It simply is the right thing to do. The two
men, old and young, Trojan and Greek, enemies in war, sit weeping in the
twilight. They are one in their humanity, one in their suffering and loneliness.

The Greeks derived their sense of right-dealing from a hardheaded look
at man's frailty. They had the most advanced medicine in the West until
the late nineteenth century, they lived in the open air and the sun, they
ate a healthy diet, they exercised even as old men; so they lived a long
time. But "health care" was something they had to provide for themselves, and eventually all the care in the world will be in vain. Death
looms over our glory, and should instruct us against *hubris*, literally
"haughtiness" or "uppityness." So when Odysseus, disguised as a beggar, goes round the table at his house, asking for bread from the men who
are suing for the hand of his wife Penelope, he approaches the ringleader

Athens' Athletes II

"No Greeks ever shook hands after a fight, no Greek ever was the first to congratu-
late his conqueror; defeat was felt as a disgrace."

> From **E. Norman Gardiner**, *Athletics in the Ancient
> World*

Nor were the Greeks unusual in this regard. The only dew to soften the dry, hard heart of man fell
from one apparently defeated, upon a cross.

Antinous, and asks him to consider how the Fates that set a man high can ruin him too:

> I, too, was once a man of means; my house
> was rich; I often gave to vagabonds,
> whoever they might be, who came in need.
> There I had countless slaves and all those things
> that grace a man whom men consider blessed.
> But Zeus, the son of Cronus, then was pleased
> to ruin me. (*Odyssey*, 17.419–24)

Antinous replies by requesting the "pest" to get lost, flinging a footstool at him when his back is turned. Fittingly, he will be the first suitor to die when Odysseus begins his avenging slaughter. The drinker and slick talker will take an arrow sunk in his throat up to the feathers, just as he is raising a goblet of wine to his lips.

Even a relativist may toss a beggar some bread—especially if, as was the case for Antinous, it is somebody else's bread. What's hard is to admit that a whole people, a state, must submit to the right. It's not politically correct to talk that way, now. It's not "democratic." But we should listen to Sophocles. A close friend of Pericles, he was fascinated by the tension between the popular and the eternal, or between political expediency and justice. In *Oedipus at Colonus*, he shows that blessings come to the pious and *not* to those who act from temporary, utilitarian motives. And the primacy of the natural law is at the heart of his brilliant *Antigone*.

The play is often read as a protest against the bullying power of government, or against patriarchy. It is actually a conservative warning against radical democracy, and a reminder that reason too can be puffed up with hubris and, like a tyrant, usurp the authority of laws that we intuit rather than deduce.

The situation is this: Eteocles and Polynices, sons of the exiled Oedipus and rivals to the throne of Thebes, have slain one another in battle.

Creon, the uncle of the two young men, is left in power. His only consideration, so he says, is the welfare of the *polis*:

> No man who is his country's enemy
> Shall call himself my friend. Of this I am sure—
> Our country is our life; only when she
> Rides safely, have we any friends at all.

So he commands that Eteocles be buried with full military honor, while his brother Polynices must lie to rot outside the city walls, his body guarded by sentries. Creon considers only the day's politics—justice is defined according to the city's advantage. One brother must be elevated as a hero and the other condemned as a traitor. Morally, though, there is not much to choose between them, as the audience knew. Eteocles had gained the popular allegiance and ousted his elder brother in a coup. Polynices would not sit content, but roused up six other kings to help him attack his own city. Clearly an unnatural act; but then, the younger brother should not have driven the elder into exile, nor should the two now be lying dead, each slain by the other's hand.

Such considerations mean nothing to Creon. But it is the welfare of the city that seems not to enter the mind of the young Antigone, sister to the two dead men. Her world at first glance appears to be narrower than Creon's: a world of intense loyalty to family and blood. I doubt that it is narrower, but it is a dreadfully real world, more immediately present to the human heart. She knows only that a beloved brother lies unburied. So she steals past the sentries to scatter a little ritual dust upon the body. Caught in the act, she is haled before Creon.

We might expect the passionate woman to fly into speeches of frenzy. Antigone is certainly capable of it. And we might expect Creon, the clear-sighted, manly ruler, to speak dispassionately about reasons of state, and why we must set personal motives aside. It doesn't happen. What Sophocles gives us is startling. It is Creon, the "democrat," the political man, who gradually reveals motives of insecurity and hunger for power, lurking beneath his city boosterism. "There's a party of malcontents in the city," he grumbles, "rebels against *my word and law*" (emphasis mine); you might call it a vast right-wing conspiracy of tradition. Meanwhile, Antigone affirms with rational clarity our duty to revere eternal laws which we *have not deduced by reason* and cannot alter by civic assembly:

> That order did not come from God. Justice,
>
> That dwells with the gods below, knows no such law.
>
> I did not think your edicts strong enough
>
> To overrule the unwritten unalterable laws
>
> Of God and heaven, you being only a man.
>
> They are not of yesterday or to-day, but everlasting,
>
> Though where they came from, none of us can tell.

Creon will not be budged. He condemns Antigone to go down to the underworld gods—to be buried alive in a tomb: "Go then, and share your love among the dead." In doing so he asserts a radical democratic claim: the old gods may be ignored. Tradition be damned. We can pass laws as we wish. Family rights mean nothing. But the people of Thebes begin to turn in sympathy to Antigone, whom they do not like, but who appeals for a justice beyond self-interest. Even Creon's son Haemon, Antigone's betrothed, warns the king that disaster hangs over him. At that, Creon calls upon the same natural law he has been abrogating. For the young should revere their elders: "Am I to take lessons at my time of life," he scoffs, "from a fellow of his age?" Haemon's reply cuts to the heart: "It isn't a question of age, but of right and wrong."

Not until his niece Antigone, his son Haemon, and his wife Eurydice have all committed suicide does Creon see that his wickedness, clothed in the garb of civic virtue, has destroyed him. In denying the fundamental rights of family and blood relation, he condemns his own family to death, and becomes a man accursed, unfit for rule of the city. "I am nothing," he weeps. "I have no life."

Creon's mistake is not that he is male. He happens to be male, prone to boastfulness, aggressiveness, and a love of power. He clearly also treats women with contempt. Haemon's love for Antigone he dismisses coarsely: "Oh, there are other fields for him to plough." Those are character flaws, and they play a part in his downfall. But the mistake, the trigger, is his abrogation of the natural law. He might have been female, prone to touchiness, guile, timidity, and hatred of men. The Nanny of today's American politics comes to mind. Make the same mistake, suffer the same fate. The trigger cannot tell whose finger squeezes it.

Beauty is not merely in the eye of the beholder

We cannot understand the Greek desire to discover the moral and physical laws that govern the world unless we entertain a few claims that our schools ignore or reject:

✦ The world is a *cosmos*, an ordered whole of surpassing loveliness, wherein man, surpassingly beautiful, occupies an especially interesting place. The most inter-

When Patriotism Was Real

"When [the Spartans] fight singly, they are as good men as any in the world, and when they fight in a body, they are the bravest of all. For though they be freemen, they are not in all respects free; Law is the master whom they own; and this master they fear more than thy subjects fear thee."

From **Herodotus**, *The Persian Wars* (7.104)

So said a Spartan to the king of Persia, Darius, as he prepared to invade Greece. The Spartans did not produce much poetry or art, and they knew little ease in their lives. But it is not only by poetry and art that a culture can make its impression on the world. For more than two thousand years—until our own slack, effete age—we have had the example before us of that small *polis* and its men who were free because they acknowledged the law and feared disgrace more than death.

esting thing about the world is that it is a *world*, not a chaotic soup.

* Beauty is not merely a matter of opinion or social convention.
* Love, inspired by beauty, possesses a spark of the divine. Love is more than appetite.
* Our study of the physical world and of the moral world are not to be severed from one another. They are part of the same longing for wisdom which we call *philosophy*.

Together, these claims constitute a potent attack on our schools and our politics. Good and evil exist. Truth exists, and we can come to know it. The beautiful exists, and we are meant to love it. For the world cannot be reduced to matter alone.

The first Greeks to call themselves philosophers strove to understand the physical world, to see what prime element underlay clouds and lions and marble and blood. We should not take for granted their bold assumption that such an element could be found, and that the world was intelligible! Thales of Miletus[14] reasoned that such an element must be capable of assuming the three phases of matter: solid, liquid, and gas. Hence he posited that water was somehow the *arche* or foundation or origin of all things, though he knew well that you couldn't squeeze water to make iron or clay. His successor Anaximenes voted for air. Others named earth or fire or some combination of the four so-called elements.

But there's a logical problem with all explanations of the world that resolve it into such stuff as water or air.[15] To say that the *arche* of the world is water doesn't explain anything, since water is itself one of the things that requires explaining. It is circular reasoning. Nor does it help to stretch the circle as wide as the cosmos. The philosopher Anaximander, therefore, reasoned that whatever the *arche* is, it cannot be like the things it explains. It must be beyond predication. So he called it the *apeiron* or the boundless.[16]

Historians of science now mutter. "If only the Greeks had remained on the materialist track! They might have made fantastic discoveries in chemistry and physics. But instead we lose ourselves in metaphysical speculation and theology." They too might have had plastic cities and hearts, centuries before our time.

Yes, the Greeks might have made impressive discoveries. Thales noticed that certain signs always preceded a bumper crop of olives. So one year he bought up every oil-press he could find, and made a killing.[17] But let's pardon the Greeks for assuming that the world, and man, present more important and interesting questions than can a vat of olives. Anaximander's objection demands to be answered. If there is a cause of the world, it cannot be one of the objects in the world—that collection of things no one of which is the cause of itself. Then it must be radically different from those objects. Then it cannot be material.

That observation seems self-evident, but today it would be derided as "unscientific." "We can have no knowledge of things unless they are material," says the modern professor. Is that so? Pythagoras, for instance, discovered that strings whose lengths were of certain ratios would sound notes of a certain harmony: a string half as long as another, of the same girth and stretched to the same tension, would sound a note exactly one octave higher, the so-called diapason. He saw such harmonies in all the world, and concluded, with the soul of a mathematical physicist, that all the world was made of immaterial *number*. When we recall that Pythagoras had no numerical system to work with, and that for him and his fellow Greeks the sentence $3 \times 2 = 6$ meant that "a rectangle made by segments three units long and two units wide will have an area of six square units," we sense that for him "number" meant *ratio*, exact relationship. We might say, more poetically, that the world is made of harmonic law. Such was the awe with which Pythagoras contemplated this truth, that he attracted a group of devoted followers, who joined him in religious devotions inspired by the laws of numbers. They revered him as a saint.[18]

It's easy to laugh at their innocence, but Pythagoras has rolled an engine of war into the camp to stand alongside Anaximander. What is the status of such mathematical objects as a triangle? The Greeks were too enthusiastically discovering the laws of geometrical objects to relegate them to mere human invention, the tics of certain minds in flight from the "real" world. When Euclid showed how you can prove the theorem of Pythagoras by constructing a set of parallelograms, with only a straight-edge and a compass—that is, with no *numerals and no calibration*—and by the rules of strict reason, he did not believe he was dissecting an unreality. More than that. He knew he had shown with absolute certainty that the theorem was correct, although neither Pythagoras nor he had ever seen or could ever see a line of infinitesimal thinness, or a circle exactly circular, or a right angle that was just right.

After Socrates had needled his fellow Athenians for claiming to know what they had only heard, his pupil Plato strove to discover how we could come to certain truth, rather than accept convention or give up altogether. Naturally, then, he turned, as Immanuel Kant much later, to mathematics. But Plato did not make the tremendous error that has kept much of modern philosophy bottled up in symbolic logic and linguistic analysis. Plato didn't assume that everything had to be demonstrated in the same way as the Pythagorean theorem was. Instead he asked about the nature of various kinds of objects, including mathematical objects, and about the various ways we have of knowing them, some more reliable than others. That's why, according to one ancient account, he caused a sign to be hung over the door of his Academy: "No one ignorant of geometry may enter here."[19]

Plato saw that the knowledge we have of a triangle was knowledge of a genuine thing, not a figment of the imagination. Such knowledge lay waiting for discovery. It was also knowledge of a universal. When we prove Pythagoras' theorem, we know something about all right triangles, not just this one or that one. That led Plato to consider a mysterious property of language and the world. We say "cat" and "tree" and know that we are not talking necessarily about any particular cat or tree, or any cat or tree we have materially seen. We mean something other than "Tabby" or "the oak tree in front of my house." But how can this be? What does the term "cat" denote? There are many cats, but what do I mean when I say "cat," if I don't intend any particular one, dead or alive?

Plato concluded that knowledge could not be simply of matter, because we have knowledge of immaterial objects such as triangles, and because such words as "cat" are universal in their signifying, and not particular. Plato concluded, as had Anaximander, that material causes were not sufficient to explain the world or even to speak intelligibly about the things in it. So he developed his theory of the *Forms* or *Ideas*, universal, intelligible, immaterial, and immutable. We may see all the horses in the world, but unless we conceive of the idea of What It Is Essentially to be Horse, then we don't know what a horse is.[20]

The universal Good

We can then, he argued, apply the same insight to morality, aesthetics, and politics. We may see this or that good deed. We agree that it is prudent for Themistocles to persuade the Athenians to use their new-found money to build a navy, and that it is courageous of Leonidas to stand with his small Spartan contingent

Politics Before Polling

But in other things [Pericles] did not comply with the giddy impulses of the citizens, nor quit his own resolutions to follow their fancies, when, carried away with the thought of their strength and great success, they were eager to interfere again in Egypt, and to disturb the King of Persia's maritime dominions.

Plutarch, *Life of Pericles*

Pericles was more than a politician: he was a leader, a manly yet modest ruler of a people that had the power to overrule him if their orators could carry the day. He knew what the people wanted, yet always did what he believed was best. But there were no pollsters back then.

to delay the Persians at Thermopylae. But what makes these actions good? What is the form of the good?

A college student I met once gave me the politically correct answer in a startlingly politically incorrect form. "There is no such thing," she said, and then gave an example. "What was good for the Nazis, was good for the Nazis. It's all a matter of opinion."

That was the single falsehood Plato gave his life's work to put to rout. Is good simply a matter of material advantage—of the survival of the *fattest*? As we saw in *Oedipus at Colonus*, Theseus should welcome the aged Oedipus into the holy grove, because Oedipus is a man humbled by unimaginable suffering. So Theseus does, though he knows the Thebans will hate him for it. The good cannot depend on what gives most pleasure to the greatest number of people at the lowest cost of suffering, since the good directs what we should find pleasure in, not the other way around. Handsome Alcibiades wants to make love to Socrates. He wouldn't be harming anyone by it, and besides, he might gain a little wisdom. But Socrates knows it would be better for Alcibiades if he learned to desire things nobler than sexual pleasure. "For anything that had happened between us when I got up after sleeping with Socrates," says Alcibiades, "I might have been sleeping with my father or my elder brother" (Plato, *Symposium* 219d).

Even if what we delight in is innocent, it might prevent us from knowing the good. A man may spend his days jittering his fingers at a video game, or playing checkers with his friend Cleon. If he does little more, he is hardly a man, and no judge of the good. It would be better for him to master an art, and even better, to pursue wisdom. That is both a moral and an aesthetic judgment: as a man who throws the javelin in the fields against well-trained opponents will have a more beautiful, well-proportioned body than one who indulges himself always in the low pleasures of drink and ease.

The good of man, for both Plato and his brilliant pupil Aristotle, must involve perfection, the result of difficult moral training. This holds true for the State as well as for the individual. Here again we touch upon lessons that modern man has forgotten—lessons that Sophocles attempted to remind his fellow Athenians to heed. When, in the *Republic*, Plato's Socrates is asked to define justice, he contends that an analogy must be drawn between the *microcosmos* of an individual man and the *cosmos* of the city. He notices that there are three principal faculties in man: the intellect, by which man judges what is true; the "spirit" or "drive" by which he is moved to possess and enjoy what is noble and beautiful, and the appetite, by which he desires what seems good at the moment, such as food or sexual release.[21]

Now in a virtuous man these faculties must cooperate in a hierarchical harmony. No slovenly egalitarianism here. The appetite should not govern, since it does not look ahead, and does not judge the better and the best, but only seeks to gratify itself with what is present. The intellect must rule, but it cannot rule effectively without the energy of the ambition and the appetite. The "spirit" is the passion that bridges intellect and appetite. It is a reason-loving movement of the heart, full of fire and zeal.

So if you're going to raise a virtuous child, you must not only teach him what happens to be good, you have to train him to long to possess the good. You fire his imagination with accounts of noble deeds. You set before his sight a beautiful soul: Achilles thirsting for glory, Socrates thirsting for the beautiful. Such training in virtue must prevail in the just state. Eros must be enlisted not in the pursuit of a Helen of Troy, or the wealth of Croesus, or the power of the Persian king, Xerxes. It must be enlisted in the pursuit of the justice that knits together all the classes of the state: those spurred mainly by appetite, who produce goods to buy and sell; those spurred by glory, who become valiant warriors or "guardians"; and those rare few who long for wisdom, the philosophers, who must govern the workers and merchants by means of the guardians.

The curse of democracy, as Plato saw it (and de Tocqueville, and the Adamses, as we shall see), is that the appetite may come to rule, both in

A Book You're Not Supposed to Read:

Who Killed Homer? The Demise of Classical Education and the Recovery of Greek Wisdom by Victor Davis Hanson and John Heath; New York: Encounter Books, 2001.

Classicists now "privilege," "uncover," "construct," "cruise," "queer," "subvert," and "deconstruct" the "text." Titles abound with the words "construction," "erotics," "poetics," "rhetoric," and "discourse" randomly joined by the preposition "of" to the following (it makes little difference which): "manhood," "the body," "masculinity," "gender," and "power." (136)

A brave defense of the impressive accomplishments of the Greeks, overcast by a certain sadness that anyone should have to be reminded of them. It is also a savagely funny exposé on contemporary teachers of the classics, who seem to loathe what they study, and who despise all but the most intelligent of the students they are paid to teach.

the State and in the common people. We misunderstand him if we conclude that he does not believe in a vibrant civic life. Democracy, untempered by higher ideals, will rot the pith and marrow from civic life, as its tendencies are to efface all exclusive institutions—clubs, families, guilds—and leave the arena naked of anything but State power and individual will. Freedom and the franchise are not the same thing.

Yes, Plato was an elitist, but that does not mean he would favor government by graduates of Harvard. It all depends on how you choose your governors: "elite" means nothing else but the object of discriminating choice. I do not love Plato's ideal republic (which, let's note, he confesses to be impossible), but surely he is right to see something self-destructive in pure, appetite-driven, egoist democracy. Its people will lack the patience to be corrected by traditions and laws that delay or prohibit the gratification of their desires. They will be too shortsighted for visions of beauty or justice. Such things matter little when the wallet, or the boudoir, calls: "How superbly [democracy] tramples down all such ideals, caring nothing from what practices and way of life a man turns to do politics, but honoring him if only he says he loves the people" (*Republic* 8.558b). Besides, the rulers in Plato's imaginary republic are not supposed to be cleverer than everyone else, but wiser, more deeply in love with the good, the true, and the beautiful. That would rule out our academic elites, who cannot be in love with those things, because they do not believe they really exist.

On the dark side, we see in Plato the first inventor of a Utopia, and, not coincidentally, the first man to suggest, it is hard to tell how seriously, that the State should take over all childrearing and should officially recognize no differences between the sexes. But Plato's critique of democracy, bolstered by the ineptitude of the Athenian demagogues who parlayed incomparable prestige and wealth and naval might into a surrender from which Athenian democracy never recovered, underlies all later criticisms of the liberal, secular, and soulless state.

The State and the end of man

Plato's pupil Aristotle learned from that critique, and adjusted it to suit his understanding of physical nature and of man. Aristotle was not a mathematician by hobby, but a biologist. The difference is intriguing. He could not conceive of immaterial objects existing separate from their embodiment in actual things. But he was not a materialist. Ultimately, the materialist can only talk sensibly about underlying matter, and not about discrete objects, what Aristotle called "substances," made up of that matter. For Aristotle, the genuinely real are neither the forms shimmering somewhere above or beyond this world, *nor* the unseen atoms whose combinations make flint or oil, but the things around us: trees, rocks, birds, man. This flatfooted insistence upon seeing the obvious, before we talk of contemplating the good, characterizes Aristotle's views of individual morality and the State.

Aristotle notices that of all things natural and man-made, we can predicate four "causes," or characteristics, essential to its being:

+ The *material* cause: what it is made of
+ The *efficient* cause: who or what made it

- ❖ The *formal* cause: what kind of thing it is
- ❖ The *final* cause: what it is for, to what end or perfection it inclines[22]

An oak tree is made of wood, its material cause. It has germinated from an acorn produced by the parent tree, its efficient cause. It is an oak tree, with a certain identifiable structure, including shape of limbs and leaves and pattern of growth. It is not simply "something it pleases us to call, for our convenience, an oak tree," but really that kind of thing and not another. That is its formal cause. And it has found good soil and matured to a grand height, producing acorns of its own. That is its final cause.

What about man? Aristotle knew that some philosophers, like Democritus, reduced man to his constituent atoms, but such reductive materialism evades the question. It identifies the material cause, but that alone cannot describe what the fullness of our experience suggests when we meet the thing called man. The efficient cause we all know, and our public schools seem itchily driven to reveal it these days to little children. The formal cause includes not only the physical shape or structure, but the encoded instructions regulating our growth and development. What about our final cause? What are we *for*? In what state do we attain perfection as man?

Again Aristotle reasoned by beginning from experience. For us, an "empiricist" is one who will admit as evidence only what can be quantified or measured, but Aristotle saw that in most cases quantification is beside the point. So with the final cause of man. If we are talking about man, not dog, not maple, not quartz, we must ask what distinguishes him from all other things. If he is no more than certain combinations of carbon and other elements, then his perfection might be simply to *exist*, to take up space, to be heavy, like a lump of quartz, or a senator. If all he does is grow, he might find his perfection in taking in nutrition and expelling waste, as the oak tree does without moving or sensing, or as the dog does, hunting down its quarry.

But man possesses an intellect. Therefore man's final cause, his perfected state, must lie in the perfection of that intellect which distinguishes him from all other substances. But we also notice that man pursues many objects because he believes they are good. He wants food, riches, sex, honor. What do these pursuits have to do with his final cause? Again Aristotle begins from experience. Why do I want money? So that I can buy a raccoon coat. Why do I want a raccoon coat? So that I can look debonair on campus. Why do I want to look debonair? So that Suzy will marry me. Why do I want Suzy to marry me? So that I will be happy. Why do I want to be happy?

The last question makes no sense. Happiness has no purpose beyond itself. Many people will say, "I want money, because money will make me happy," but no one says, "If only I were happier, then I might be rich!"

Happiness is the end we pursue: it is the intended goal of all our action. But our perfection must reside in the perfection of the intellect. Therefore, *happiness is the enjoyment of the good of the intellect*. It consists in contemplating what is good, and developing the habit of action in accordance with it. This is a conclusion of tremendous significance for medieval Christianity, as we shall see. And of all the good things we can behold with the mind, the intellect's highest object of contemplation is what does not change. It is what Aristotle calls the Prime Mover, the (impersonal) unmoved mover or uncaused cause of the world, without which there could be neither motion nor cause. This too is a conclusion of tremendous significance.[23]

Both Plato and Aristotle, then, are deeply theological thinkers. Aristotle's ideal State must be one wherein man stands at least a fair chance of achieving the fullness of his intellectual growth, both contemplatively and practically. Those who are capable of contemplation must have some opportunity for calm reflection, while everyone else, capable of exercising the practical good, must have a free field for developing and displaying the moral virtues of temperance, courage, justice, and wisdom.

Note what such a State cannot be. It cannot be an empire, because empires steal from men the opportunity to govern themselves. It cannot be anarchy, because lawlessness makes one's life too uncertain for the leisure to pursue the good of the intellect. It must somehow take into account human nature as we find it. The *family*, that schoolhouse of virtues, cannot be abolished, says Aristotle.[24] The State cannot be so vast that we fall into anonymity, and government is imposed upon us rather than created by us and for our purposes. Thus the modern "democracy," neither republican nor democratic but bureaucratic, distant, imperial in its all-encompassing demands, leaving little for the common people of a Colonus or Corinth to determine, is poor soil too for man's thriving. That is, unless we believe in the *Oliver Twist* model of citizenship, wherein each of us must timidly approach the great fat beadle the State, and mumble, "Please, sir, I want some more."

Human Nature

The very first sentence of Aristotle's *Metaphysics* would earn him an instant F from a college professor today: "All men, by nature, yearn for knowledge." Positing a human nature would make him closed-minded today—but it also made possible some of the best philosophy the world has ever seen.

What then? "Man is a political animal," says Aristotle. He thrives in a community of families and clans who govern themselves freely and well, providing for more than a basic subsistence. What they mainly provide is *freedom*: free time, leisure for conversation, an arena for debate, for struggles that have consequences, for reading and arguing, for sport, for contemplation, for honing all the practical and intellectual virtues. True civility has more to do with a well-ordered fight than with the bonds of niceness.

Both philosophers saw that if freedom means "being free to take what you like, within the law," then no nobler faculty of the soul beyond the appetite will be developed. People whose votes are bought by enticements of appetite are not free, regardless of how often they throng the assemblies, or the academies. For man in a corrupted democracy, says Plato,

> goes in for politics and bounces up and says whatever enters his head. And if military men excite his emulation, thither he rushes, and if moneyed men, to that he turns, and there is no order or compulsion in his existence, but he calls this life of his the life of pleasure and freedom and happiness and cleaves to it to the end. (*Republic*, 8.561d)

The disorder penetrates into the family:

> The father habitually tries to resemble the child and is afraid of his sons, and the son likens himself to the father and feels no awe or fear of his parents, so that he may be forsooth a free man. And the resident alien feels himself equal to the citizen and the citizen to him, and the foreigner likewise. (8.562e)

Teachers fawn upon their students; students ignore their teachers. A lawless egalitarianism descends upon all, along with a great touchiness, an inability to bear any restraint, until finally, slaves to their appetites and plunged in chaos, the people choose to be slaves to a "protector" who can rein them in. Hence tyranny—welcomed!—puts an end to corrupt democracy. Napoleon cleans the blood from the streets of Paris.

But at their healthiest and noblest, the Greeks retained their confidence that somehow the good and the beautiful were one—*to kalon*, the greatest of all things in that splendid, lawful, and harmonious world they called *cosmos*. Somehow man's reason played a part in it, but then too there were truths accessible to the inspired madness of poets and lovers and those greatest lovers of all, the lovers of wisdom, the philosophers. Such truths might call upon Plato's breathless dialogues of love, the *Phaedrus* and the *Symposium*, but they might well be rooted in what any man should know, by his own ordinary nature. We would do well to take heed. Sophocles was a democrat, but he knew that man by himself can only obey or disobey the good, not invent it:

> I only ask to live, with pure faith keeping
> In word and deed that Law which leaps the sky,
> Made of no mortal mould, undimmed, unsleeping,
> Whose living godhead does not age or die. (*King Oedipus*)

A city's fate may hang upon a bad harvest or the whims of a madman with an army across the sea. But if its people forget wisdom, there will be no need to wait for weather or war.

They Had Hippies Then, Too

Like a dog, [Diogenes the Cynic] performed any bodily act without shame, when and where he chose. He obeyed no human laws because he recognized no city. He was *Cosmopolites*, Citizen of the Universe; all men, and all beasts too, were his brothers.

Gilbert Murray, *Five Stages of Greek Religion*

Chapter Two

ROME: AN EMPIRE OF TRADITION AND PATRIARCHY

In some ways ancient Rome, especially during the centuries of the Republic, was as politically incorrect a place as you can imagine. Our feminists, who consistently uphold the demands of a minority of well-heeled women against the common good, the family, and every freedom recognized in our Bill of Rights, would hate the patriarchy of ancient Rome, and not least because that patriarchy worked. Nowadays, gripped in our great national passion of envy, we demand all sorts of equality: economic, social, and political. We'll destroy the family to attain this equality, and never mind the prisons that result. The Romans instead first sought the good of the family and the city. For the most part, they found that good not in leveling distinctions but in revering them. Let's see how.

Guess What?

◆ Patriarchy worked.

◆ Gridlock, resistance to change, and other anti-democratic features helped make the Roman republic strong.

◆ Tax hikes, slavery, and moral depravity brought Rome down.

Respecting your elders

You're a small child growing up under the watchful eyes of your grandfather, his father before him, his father's father, and a host of great-uncles to boot. But you won't see them pottering about the garden, tending the fig tree, and telling stories. They have gone down to the shades, and are all the more potent for it. You see them every day, though. They stand upon the mantel above the *focus,* the hearth, where your family will take

39

meals, talk, and gather for the holy rites. They are your household gods, these ancestors. When they died, their kin made a plaster or wax impression of their faces, or small figurines. In later centuries, a rich family might hire someone to sculpt their busts in marble. They are holy. They are the guardians of the family and of ancient traditions. They define for you, the child, what it means to be a Roman.

Such a religion, like Shinto among the Japanese, befits a strongly patriarchal society, with well-established lines of authority and a deep suspicion of innovation. Now, all societies, without exception, have been dominated by men; they have had to be, if they wanted to survive. But the *father* was central to Roman order. Not so in Greece, where the all-male club, at the *gymnasion* or the assembly, tended to shoulder aside the family as the ruling institution of civil life. The Roman head of household, or *paterfamilias,* possessed an astounding authority. His word was law. In the early days he could, legally, commit his children to death.

That was no idle power. Various Roman historians tell the story of one of Rome's legendary heroes, nicknamed Torquatus, or "The Man with the Neck Chain," because in the middle of battle he raced up to a gigantic Gaul, killed him, and ripped the chain off the man's neck. This same Torquatus later led the Romans against the Latins. By then he had a son of his own, commanding a small company of soldiers. This son, using some independent strategy, or hankering after glory, broke the orders of the consuls and, challenged to single combat by a Tuscan nobleman, slew him. For breaking orders, Torquatus had that son executed. An army without discipline is no army. A city without an army will soon be no city. And a father who is not obeyed is no father.[1]

In 509 BC, Lucius Junius Brutus freed the city from its last Etruscan king, but then learned that his grown sons were conspiring to return Tarquin to the throne. He sentenced them to death.[2] In the Roman imagination, the city was an extension of the family, and treason against the *patria* was tantamount to parricide. We see this identification everywhere, this rule by fathers. The historian Livy preserves for us the language of an archaic oath between warring factions: the legate entrusted to act for one of the sides in a controversy is called a *pater patratus,* a "father enfathered," a father endowed with the full authority of a father.[3] The members of the Senate, a body that predates the establishment of the Roman Republic, are literally "old men," seniors. They are the revered heads of the most powerful families.

This preference for a severe wisdom and the performance of duty, as opposed to the glow of a moment of individual triumph, is easy to see in Roman art. The Romans, who mostly looked down upon free men who competed in sports, did not idolize the young athlete. When they finally learned a little bit about sculpture, their tastes did not run to the buff bodies of nude youths, as in Greece. They preferred bald heads and jowls and warts and all, the serious busts of old men. What you see in a Greek youth

Collapse of the Family, Fall of an Empire

Whether because of voluntary birth control, or because of impoverishment of the stock, many Roman marriages at the end of the first and the beginning of the second century were childless.

Jerome Carcopino, *Daily Life in Ancient Rome*

It is the mark of a society in decline, this living for one's present. It accompanies feminism, since bearing and caring for children keeps women from donning helmets and play-acting at being legionnaires. Carcopino added:

The feminism which triumphed in imperial times brought more in its train than advantage and superiority. By copying men too closely the Roman woman succeeded more rapidly in emulating man's vices than in acquiring his strength.

Sound familiar?

sculpted in the golden age of Athens is the ideal of youth: a young man at the height of his strength, about to hurl a discus, or striding forth to throw the javelin; looking like a god, and enjoying for a brief moment the blessedness of the gods. What you see in the Roman bust of a jowled Cicero is hard public thought, experience, determination, responsibility.

What is the politically correct line on such a society? If today's assumptions are correct, what should we expect of ancient Rome? It must have been violent, ruled by despots, and oppressive to women. But Rome was none of those things.

Women enjoyed more freedom and higher esteem in the Roman family than anywhere else in the Mediterranean world, outside of Israel. The woman was the heart of the home, and the home was holy. Roman women did not have to endure being shunted aside for second and third wives: the Romans were monogamous, and, especially early in their history, they looked down on divorce.

The histories are full of accounts of noble women, like Cornelia, the mother of the reformist tribunes Tiberius and Gaius Gracchus, or Portia, the daughter of the moralist Cato and wife of Brutus, or Cloelia, the woman who escaped from her captors by bravely swimming across the Tiber under enemy fire.[4] Greece was more male-dominated than Rome, but Rome was more committed to the rule by fathers, and that seems to have been a good thing for Roman women.

Despots? From the time they expelled Tarquin, the Romans abhorred one-man rule. Occasionally they did delegate dictatorial powers to a single man, as they did with Cincinnatus, the farmer who took command of the armies, defeated the enemy in a couple of weeks, and resigned his commission.[5] But that was for an emergency, and only for a specified term; and when the term was out the ex-dictator had to face the people, should anyone come forth to accuse him of abusing his authority. The Roman devotion to the family set up a strong buffer *against* the State, even as it helped to create the State. It is interesting to note how this buffer worked, because it helps explain why America's founders established the checks and balances of its apparently unwieldy government.

Suppose I'm a Roman of the noble class, a patrician, and I want my son to be elected consul. I call in my markers. I've done many favors for the heads of lesser families: I am their *patronus* or patron, literally their sort-of-father, and they are my clients, literally the people who call on me for assistance. They repay me by supporting my candidates. Now if there were only one consul, we'd have a recipe for constant civil unrest; but the Romans relieved the pressure by establishing *two consuls*, parceling out the executive power month by month, by turns, for one year. Consider the disadvantages, if one believes that government should be a laboratory for, as Edmund Burke put it, "men who are habitually meddling, daring, subtle, active, of litigious dispositions and unquiet minds" (*Reflections on the Revolution in France*). The consul serves for one short year, and at that it's a month on and a month off. It's a system designed to prevent anything abrupt from happening; the more so, as one consul can veto the other. Then, when the year is out, said consuls may not immediately run for reelection. They become members of the Senate, a consultative and legislative body, and historically a brake on hasty measures.

Rome was set up to ensure precisely what is decried today: gridlock, infighting, and obstacles to "solving" problems—solving them, that is, by creating others that are new and worse. Our media buy wholesale the effete leftist line that we need to "put our differences behind us," "get together and work towards solutions," and fearlessly bring about some utterly undefined "change." These notions, self-evidently good in the eyes of today's media, were exactly the things the consuls and the Senate were created to block. The Romans had set up their government to prevent the newest ideas, however popular, from winning out over the traditional way of doing things and the wisdom of old men.

So we have a Roman state, suspicious of change, which still manages to change with the times, and survives and grows as a republic for *five hundred years.* And even after it lost a truly republican government, it continued in imperial form for yet another five hundred years in the West, and another fifteen hundred years in the East. It did so, unquestionably, with a lot of civil strife, but, during the centuries of the Republic, without any full-scale civil war, such as convulsed France twice in one century, England under Charles I, Spain under Franco, the United States in the War Between the States, and ancient Athens. It did so even though the geographical position of Rome made it vulnerable to attacks from north and south, and from the sea. Why?

Father knows best

One reason was that they understood the truth of a proverb that now we can only snicker at: father knows best.

We can't underestimate the importance of the father and the family in the Roman mind. When the great national poet Virgil wrote to legitimize the rule of Augustus—the first Roman ruler to be called "emperor," and the reinventor of Roman government after the Republic collapsed—he compared his saving his country from civil war to its founding by the legendary Aeneas, a refugee from Troy. But Aeneas is no swaggering warrior or privateer like Odysseus, taking twenty years to get back home to Ithaca. Aeneas is Roman at heart before he ever leaves Troy. He is called *pater Aeneas* and *pius Aeneas,* meaning Aeneas the father who performs his duty to *his* father, to his fatherland, to his household gods, and to the great gods. Now Virgil is a great and humane poet, not just a propagandist. He extends the definition of such piety to include humaneness and mercy towards those who suffer. Rome must obey the right. But the bedrock definition of piety remains fatherly duty and duty towards the father. We see a perfect picture of Roman piety when Aeneas, instructed by the gods, prepares to leave the burning city of Troy. He sets his crippled old father Anchises upon his shoulders, and takes his little boy Iulus by the hand, while Anchises carries the "household gods," that is, the ancestral images.[6] It is a picture of being rooted steadfastly in time, taking nourishment from the past, and placing one's hope in the descendants to come.

That rootedness in the past, and that firm trust in the perpetuity of one's line, can help us distinguish Rome from Greece, from the imperial governments of Persia and Egypt, and from the follies of our day. Unlike the Persian, the Roman in the days of the Republic never bowed before the glory of a self-styled King of Kings. He was a free man. His family too, though it might not be influential, was holy. Each family possessed its own *genius* or guardian spirit, passed along from one head of the family to the next. The State, a cooperative of families, could not breach the sanctity of any family without setting the precedent for its own destruction. The notion that a State could intrude upon the hearth and wrest the children from the authority of their parents, as is called for in Plato's *Republic* and as is the precondition for every modern socialist state, would strike the Roman as barbarous and blasphemous.

Unlike the Greek, the Roman never conceived that the State was just the creation of men, to be altered at will. It was holy—as was the family or clan. As such, it could resist the surges of popular appetite or willfulness. Several times Rome came close to breaking up, but did not. The people's fundamental reverence prevented it. Once, early on, the plebeian families, the commoners, grew sick of their high-handed treatment by the patricians, from whom the consuls were then chosen. So they threatened to destroy Rome, not by fire or sword, but by walking away.[7] They packed their belongings, just when Rome was threatened by the Volscians; but the Senators agreed to compromise, and Rome survived. And at a time when Rome was struggling for supremacy against nearby Veii, a powerful Etruscan port, the tribunes of the people complained that it was too great a burden upon the farmer-citizens to remain deployed through an entire year, "no longer allowed even during the storms of winter to visit their homes or see to their affairs" (Livy, 5.2). The people suspected that the protracted war was a plot by their noble rivals to keep their numbers down in the assemblies. But the senator Appius Claudius rose to remind the people that it was for this very reason that pay had been voted for military service, and that it made no sense to break up the camps and entrenchments now, only to have to establish them all over again in the spring. The heart of his speech, though, is an appeal not to money or self-interest or practicality, but to union, despite rivalry and strife:

> What [the tribunes] were afraid of then, and what they are seeking to destroy today, is—obviously—concord between the orders—between nobility and commons—as they are convinced that it would contribute more than anything else to the collapse of the tribunate. They are like dishonest tradesmen looking for work—it suits them best if there is always something wrong in the body politic, so that you can call them in to put it right.
>
> Tell me, which side are you tribunes on? Are you defending or attacking the commons? Are you for or against our soldiers in the field? (5.3)

The reader will be able to think of examples in our time, when party politics instructs people to hope that their own nation will be defeated. But the Romans cleared their heads and decided that if you are going to fight a war, you had better win it. They maintained their positions around Veii, and won their most significant victory before the Punic Wars against Carthage.

The early Romans were assisted in their political endeavors by a personal asceticism. At least before they conquered the Greek world in the second and first centuries BC, Roman men and women despised lavish displays of wealth, sumptuous meals, or an unseemly desire to gratify one's lusts. They considered it effeminate and enervating. Instead, their lives were granted meaning by family duties and patriotism. That latter virtue is hated by the politically correct, even as they pay lip service to it. True patriotism is the enemy of all utopias, the enemy of socialisms that bury the local community and the family, the enemy of a world controlled by technocrats and bureaucrats. It's the enemy of a "multiculturalism" that reduces culture to cookery and clothing, and replaces deep beliefs and old customs, "prejudices," with new-and-improved prejudices—against the family, against faith, and for the all-powerful State and its octopus arms called social services.

It's also the enemy of the opportunism or crass utilitarianism that men fall prey to when they are persuaded that neither our forebears nor our descendants mean anything to us. Here is an anecdote from the struggle against Veii. A schoolmaster in the Veian village of Falerii, hoping to curry favor with the Romans, led his boys out on a walk, as was his daily routine, only this time it was straight into the Roman camp and the headquarters of the consul, Camillus. The teachers gave the boys over and declared that, since they were the sons of the Falerian elders, the town was now in the hands of Rome.

Virgil the Chauvinist

Woman's a thing forever fitful and forever changing.

Virgil's Aeneid

Say that now, Virgil, and you've lost your job.

But Camillus spat upon the offer, claiming that Rome and Falerii, though political and military enemies, were bound by a common humanity. "We have drawn the sword not against children, who even in the sack of cities are spared," said he, "but against men, armed like ourselves, who without injury or provocation attacked us at Veii" (Livy, 5.27). So Camillus had the treacherous schoolmaster stripped and bound, and gave the boys sticks to flog him with as they beat him back into town. Seeing this, the people of Falerii, impressed by Roman honor and decency, decided to unite with Rome rather than continue in their alliance with Veii: "We admit our defeat, and surrender to you in the belief—than which nothing can do more honour to the victor—that we shall live better lives under your government than under our own."

The patriot is not the man who does whatever he wishes, even if it is for the apparent advantage of the country. Honor and mercenary calculation are different things. To illustrate, here's another favorite story of mine—and it hardly matters whether it's only a pious legend, since it was the sort of thing that defined for the Roman boy what it meant to be a Roman and a man. The Romans have just thrown off the yoke of Tarquin the Proud. Wishing to return to power, Tarquin enlists the aid of another and more powerful Etruscan, Porsena, who lays siege to Rome, preventing anyone from getting in or out. He aims to starve some sense into them.

Then a youth named Mucius, after telling his plan to the "Fathers," that is the senators, sneaks over the walls and makes his way to the Etruscan camp, a dagger hidden beneath his cloak. There he sees a group of squadron leaders gathered around a man giving orders. He rushes the man and buries the dagger in his chest, killing him instantly. But it was Porsena's secretary he slew, and not Porsena. At once he is bound and brought to the commander, who asks him what he was doing. His reply ought to be known by every American schoolboy—and once was known, by many:

"I am a Roman citizen," he cried. "Men call me Gaius Mucius. I am your enemy, and as your enemy I would have slain you; I can die as resolutely as I could kill: both to do and to endure valiantly is the Roman way. Nor am I the only one to carry this resolution against you: behind me is a long line of men who are seeking the same honor. So if you think it worth your while, gird yourself for a long struggle, in which you will have to fight for your life from hour to hour with an armed foe always at your door. Such is the war we, the Roman youths, declare on you. Fear no serried ranks, no battle. It will be between yourself alone and a single enemy at a time" (Livy, 2.12). Porsena, enraged, ordered Mucius flung into the flames, but the Roman in scorn thrust his hand into the fire, saying, as it burned, "Look, see how cheaply we value our bodies, we whose eyes are fixed upon glory!" Moved by the lad's nobility, Porsena set him free, unharmed. And ever after the good Romans honored Mucius with a jocular nickname, "Scaevola," meaning "Lefty." It became his family's surname, one of the most highly esteemed in Rome.

The Romans could not have survived had they not fostered such manhood in their youths; the Etruscans were stronger than they were. But that was their ideal: scorn for pain, scorn for death, a determination to do what is right, a love for country, and a refusal to surrender.

That refusal is at the heart of the Roman success. The Romans did not produce a lot of military geniuses before Julius Caesar. They did not always have more efficient weaponry, or greater numbers of soldiers. What they did have was an uncompromising belief that the city must survive, and that surrender meant annihilation or servitude. Surrender was not an option.

So the Romans lost plenty of battles, but for many centuries did not lose a single war. Consider one of their worst military disasters, the battle of Lake Trasimene in the second Punic War.[8] The Carthaginian general Hannibal—perhaps the greatest military genius of all time—had ravaged Italy with his armies. One of the Roman consuls longed to engage Hannibal in a pitched battle once and for all. Against the judgment of his fellow consul, he allowed himself to be lured by Hannibal into a trap. The Carthaginian ordered his archers to attack the Romans and then to appear to be repulsed, retreating along the narrow shores of a twenty-mile long lake. They were bounded by water on the right and a mountain ridge on the left. When the Romans had been lured in far enough, Hannibal sent reserves from their ambush on the far side of the mountain round to press the enemy from the rear, while his "retreating" troops turned suddenly against their pursuers from the front. The Romans were caught in a vise. Both consuls died in the battle. Almost all who were not slaughtered on the shore drowned, or were cut down as they tried to swim to safety. According to Polybius, Rome lost 15,000 men on that day, one-quarter as many men as the United States lost during the entire Vietnam War. Even supposing the numbers to be exaggerated, it was a devastating loss.

What was the national reaction? The Romans saw immediately that it was a rash, foolish, glory-spurred, and un-Roman thing for the consul to do. Yet they gave him full military honors, because even a rash fool may die for his country and deserves his country's gratitude. The Romans did not send ambassadors to dicker with Hannibal, brokering a truce from a position of weakness. They also did not back down. *They changed tactics.* No doubt they fought over it in the Senate, and it caused recriminations between two unquestionable patriots, Fabius and Scipio. But for the next two years, the Romans held their ground patiently. They were content to lose battles, so long as Rome herself remained untouched. They waited Hannibal out, harassing him, cutting off a platoon here and there, laying waste to the fields whose produce the Carthaginian would need to feed his armies. There were, at that time, no news reports friendly to the enemy, and no daily body count to dishearten morale. Quintus Fabius Maximus, nicknamed Cunctator or "The Delayer," saved his nation without winning any important battles, buying Rome enough time to destroy Carthaginian enemies in Spain, and to send legions by sea to Carthage itself. That forced Hannibal to return to Africa, where the young Scipio handed him his only defeat in a pitched battle, at the desert sands outside of Zama, in 202 BC. Rome did not win that war because she was richer, or smarter, or mightier. Rome won because she would not lose.[9]

Tradition's wisdom vs. democracy's fickleness

If you stroll about the Roman Forum or her port of Ostia and look at the ruins, you will see a common inscription, "SPQR," standing for *Senatus Populusque Romani,* or "The Roman Senate and People." It's a phrase that resonated in the hearts of the old Romans. Virgil uses it at a critical moment in his *Aeneid.* He has been describing Aeneas' shield, which tells the future glories of Rome, leading up to the great victory memorialized in the center, the naval victory of Augustus over Marc Antony and Cleopatra at Actium (31 BC). Antony and Cleopatra have priestesses in their luxurious boats, shaking their tambourines in honor of the dog-headed god Anubis and other strange deities, while in the Roman ship, behind Augustus, are the Senate and the People of Rome, with their household gods and the great gods. The victory at Actium is thus a victory of Roman piety over the self-gratification and effeminacy symbolized by the debauched Antony and his entourage.[10]

But why "The Senate and the People"? Why not just the Senate, or just the People? Here again we find the practical political wisdom of the Romans, emulated (after much healthy debate) by our Founders, and forgotten by us, their descendants. It is that the Senate and the People are not the same.

The Roman constitution was neither monarchical, aristocratic, nor democratic, but a fascinating and tangled combination of all three. The consuls had nearly unlimited authority in the battlefield, but there were two of them and their terms were short. The Senate, too, could restrain the military power of the consuls, because it was the Senate that voted appropriations for their campaigns, nor could any war succeed without the hearts and arms of the common people. Then at the end of their terms the consuls had to stand scrutiny for their comportment in office. In the last two hundred years of the Republic, the tribunes of the people (whose proposals in the popular assembly could not be vetoed by any consul) would lead the prosecution against corrupt executives. The Senate controlled the purse, foreign affairs, and the prosecution of crimes against the state, such as treason.

As for the people, they were eventually granted the authority to propose laws of their own, and they possessed a potent veto on the actions of the Senate. The Roman constitution compelled various elements in the society to depend upon one another; or, rather, taught by their piety and patriotism, the Romans resigned themselves to depend upon one another. Their constitution was more the *result* of their traditional virtues than the *cause.*

Polybius, a Greek, gives a short and admirable description of the moral value of the Roman system. It was not dreamed up by a philosopher, but was the result of centuries of compromise and of devotion to tradition. Even a true democracy, as described by Polybius, partakes of the nobility demanded by aristocracy and the obedience demanded by monarchy:

> A state in which the mass of citizens is free to do whatever it pleases or takes into its head is not a democracy. But where it is both traditional and customary to reverence the gods, to care for our parents, to respect our elders, to obey the laws, and in such a community to ensure that the will of the majority prevails—this situation it is proper to describe as democracy.

The virtues of the Senate, meanwhile, were partly the result of its *distance* from the people. The people did not elect senators. Nobody elected senators; a senator is a former consul or other high officer. And senators (unless they disgraced themselves) served for life. They were therefore protected from the changes of mood that can sweep through a body politic. They felt those changes, and they dared not ignore them, but they need not act in haste. Indeed, their sluggishness to enact land reforms in the time of the Gracchi brothers (133–121), reserving huge tracts of conquered territory for themselves rather than relinquishing them to Rome and to the soldiers who had abandoned their farms to fight Rome's wars, was decisive in the Republic's slide into despotism and chaos, before Augustus and his reforms. But haste is usually more dangerous than caution, as there are many ways to get something wrong, and few ways, sometimes only one way, to get it right. Rome's built-in conservatism generally served the state well. The senators did not have to worry about election, so they did not have to pander to the people. Our word "ambition" comes from the Latin *ambitio,* which literally meant "running around," that is, scrambling for votes. It was a term of reproach. Most often the Senators resisted the people, until the people compelled them to yield to measures that the senators themselves confessed were just. If the senators were sometimes hard of hearing when the poor came to plead, their wealth enabled them, at least until the end of the Third Punic War, to resist the temptation to use state power to enrich themselves.

An anecdote from the early Gallic Wars (ca. 386 BC) shows what virtues a patriotic Roman wanted to see in his senators. The Gauls had

come pouring down from the Alps, attracted by the wealth and the warm climate of Italy, to storm the city. But Rome was undefended; the bulk of the army was stalled in northern Italy. The senators took the situation in hand. Rome must be saved. They ordered the few soldiers they had to take the women and children and the infirm to the citadel—a little walled city within the city—before the Gauls came. They themselves would remain in their homes, so as not to strain a tight food supply. The Gauls came, and found empty streets. Taken aback, they peered into the houses, where they saw, here and there, old men in togas and the purple stripe of the senatorial class, sitting at tables, waiting, "the robes and decorations august beyond reckoning, the majesty expressed in those grave, calm eyes like the

A Book You're Not Supposed to Read

The Inevitability of Patriarchy by Stephen Goldberg; New York: William Morrow, 1974.

It's not about Western civilization, or religion, or literature, or politics. All this book does is to claim that not one instance of genuine matriarchy has ever been discovered—and then it shows why that is not surprising, given our hormonal makeup. Recommended for all students whose professors deride Greece or Rome for their patriarchy, without ever suggesting an historically or anthropologically feasible alternative. One might as well take leave of the whole human race.

majesty of gods" (Livy, 5.41). At last one soldier pulled a senator's beard to see what would happen. When the old man cursed him and struck him, the spell was broken, and the massacre of the senators, who in noble scorn gave their lives for their people, was underway.

I'm not implying that the senate was filled with heroes. Roman political history is marked by the conflict between the classes, the slow squeezing by the plebeians of political rights from the patricians, and, later, the securing by the poor of something like lawful treatment from the rich. But for five hundred years the Romans never collapsed into civil war or civic degeneration. The patricians agreed, grudgingly, to have the laws written down, as a protection for all: hence the famous Twelve Tables (450). They agreed, in the Lex Canuleia (445), to allow patricians and plebeians to marry. They finally agreed to open up the consulate to plebeians, to limit the acreage of public land a man might hold, and to temper their measures for exacting payment from debtors (367). They bowed to the office of the tribunes, and conceded that the person of a tribune should be held sacrosanct. But, with all their faults, they acted as a healthy check upon the passions of the people. Unlike Athens, Rome could not slide into mob rule. There were too many senators in the way.

Another anecdote will illustrate the point.[11] The plebeians had been stoked to rebellion by their tribunes, just when Rome was vulnerable to the Volscians, their rivals in central Italy. Then Menenius Agrippa, a shrewd and eloquent senator, rose to settle them down. He compared the state to a body, with the rich—who seem to produce nothing, but consume everything—as the belly, without which the other members of the body could receive no nourishment. It's a metaphor that reflects poorly upon the rich, but the people are swayed by it. They do not erupt in violence. Such scenes are repeated again and again in the histories that helped fashion the Roman imagination. We see it in Virgil's famous simile, comparing Neptune's calming the raging sea with the calming of the people by one man, one leader, marked by piety:

> And just as, often, when a crowd of people
> is rocked by a rebellion, and the rabble
> rage in their minds, and firebrands and stones
> fly fast—for fury finds its weapons—if,
> by chance, they see a man remarkable
> for righteousness and service, they are silent
> and stand attentively; and he controls
> their passion by his words and cools their spirits:
> so all the clamor of the sea subsided. (*Aeneid,* 1.209–217)

The point is that republican Rome survived. Neither the Etruscans, nor the Gauls, nor her Italian rivals, nor Hannibal, nor even her own strife between the classes, brought her down, until her victories and her wealth corrupted her, requiring an Augustus to set things in order again. Roman commitment to tradition provided a check on the power both of the wealthy and of the mob. Rome retained a dread of both tyranny and untempered democracy, and the bastion against both was that fatherly virtue of piety. The American Founders took the lesson, modeling their state not after Athens—for Athens fell too soon—but after the more stable, more unwieldy, more Stoical, and more agrarian Rome. It is why George Washington was called the Cincinnatus of his country, after the rather poor gentleman farmer who saved Rome, profited nothing, and returned to his land. He was not called the Pericles of his country.

Peace through strength

But weren't the Romans warlike?

Yes, they were. They wanted to survive. A small consideration, easy to overlook.

They were not, for most of their history, aggressive. A strange thing to say, given that they rose from a village in the hills near the mouth of the

Tiber, to the capital of the Mediterranean world and beyond. But it's true. Until the late and decadent years of the Republic, when generals like Marius and Sulla commandeered professional armies loyal to themselves (for they, and no longer the Senate, paid them in plunder and land), Rome usually didn't go forth to seek wars. But Rome also didn't duck any, either. This conservative attitude calls for explanation.

Unlike most peoples at the time, Rome was not governed by a king who could increase his wealth, consolidate his authority, and win an immortal name by military conquest. The consuls served for far too short a time to conduct a war of any magnitude; besides, there were *two of them*. And, as Polybius notes, it was the Senate's prerogative "either to celebrate a general's successes with pomp and magnify them, or to obscure and belittle them."

Until Rome was flooded by the wealth from the east after the Third Punic War (146 BC), the state depended for its economy and its political stability on the small landed farmer. This ideal is ingrained so deeply in the Roman mind that, even after the rise of the empire under Augustus brought in cheap grain from Egypt and undercut the Italian farms, the poets Horace and Virgil still look upon it with nostalgia, Virgil writing four stupendous poems, his *Georgics*, on farming, animal husbandry, winemaking, and beekeeping, always with an eye to the political and theological lessons they suggest. But people who farm have little opportunity for professional warfare.

The Romans expressed their deep conservatism by a reverence for limits: one of their more important (and unusual) gods was Terminus, god of boundary stones. This reverence extended to their oaths and treaties. Not that they didn't *interpret* treaties favorably to themselves, and act accordingly. This they did most notoriously when they sought cause against their nemesis Carthage, picking the fight in the Third Punic War. But that reverence restrained them from engaging in the trickery they associated with Greece. Consider a story from the First

Punic War.[12] A Roman general named Regulus was captured by the Carthaginians and brought to Africa. The senate of Carthage charged him to return to Rome to present terms for peace. Regulus was to swear that, if Rome refused the terms, he would return to Carthage as a prisoner and be executed. The Carthaginians depended upon his oath, and figured that, since he might prefer living to dying, he would persuade his fellow citizens to accept the treaty. Regulus went to Rome, persuaded his countrymen to *reject* the treaty, and returned to Carthage, where he was tortured and put to death. Is the story true? There's no evidence to suggest that it is *not true*. The Romans believed it, and held Regulus up as a model of Roman integrity and manhood. By contrast, they considered the mythical Odysseus, whom Homer calls "the man of many turnings," a liar and a villain. "The inventor of impieties," Virgil calls him (*Aeneid* 2.233).

Rome won her wars and increased her territory. But it was centuries before she claimed control over Italy: as late as the fourth century BC, Gauls from beyond the Alps set fire to the city, assisted on their way by Gauls on the Italian side. But the real story in the Roman conquest of Italy

Another Local Culture Squelched by Christianity

When the conquered man was thought to have defended himself bravely, the spectators waved their handkerchiefs, raised their thumbs, and cried, "Mitte! Let him go!"...If, on the other hand, the witnesses decided that the victim had by his weakness deserved defeat, they turned their thumbs down, crying, "Jugula!"

Jerome Carcopino, *Daily Life in Ancient Rome*

Meaning, "Give it to him in the throat!" Those who decry the ascendancy of Christianity should ask what kind of society imperial Rome had become, empty of any religion which stirred the depths of human imagination and devotion. They might apply the lessons to ourselves, too.

is political, not military. That is, the Romans—unlike the Athenians—did something sensible after their victories over the Samnites, the Aequians, the Volscians, and most of the other rival states on the peninsula. They cleared out the few genuine enemies of peace, ruthlessly punishing those who led armies against them. Then they incorporated the lands into the Roman state, usually granting citizenship to the leading families, and extending citizenship, on evidence of good behavior, to the free men of the city. *They made them Romans.*

That didn't mean the people couldn't keep their local gods. The Romans were too pious and practical for that. You never know when you have overlooked a deity, so it's better to have the Rhegians praying to a god you don't know about, so long as they also pray to the state gods. The results were remarkable. When Hannibal came marauding over the peninsula for fifteen years, he expected that most of the "allies" of Rome, the other old cities, would revolt. They did not. Fear kept some in line, but most had long simply identified themselves as Romans.

To put it simply, a Roman citizen was a *Roman* citizen. We now associate citizenship with geography. "I am an American" means simply "I was born within the borders of the United States," and suggests very little about devotion. The Romans prized citizenship far more highly than that. Yet at the same time they were generous in bestowing citizenship upon conquered peoples, without regard for race or ethnicity or religion. None of that mattered. Being Roman was what mattered. So when Saint Paul's enemies had him arrested for insurrection, he appealed directly to the emperor to try his case, as was his right as a Roman citizen. It is as if an islander in Samoa should invoke the name of the President, calling a halt to local proceedings. The centurion immediately ordered Paul's safe conduct to the Roman governor, and thence to Rome. Paul was a diminutive Jew from Tarsus on the coast of Asia Minor. He probably never set foot in Rome till he was brought there under arrest. Yet a citizen is a citizen, and the centurions obey the rules.

After the fall of Nero in 69, only one or two of the succeeding emperors hailed from Italy. No one cared. Saint Augustine was born in North Africa in 354. He too was a Roman citizen. Was he black or Caucasian? Berber, or Semitic? We don't know. No one cared to notice.

In short, when it came to governing conquered peoples, no one did it more efficiently than the Romans did, with remarkably little brutality (there are important exceptions: the destruction of Jerusalem in 70 AD). Their form of tolerance was simple. Swear loyalty to Rome and keep the peace, and they'd eventually make you Romans, with the same rights as anyone. You might enjoy a measure of home rule, if you abided by the law and kept the taxes coming in. But you wouldn't be Spanish-Romans, or Parthian-Romans, or Greek-Romans. You'd be Roman Romans. Only one nation in the history of the world has managed to follow that wisdom consistently: the United States, until about 1970 (apart from its shameful treatment of blacks). After that, the numbers of illegal immigrants with no emotional ties to America grew, as the value of citizenship among the native people fell.

And the Roman armies, from the time of Augustus till the German takeover of the western empire in 476, brought considerable advantages to the frontier lands. I'm not ignoring the brutal efficiency of the army: when the Romans turned against the rebellious Jews of Palestine, they overran Jerusalem, destroyed the Temple, and plundered the Holy of Holies. That desecration is celebrated in relief on the Arch of Titus, near the Coliseum. Nor do I ignore how bloody army discipline could be. If a company of men had shown unseemly cowardice, their commander could order them to be "decimated." The soldiers stood in a line. One tenth would be chosen by lot, to be clubbed to death by the rest. It was an effective deterrent.[13]

But at its height the Roman army numbered about 400,000 men, guarding a frontier stretching thousands of miles, from the walls behind the Roman outposts in Britain, to Gaul and Germany along the Rhine, across the passes of the Alps and into eastern Europe along the Danube to the Black Sea, from there beyond Asia Minor at the Parthian and Persian borders, circling south and west to Arabia and the Sinai, then across North Africa. They could not have done it without discipline. The Romans left little to the whims of their commanders. They had clear lines of authority, and clear military traditions. They pitched camp when it was time to pitch camp, and their camps were laid out in exactly the same fashion everywhere. They knew too that many men will be lazy and careless without the fear of punishment. In the Roman army you risked your life if you fell asleep on sentry duty, or if you failed to pass on orders to the next patrol. Also if you committed those deeds that would sap the morale of your squadron: "The punishment of beating to death is also inflicted upon those who steal from the camp, those who give false evidence, those who in full manhood commit homosexual offenses, and finally upon anyone who has been punished three times for the same offense" (Polybius).

Nor could the Roman armies have succeeded if they had made themselves hated wherever they went. Augustus ensured that the armies would be paid by the State, relieving them of the need to plunder for food. He also gave twenty-year veterans a pension and a parcel of land in the provinces. The result was that many non-Romans determined that serving in the army was a good way to gain modest wealth and the privileges of Roman citizenship. Increasingly, recruits were taken from the provinces, and veterans settled there. And in those provinces the armies did not merely eat, drink, pick up whores, and fight. They built roads, some of the most durable ever, with gravel foundations many feet deep, to prevent buckling under loaded wagons and companies on the march. They built aqueducts. They dredged harbors. They cleared mountain passes. They contributed manual labor to civic works that had nothing to do with an army's needs: temples, theaters, places of government. They were an ancient Army Corps of Engineers.

The real reason Rome fell

Edward Gibbon suggested that it was because Christianity weakened the pagan militarism that kept Rome strong. The philosopher Nietzsche accused the Christians of the same thing. That was one of the things that led G. K. Chesterton to wonder whether there might not be something to Christianity. On Monday its critics reviled it for its pacifism, and on Tuesday for the Crusades and the conquest of the Americas.[14]

Gibbon was wrong. Christians formed a significant portion of the legions, even before Constantine legalized the religion in 313 with his Edict of Milan. There's nothing in the Bible that says that you cannot fight in the defense of your country, and so long as the commanders looked the other way, a Christian lad in armor might dispense with the "required" sacrifices to the gods Augustus and Rome. As early as 180, under the command of Marcus Aurelius (who permitted Christians to be persecuted in Rome), Christians served in the armies defending Rome against German invaders.

The fall was not caused by rampant immorality, either, at least not in the way that novels like *I, Claudius* might lead us to believe. That's because the way the aristocracy and the rabble lived in Rome was not the way people lived out in the countryside, not to mention in the provinces. By the first century AD, the *city* of Rome was a cultural sinkhole. Petronius laughs at the emptiness of Roman life during the reign of Nero. In his *Satyricon,* a former slave rises to such wealth that he invites his banquet guests to wash their hands in wine, while he is flattered by "educated" Romans and Greeks, who elbow one another for a place at his table. Meanwhile, the "hero" spends an idle hour eyeing up boys playing ball near the baths. He squabbles with his friend over who gets to sodomize their pretty favorite, an effeminate slave boy. He is reduced to paying a sorceress to assist him when a certain member of his body won't raise itself up anymore. Or the poet Juvenal can lend us a sour look on Rome's filth, its firetraps, its noise and idleness—where every imaginable sin and stupidity festers, and where the poor man's "liberty" is to be beaten senseless in the alleys, where he can beg his assailants to let him go home with a few teeth remaining in his head (Satire 3.299–301).

But that was the city, a magnet for people who wanted, as Juvenal put it, "bread and circuses," free food and bloody games provided by the state. If the welfare-state mentality of the capital had prevailed throughout the empire, Rome would have fallen in a generation or two. It didn't, partly because the money wasn't there, and partly because the evil manners of the cities had only limited influence. People in the country preserved the old traditions, worshiping their household gods and living modestly, such as Italian peasants have done almost to the present day. They ate lentils, chickpeas, vegetables with olive oil, bread, cheese, some fruit, and a little bit of meat, not the fancy and uncomfortable dinners that Horace satirizes (e. g., in Satire 2.6, the source of the tale of the city mouse and the country mouse). So conservative were these farmers that they proved resistant to the new Christians, who were most numerous in urban areas, where they could most quickly find work. Hence the word "pagan," from Latin *paganus,* meaning, loosely, somebody who lives in the sticks.

An economic slowdown did help bring about the fall. It is one of the just ironies of history that empires that depend upon slave labor can get a lot done with it, but then they stagnate, since slavery removes the incentive for technological development and efficiency in production. Of all the peoples of the ancient world, the Romans could have had an industrial revolution. Their tradition had ennobled manual labor (though the rich came to view that as quaint, from the dusty past).

Someone Tell This to Congress

[Tiberius] answered some governors who had written to recommend an increase in the burden of provincial taxation, with: "A good shepherd shears his flock; he does not flay them."

Suetonius, *The Twelve Caesars*

Of course, this assumes the shepherd is thinking past tonight's meal.

They imitated the accomplishments of other peoples, learning the use of the arch from the Etruscans, the colonnade from the Greeks. They were remarkably inventive in their uses of building materials. They used the volcanic ash of southern Italy to form a mixture we know as concrete— cheap, much lighter than marble or granite, and pourable into forms to make slabs or columns as needed. The concrete could also be mixed by various formulas, depending on the use. One kind would set up underwater, for bridge-piers, which could be driven deep into a riverbed by pile drivers.

But slaves there were, and Rome depended upon them too heavily for produce from the land. Hence, when the climate cooled in the third century and harvests were poor and the plague returned from the East, there was no way, by means of technology, to make up the economic shortfall.

The emperors had no easy way out. In the third century, they were men who had come to power mainly by military coups. They had been set up by their soldiers, so they were beholden to them, and needed to pay them back. But, what with the shrinking economy, people hoarded their cash. Money went out of circulation. You could sometimes rely upon payment in kind: you could give the common soldiers a *salarium,* or payment in salt (cf. English *salary*), which they might keep for personal use or to barter for other items. But commanders needed to be paid in more than salt, or else they will choose another man to follow. Of the Roman emperors from 235 to 284, only two died of natural causes; most of the other twenty were assassinated, usually by their own soldiers. What do you do?

Had the Roman emperors had the opportunity to *lower taxes* so that people could invest greater capital to produce better crops and more revenue for the state, they probably would have done so. People will always complain about taxes, and Roman tax collectors could sometimes be vile customers: Rome "farmed" her taxes, meaning that she would set somebody, often one of the locals (Matthew, for instance, in the Gospels, or

Zacchaeus), the task of squeezing a fixed take from his district. Anything above that take, he could pocket. It's a system that invites corruption. But, all in all, the people were not taxed too heavily. Rome knew better. She had all she could do to maintain the frontiers, and had no interest in kindling popular revolts in long-pacified Gaul or Spain. If we could trade our tax rate for what the Romans paid, we'd do it in an instant. The more so, as the Romans used the money for practical ends, to build roads and public works, and to maintain the standing army, the empire's greatest expense.

But there wasn't any point to lowering taxes, since slave labor on the land made capital improvements unthinkable. So Rome *raised taxes,* and the consequences were bad. For a while they collected more money; but the higher rates made it no longer profitable for a private citizen to collect them. Soldiers then had to be employed to do it, and so one of the props of citizen government fell. Meanwhile, higher taxes lowered the birth rate, already lowered by poor living conditions and the scarcity of land to bequeath to children. That's because, in good times, or among a people with something to hope for that transcends themselves, large families thrive. When times go bad, or when a nation falls to cynicism or a practical atheism, people decline to marry, and those who do marry have fewer children. To raise taxes then is to rouse an alcoholic by giving him a drink. Europe is learning this lesson now—or failing to learn it. So Rome fell for lack of men. It was already happening, among some of the conquered peoples, at the time of Plutarch. "We are not replacing ourselves," says a Spartan.[15]

So Rome fell into an economic sludge from which she never emerged. The emperor Diocletian in 301 attempted wage and price controls; they failed. To avert odd shortages of goods, he ordered sons to follow the professions of their fathers (with some exceptions, for talented boys who could serve the government). Another prop of citizen government fell. To unite an increasingly restive empire, he—who probably didn't believe a word of it—commanded all citizens to adore the gods Augustus and Rome as the highest of their pantheon. He himself was "Augustus." Men entering his godly presence had to prostrate themselves. So fell still another prop. The Christians, who would offer no sacrifices to any such god, were persecuted. It was the last great persecution they suffered. Constantine, the man who came out on top in the struggle to succeed Diocletian, then lifted the ban on Christian worship. But the economic and military troubles of the empire remained.

It didn't help that the Roman frontiers were invaded. Why were they invaded? Why not? Who would live on the steppes of Russia, if you could have Greece or Italy instead? And a materially better life: fine linen and basilicas and rich food. The telling thing about the invasions by Germans, Celts, and Huns was not that they wanted to conquer the Romans, but that they wanted to *be Romans.* They admired the land they were invading—not all of them, but enough of them to save Rome for another century or so. The Roman legions on the frontiers were, more and more, manned by recent invaders.

Three dates stand out for me. In 378, the Visigoths, a Germanic people fleeing the Hun, asked permission to settle within the bounds of the empire, but then rose in revolt against their abusive Roman commanders. The emperor Valens went east to settle the matter, but was slain in battle at Adrianople (modern day Edirne, in European Turkey), and Valens' successor, Theodosius, came to terms with the enemy, to Rome's disadvantage. Rome had lost battles on the frontier before, and had managed to close off the breaches. At Adrianople it may be said that she lost her first war. Then in 406 there was a particularly cold winter—global cooling makes for rough times—and the Rhine froze over. Rome had only had to post troops at the fords, but now the Germans crossed the ice with their herds and families wherever they pleased. The western frontier was thus breached. Finally, in 410, the Visigothic chieftain Alaric, disappointed of his hope to be granted political authority by emperor Honorius, swept into Rome and put it to the sword and flames. It was not long before those Germans, filled with a vigor and manly freedom that the Romans had lost, concluded that one of their own should govern the West. Hence in 476 Odoacer "encouraged" the lad Romulus Augustulus, last emperor in the west, to retire to a monastery. The last prop was kicked out, and the edifice fell.

Or did it? Did Rome fall? In the East, at the capital that Constantine built for himself, Constantinople, an emperor still reigned, and an emperor would continue to reign until 1453. And in the West, those German warlords still acknowledged, in polite words more than in deeds, the supremacy of the emperor. More than that, they long preserved the old Roman forms: consuls and senators, for example. And some of the reality was preserved, too. What did Rome bequeath to the West? A powerful compromise between democracy and aristocracy; a long tradition of citizen government, even during the rule of the emperors; a military ideal emulated by nations ever since, and an example of almost two centuries of peace; the spread of Latin and Greek learning to the hinterlands; and, most important, the spread of Christianity. For Europe is not Europe without the faith, as we shall see.

Chapter 3

ISRAEL: HOW GOD CHANGED THE WORLD

Nearly four thousand years ago in the plains outside the walls of the sophisticated Chaldean city of Ur, an old herdsman who had lived there all his life heard a voice:

> Get thee out of thy country, and from thy kindred, and from thy father's house, unto a land that I will shew thee:
>
> And I will make of thee a great nation, and I will bless thee, and make thy name great; and thou shalt be a blessing:
>
> And I will bless them that bless thee, and curse him that curseth thee: and in thee shall all families of the earth be blessed. (Gen. 12:1–3)

That poor fellow probably believed in a crowd of gods, and if they were those of his neighbors the Chaldees, they were a mixed lot, many vicious, few to be trusted. He was not even given the name of the God telling him to abandon all he knew, and the land he loved. But he obeyed anyway and, according to the Old Testament, though this Abraham was old and childless, he indeed became the father of a great nation. His descendants, by blood and by adoption into his faith, have been as numberless as grains of sand on the shore, or as the stars in the sky. We are too used to the astonishing promise made in these verses, which even according to liberal theologians and skeptics were written down long before any Jews

Guess What?

* The God of Abraham was nothing like the pagan gods.

* The Old Testament God made modern science possible.

* Jesus made Western civilization possible.

could reasonably expect a day when their nation would be a blessing to *all families of the earth.* Yet that is what has happened.

A blessing? Even our professoriate, with their predictable disdain for religion and for the nation of Israel, refrain from casting contempt upon the Jews. Yes, they will laugh at the creation story in Genesis, and will revile the bloodiness of the Hebrew conquest of Canaan under Joshua and the judges, and will shade their eyes from the natural moral law so magnificently engraved in the Ten Commandments. But it is a nervous laughter. They know that there is something shattering in the confrontation of sinful and ignorant man with the Holy One of Israel. If they say that the universe is pointless, they find Job crying out the same, but with the cry of a man who has suffered deeply and who still longs for God's justice. They cannot, like Hitler, deny the Jews their glory, but then they are hard put to tell what is glorious about them, if not their tenacity in upholding their faith. Nor can they easily claim that the Jewish faith is just like all the paganisms against which it struggled. It manifestly is not. For it is the faith that claims God alone as true King, for whom kings and princes, and academicians and bureaucrats, weigh no more than dust. That means that

Someone Tell John Kerry and Other Pro-Choice Christians

Do not murder; do not commit adultery; do not practice pederasty; do not fornicate; do not steal; do not deal in magic; do not practice sorcery; do not kill a fetus by abortion, or commit infanticide.

The Didache (c. 150)

This early Christian text adds to the incontestable evidence, among all Christian communities and at all times, is that abortion is forbidden. Note the company that that crime keeps.

men need not truckle to the state, or tremble before its lackeys. The Torah is a law to set men free.

Were the Jews important for any other reason? If we consider only those material achievements that confer glory on a nation, the Jews would qualify only for a short time. So it is deeply ironic that they should have played so important a role in the development of Western civilization—indeed *the central role.* They had little to recommend them. They did not invent democracy. They were not great sculptors or painters. That was only to be expected, since God had forbidden them to make graven images (a command of crucial importance for civilization, as we'll see, but not one bound to encourage the arts). They had been shepherds and cattlemen, with little affinity for trade and the sea. Rather, when they sought an image of horror and chaos, landlubbers that they were, they looked to the ocean, where dwelt the terrible leviathan, and where Jonah found himself once in the belly of a great fish. Aside from the Old Testament and their commentaries upon it, the Jews wrote nothing of great interest. They enjoyed an early spring of political prominence during the time of David and Solomon, after which the kingdom was split in two. Both Israel in the north and Judah in the south were constantly pressed by their more powerful neighbors: Assyrians, Egyptians, Philistines, Babylonians.

We remember them for one thing alone, but it is the most important thing: the revelation of the one, holy, all-knowing, almighty, all-loving God.

Whether you believe it or not (and I do), it is a plain fact that this single revelation—with all the history in which it is embedded and by which it comes to light—has been the most important idea in the history of the world. Secular historians today explain the past in terms of accidents: Who had steel? Who bore which germs? What wind blew which ships where? But if you really ask how we got where we are today (and by "we" here, I mean almost everyone in the world), you inevitably return to the city walls of Ur, and Abraham's revelation from God.

The honest atheist must admit it. Should that atheist turn sincerely to God, it will not be to some folklore Zeus on Olympus, hurling a thunderbolt, nor to some Scythian Great Mother with fat breasts and buttocks. He will turn to the God of Abraham, Isaac, and Jacob. It may be politically incorrect to say so, but it is true nonetheless. If there is a God (and there is), it is He.

Why is this so important? How has it changed the world? To see that, let's return to ancient Mesopotamia and the lands around the Mediterranean Sea.

A God above nature, not a nature god

The people who lived in the Tigris and Euphrates River valleys had plenty of water and fertile soil, making it possible to grow surplus cereals and store the dry grain. That was the minimum requirement for a city. It freed men from the daily need to procure their own food, allowing many to become carpenters or masons or bureaucrats. But the Land Between the Rivers was no easy farming. Rain was scarce, and when it came, it came in torrents. You had to use deftly constructed canals to divert the river water into the fields, or to divert the sudden rainwater. These canals had to be pitched most precisely. That's because the land was nearly dead flat from Babylon all the way to the mouths of the rivers in what is now Kuwait, five hundred miles away.

That need for extensive and organized canals helped determine the eventual political structure of the Mesopotamian kingdoms. They had to be large states, and they had to be controlled by a single center of authority, concentrated in the person of a god-king. But the canals were still not enough to make life secure. The Tigris and Euphrates were prone to sudden and terrible floods caused by snow melt in the mountains and monsoon winds coming off the Persian Gulf. The people held their life from the fertile earth, and so it was natural that they should worship fertility gods. But nature, there even more than usual, was ferocious, capricious, wild. This disorderliness is reflected in the Babylonian gods.[1]

The great sky god Apsu and his consort, the malevolent sea-goddess Tiamat, once conspired to destroy the younger gods, who had gotten too many and too noisy. They were thwarted by the benevolent god Ea, who organized the opposition under the leadership of one Marduk, who then became chief of all the gods, a kind of emperor and personal protector of Babylon and *its* emperor. Marduk ended the war by funneling the winds into the gaping maw of Tiamat, to blow her belly up and blast it apart. From her scattered members he fashioned the physical world. Then he slew Tiamat's lover, the evil Kingu, and mixed his dripping blood with earth to create mankind. He did so not out of love, but to placate his subordinate gods, who hated the tedious work of offering incense in the temple. Man is made to do work that the gods dislike. He is a slave.

So it was with the ancient fertility cults. They were, with the partial exception of Egypt, grim and nasty affairs, governed by the iron necessity of hunger. If your life comes from the earth and the sky, and if these are so often malignant, ruining your crops with hail and withering them with drought, then you must placate the gods by offering them your own fertility. You send girls into the temples to be prostitutes; it was not flight of fancy when the prophets regularly compared idolatry to whoredom. Hence, also, human sacrifice. In Phoenicia and Carthage, economically savvy parents would make their children "pass through the fire to Molech"(cf. 2 K. 23:10), roasting them in the furnace-mouth of the idol, to ensure fertility to come. If you thought you might miss your own children and you had some ready money, you might bribe a poor man to let you "adopt" one of his. That would make you happy, the poor man happy, and Molech happy.

When, having obeyed the voice of God and traveled to Canaan, Abraham is granted a son and then is commanded by the same voice to sacrifice him on a mountaintop, the poor man must have been disappointed, but not surprised. That is the way gods of nature are. No doubt the god has to drink blood to provide blood. Abraham might have thought not that his promised line was coming to an end, but that this sacrifice must be an unfortunate part of the mercenary arrangement.

"Lay not thine hand upon the lad," cries an angel, as Abraham prepares to cut Isaac's throat on the altar, "for now I know that thou fearest God, seeing thou hast not withheld thy son, thine only son from me" (Gen. 22:12). Instead, as Abraham himself unwittingly prophesied, God has provided the sheep for the sacrifice, a ram caught by his horns in a nearby thicket. It is a test of Abraham's faith that he would slay his only son, but it is also a surprising revelation of the nature of God. There will be no human sacrifice in exchange for food and full wombs. Indeed, there will be no sacrifice of any natural good for the sake of good harvests. God is not mired in the natural world; He is above that world. The distinction is crucial. The Hebrews took long enough to get the idea, but eventually they understood, and when they turned to the Creator, they turned to the One who ordered the world "in measure and number and weight" (Wis. 11:20). That meant that they could look upon nature with a free eye. They need not cower before it. It might be terrible, as the behemoth, who "moveth his tail like a cedar: the sinews of his stones are wrapped together" (Job 40:17); but no matter how muscular his testicles were, the Jews would not fall in adoration before any such, as the Hindus would fall before the elephant god Ganesh. Nature might be as lovely and mysterious, "the work of thy fingers, the moon and the stars, which thou hast ordained" (Ps. 8:3), but when religion-hungry Manasseh "built altars for all the host of heaven in the two courts of the house of the Lord" (2 Chr. 33:5), he did evil, and his grandson Josiah smashed and burnt those altars, melted their idols, dismantled the bathhouses for ritual sodomy, and poured the refuse into a fiery pit, once a grove for the fertility cults, henceforth the garbage dump called Tophet (2 K. 23:5–15).

That rejection of nature worship is, in part, the meaning of Moses' conflict with the Pharaoh of Egypt, Ramses II (c. 1279–1213). Some time in the 1600s BC, the descendants of Abraham found themselves in the valley of the Nile, welcomed by an interregnum of Semitic rulers. But the native Egyptians resumed their empire around 1550 BC, and eventually cast the Hebrews into slavery, compelling them to make bricks for the building-works of the Pharaoh. This slavery was both economic and religious. The Pharaoh, literally "Great House," was the earthly manifestation of the just god Osiris. Now Osiris had been dismembered by his enemy Seti, but his twin sister and wife, Isis (with whom, says Plutarch, giving us a ghastly glimpse into the penetralia of the Egyptian cult, Osiris copulated *in utero*)[2], gathered his members up and re-formed him, to be the god passing judgment upon men in the underworld. One member, though, she never did find. *That* had gotten gobbled up by a pike in the Nile, and hence the fertility of Osiris was the source of the fertility of the river. Meanwhile, Horus, Osiris' son, slew Seti and assumed Osiris' place as ruler upon the earth. A Pharaoh, then, is the continuation of this imperial dynasty. He is Horus when he lives, and Osiris after he dies. He guarantees good floods and rich harvests, prosperity and justice.

So when Pharaoh stiffens his neck and will not let the Hebrews free to worship their God in the desert—in a place, note well, where nothing grows—Moses takes the battle to Pharaoh's turf. The Pharaoh is a fertility god, remember. All the people, not only the Hebrews, are enslaved to him, because all need to eat. But the Pharaoh can do nothing against the God

Christ: The Civil Rights Activist

Jesus Christ is a God whom we approach without pride, and before whom we humble ourselves without despair.

Blaise Pascal, *Pensées* (527)

He is therefore, whether an atheist will believe it or not, the great equalizer of men, who would make masters of them all by making servants of them all: the one whom it is a source of just pride to obey.

above nature. He is powerless against the flies, the gnats, the grasshoppers, the frogs, the fiery hail, the pestilence, and the darkness. His holy river turns red with blood. The flesh of his people erupts in boils—a painful and humiliating insult for the Egyptians with all their cosmetics and their embalming of the dead. Finally the firstborn of all Egypt die, while the Hebrews are spared by the blood of the Passover lamb (more about that, too, soon). The theological rout is total, long before anyone shows up at the shore of the Red Sea.

Not a political god, but the King of kings

Pharaoh's Egypt also shows us a lesson for our times that the Soviet Union understood, but many well-meaning secular liberals in Europe and the U.S. today ignore: there is no such thing as a vacuum of faith. Let Christians and other believers in human freedom take note. If man is by nature a creature who gives praise, and if he does not know the true God, he will give his heart, and perhaps his sweat and blood, to something *big* within his vision. The two biggest candidates for false gods are Nature and the State. He will drown his imagination in the swamp of natural processes, birth and growth and sex and death, or he will enslave himself to power, most clearly manifest in an emperor-god, a deified city, or an all-competent State. Often, as in Mesopotamia and Egypt, and in today's American Left, he'll do both at once.

As in Mesopotamia, geography pretty much determined the political structure of Egypt. You had to control the whole river valley or nothing, since outside of the river valley there was desert, speckled with only a few oases. If a Pharaoh held the lower Nile, and an anti-Pharaoh held the upper Nile, the one would be a constant threat to the other, a constant source of agricultural and commercial interference. The great Menes united upper and lower Egypt back around 3100 BC, and, with some periods of dynasty-change and upheaval, Egypt remained that same slender snake of fertile land, independent until Alexander conquered it in 332 BC.

So when the Egyptians adored their Great House, they were also bowing before the power of their State, embodied in the monarch and in his priestly ministers and tax collectors and slave drivers. That State brought peace and prosperity. It was the same in the more vulnerable kingdoms of Mesopotamia. That flatland was not banked with deserts, as was Egypt, so its cities had to be walled to protect the grain. That required a warrior class to defend the walls. Since no one city could stand against the might of a large army, all the cities of Mesopotamia had to be brought under a single imperial rule.

Under such circumstances the separation of temporal and spiritual power is inconceivable. Men submit to the State with the same readiness and fear as to a god. The State is divine.

The revelation to the Hebrews changes all that.

This de-coupling of God from identification with king or State or city is to be found throughout the Old Testament, from the beginning. Cain, the farmer, is the first murderer, killing his brother Abel. When he is driven from his family, he becomes the first builder of a city. Evidently that conferred no moral or religious distinction upon him; and Saint Augustine would trenchantly compare Cain with Romulus, the legendary founder of Rome who slew his twin brother Remus while they were building the city walls, and who at his death was revered as a god.[3] The solitary Enoch "walked with God," and one day was seen no more (Gen. 5:24); but the ambitious men of Babel, city builders all, wanted to construct a tower that would reach to heaven, to make a name for themselves and cause all their neighbors to cower before them (Gen. 11). God derides that statecraft, and confuses their hitherto single language, so that they can no longer understand one another. All cities, all states, all towers "whose top may reach unto heaven," are incomplete, a mockery, riven with strife.

Marduk has Babylon, Osiris has Memphis, Athena has Athens, and in all these places, to worship the god is to worship the city. It is tempting then to answer, "God has Jerusalem." Not so, as the prophets are at pains to show us. God does not bind his covenant to any city or its citizens. The commandments are given in the one place no one could mistake for a city or a fertile valley: Mount Sinai, in the desert. Indeed, when the people below miss Moses for too long and grow anxious, wishing to turn God into their good luck charm, they fashion the Golden Calf, a young bull, symbol of life and fertility. God punishes them for it. Later, when they have settled in Canaan and wish to live as other people do, in one state united under a king, the prophet Samuel tells them that God *is displeased.* Note how strange this is. Everywhere else, the union of a people in a powerful state is what a god is for—that's why you worship the

"A Little Lower than the Angels"

Curiously, the new conception [following the scientific revolution] both exalted and debased man: he was raised up against God, exalted at His expense; he was reduced through a deep desire to an object of nature no different fundamentally from an animal or a plant.

Romano Guardini, *The End of the Modern World*

How noble and liberating was, by contrast, the obedient praise of the Psalmist:

When I consider thy heavens, the work of thy fingers, the moon and the stars, which thou hast ordained;
What is man, that thou art mindful of him? and the son of man, that thou visitest him?
For thou hast made him a little lower than the angels, and hast crowned him with glory and honour.

Psalm 8:3–5

immortals! But God sends the prophets to teach the people the reverse: He Himself is to be their "city," their bulwark, their king.

God does allow Samuel to anoint a king for the people, after the prophet advises them about the misery that such concentration of power will cause, for the king "will take your sons, and appoint them for himself, for his chariots," and "will take your daughters to be confectionaries, and to be cooks, and to be bakers," and "will take the tenth of your seed, and of your vineyards, and give to his officers, and to his servants" (1 Sam. 8:11, 13, 15). If only our potentates in America would take but one tenth! But the real harm of bowing at the political altar is spiritual. One comes to believe that salvation lies in statecraft. Then every tin dictator with armies in bright uniform will look good. Ezekiel is unforgettable in his attack on this stupidity:

> And [Jerusalem] played the harlot when she was mine; and she
> doted on her lovers, on the Assyrians her neighbors,
>
> Which were clothed with blue, captains and rulers, all of
> them desirable young men, horsemen riding upon horses.
>
> Thus she committed her whoredoms with them, with all
> them that were the chosen men of Assyria, and with all on
> whom she doted: with all their idols she defiled herself.
>
> Neither left she her whoredoms brought from Egypt: for in
> her youth they lay with her, and they bruised the breasts of her
> virginity, and poured their whoredom upon her. (23:5–8)

Indeed, the whole notion of rulership and political power is being redefined. God makes a covenant with the second king of the Jews, David, promising that his line will reign forever—a promise that Christians believe is fulfilled by Jesus Christ, descendant of David, who affirmed that his "kingdom was not of this world" (Jn. 18:36). But God never promises protection for David's sons (cf. 2 Sam. 12:10–11), or for Jerusalem. No earthly dynasty should the people expect. Quite the reverse: David's grandsons split the kingdom into Israel in the north (falling to the Assyrians in 732 BC) and Judah in the south. Then God sent the prophet Jeremiah to warn Zedekiah, the last king of Judah, to surrender to the Babylonians, or the city would be overrun. The king and his advisors declined, thinking that the Temple built by David's son, Solomon, would be their talisman, their charm. They reversed the relationship of trust: if God wanted to save His Temple, He had to save them to do it. But the true temple of God is in man's heart, as Jeremiah had tried hard to teach. So the armies of Nebuchadnezzar ravished Judah, leading thousands of Jews into slavery in Babylon, and razing the Temple to the ground. "How doth the city sit solitary, that was so full of people! How is she become as a widow, she that was great among the nations," cried Jeremiah (Lam. 1:1).

Knowing God yields science

It's fascinating to note what the God of Israel is *not.* He is not one god among many. He is not a god tied to a particular city or even culture (the prophets will see God, not Israel, as the ruler of all peoples). He is not a god of nature. He is not personified more than is necessary to make sense of his deeds to a half-barbarous people. We hear nothing of any amours or private life. He decides, but we never stumble upon him worrying, pondering, or reasoning with himself. His right arm is strong to save, but we never hear of his bending it, or cracking his knuckles. He does not move from place to place, like Hermes delivering messages from snowy Olympus. He forbids his people to carve any images of him, lest they confuse him with the power-broking kings around them, or with the beasts. The people are informed not that he looks like them (only with curly locks and a perfect torso), but that *they* resemble *Him.* He has made them in *His image and likeness,* and that cannot be a physically imaginable resemblance.

Who is this God? The revelation strikes like a thunderbolt. He is the God Who Is, beyond specification. He's not simply a maker, a muddler of slush and soil, who takes some always-existing stuff and molds it into trees and birds and people. He *creates*, because he wills it. Recall the scene in the Sinai, when Moses approaches the burning bush that is not consumed (Ex. 3). When God speaks to him from that bush, Moses asks him his name, something understandable, something to define or limit. The reply shatters expectations: "Tell them that I AM WHO AM sent you." God does not say "I am the God of fire," or "I am the God of the mountaintop," or "I am the God of the sea." He says, "I am the God who essentially *is.*" To put it in philosophical terms, as later Jewish and Christian thinkers would do, God is Being itself. The Jewish translators of the Septuagint (the Old Testament rendered into Greek in the second century BC) struggled with the name that transcends names. *Ho on,* they rendered it, *The Being,* the One whose nature it is *to be,* and in whom all things that exist have their being.

Now this revelation made all the difference in the world. It allowed the Jews and Christians to view creation as God's handiwork, while holding him infinitely superior to that creation. Because there is nothing more fundamental than Being, it taught them that God is the maker of laws both moral and natural, who need not submit to some overarching Fate.

It may needle the intellectual elites, but it is historically unassailable: by showing that the universe was ordered and not arbitrary, the God who revealed Himself to Abraham—the same God worshipped by Christians—cleared our way for the farthest reaches of pure science. Yet since God is a Person and not a force, a Being who loves, and not a bundle of physical laws, the Jews and Christians could never look upon that ordered world as distant and amoral. The revelation opened their imaginations to a God whose very limitlessness allows him to be intimately present everywhere, at all times, embraced by all things, working mysteriously in all lives. Their insight into that immanence in turn helped them to bridge the chasm between the particular and the universal, this man and mankind, this moment and all of history. And the revelation was, as Christians believe, made flesh in the person of Jesus, and dwelt among us.

Which leads us to several politically incorrect considerations, as we shall see.

They that humble themselves shall be exalted

"Empower yourself!" say the voices of the World, because the World bows down before power and scorns the weak. The Hebrews would have done so too, if they'd had their history and worship all their own way. But God consistently reveals that He is no idol tangled up with human authority. Rather He shows that man is most Godlike when most humble; for God "humbled" himself, for love, to create a universe he did not need.

So He makes Adam and Eve in His image and likeness: they are *already* like God, divine in their intelligence and their dominion over the physical world. They would remain in God's favor, would remain most like God, if they would remember to acknowledge gratefully that He is God and they are not. When they eat of the forbidden fruit, violating the minimal condition of their vast and kingly freedom, they not only seek to be gods; they mistake what true divinity is. They seek to be not like God, but like god, like man's petty imagination of what a god is: a being who does as he pleases, and makes everyone else do as he pleases, too. They do not humble themselves. They humiliate themselves; they sever themselves from the giver of life, and subject themselves to death, whose greatest terror is nothing other than the emptiness of separation and alienation. But God (not god!) has mercy upon them. He utters a mysterious promise of redemption and clothes them with skins to protect them against the cold.

That is the fundamental narrative of Scripture: weakling man falls in envy of what he mistakes for power, and God the almighty saves him through those whose strength man has overlooked.

God accepts the sacrifice of the younger brother Abel, who offered his lamb with a full heart, but rejects the sacrifice of the brooding, envious Cain. It is from the younger and weaker twin Jacob, not the hunter Esau, that God will raise a great nation, and their old father Isaac, blind in more ways than one, cannot see it. That same Jacob will rouse envy among his sons when he favors the young dreamer Joseph. They throw their brother down a well and sell him into slavery. But from the slave Joseph will come their deliverance when, years later, they must travel to Egypt to barter for grain during a famine. God will choose Moses to deliver His people from bondage, a man in exile from Egypt for homicide. Moses, a

PC Myth: Jesus Was Homeless

Just as the Devil uses scripture for his purposes, liberal presidential candidates use Baby Jesus to justify their big-government programs. Only they're not always scripturally sound.

This is the time of year, as Hillary Rodham Clinton once put it, when Christians celebrate "the birth of a homeless child"—or, in Al Gore's words, "a homeless woman gave birth to a homeless child."

Just for the record, Jesus wasn't "homeless." He had a perfectly nice home back in Nazareth. But he happened to be born in Bethlehem. It was census time, and Joseph was obliged to schlep halfway across the country to register in the town of his birth. Which is such an absurdly bureaucratic overregulatory cockamamie Big Government nightmare that it's surely only a matter of time before Massachusetts or California reintroduce it.

But the point is: The Christmas story isn't about affordable housing.

Mark Steyn, "Children? Not if you love the planet," Orange County Register, December 14, 2007

stutterer, pleads at first that someone else be sent. Yet this same Moses will be hailed as the greatest of the prophets.

The Lord sends Samuel to anoint one of Jesse's sons as the next king of Israel. The seven eldest troop before him, but on none of them does the Lord's favor rest:

> But the LORD said unto Samuel, Look not on his countenance, or on the height of his stature; because I have refused him: for the LORD seeth not as man seeth; for man looketh on the outward appearance, but the LORD looketh on the heart. (1 Sam. 16:7)

Finally Samuel asks Jesse if that is all the sons he has. Jesse replies, almost as an afterthought, that he does have one more, a mere lad tending the sheep. So David comes forth, ruddy and handsome, and Samuel anoints him. Not that everybody took that anointing seriously. After all, the king Saul was still alive and crowned. And when Saul led his armies against the Philistines and their great warrior Goliath, none of the Israelites dared to take the giant on. But David, still too skinny to wear armor—with his brothers grumbling and wishing he were back home—steps forth with nothing but a sling, some smooth pebbles from the brook, and his boyish and bold faith in God. Those prove to be enough.

God's favor rests with the lonesome Elijah, a mountaineer of a prophet, inveighing against the citified fertility cults of Baal, practiced by King Ahab and his consort Jezebel and everyone who is anyone. He chooses Amos, a dresser of sycamore trees, to march before the King and the wealthy brokers at the Temple and announce that the Lord does not desire holocausts, but rather justice and mercy, and compassion towards the poor. A Homeric hero might "buy" the favor of a god by promising some great roasted heifer, and a sleek marble temple, and a gilded statue, but God hates such things. He is not the plaything of the powerful. "All our righteousnesses," cries the prophet Isaiah, "are as filthy rags," that is, as *menstrual* rags, made unclean by our weakness; "and our iniquities, like the wind, have taken us away" (64:6).

Instead, God's true servant will give himself utterly, for God and for others. He will be despised by the world; they will reckon him of no account; they will abuse him, will seek his life: "He is brought as a sheep to the slaughter" (Is. 53:7). He will cry, "My God, my God, why hast thou forsaken me?" (Ps. 22:1), yet God will not "suffer [His] Holy One to see corruption" (Ps. 16:10). For "the stone which the builders refused is become the head stone of the corner" (Ps. 118:22), and though young men may faint and warriors fall, "they that wait upon the LORD shall renew their strength; they shall mount up with wings as eagles" (Is. 40:31), because before the Lord even the great nations, the bustlers, the almighty oppressors of this world, are "as a drop of a bucket" (Is. 40:15).

Let not the cynical secularist attribute this marvelous *realism*, this refusal to bow before political greatness, to the envy of a weakling people. Weaklings too strut and boast. But the Jews, in their own chronicles of Judah (ignoring the schismatic northern kingdom of Israel, whose rulers were beneath their notice), sum up the doings of some of their mightiest kings thus:

> "And [Rehoboam] did evil, because he prepared not his heart
> to seek the LORD" (2 Chr. 12:14).
>
> "And [Jehoram] wrought that which was evil in the eyes of
> the LORD" (2 Chr. 21:6).
>
> "[Ahaziah] also walked in the ways of the house of Ahab:
> for his mother was his counsellor to do wickedly. Wherefore
> he did evil in the sight of the LORD" (2 Chr. 22:3–4).

Even the great Manasseh, who reigned for fifty-five years, no small accomplishment in a nation of intrigues and assassinations, is evaluated not according to worldly glory or leading economic indicators or political skill, but according to a standard that both judges the world and transcends the world: "But [Manasseh] did that which was evil in the sight of the LORD, like unto the abominations of the heathen, whom the LORD had cast out before the children of Israel" (2 Chr. 33:2).

The true heroes of the Old Testament reveal to us who are the true heroes of the world, if the world had eyes to see, and was not dazzled by the glare of an Alexander or a Hannibal. They are the young Gideon, who with a tiny army hurls the great Midianite force into confusion. Or Shadrach, Meshach, and Abednego, tossed into the fiery furnace by the envious courtiers of the Babylonian king Nebuchadnezzar, yet saved from harm by the power of God. Their calm defiance of the king should ring out as a motto for all men who still seek to resist the might of a smothering State:

> "Our God whom we serve is able to deliver us from the burning fiery furnace, and he will deliver us out of thine hand, O king.
>
> "But if not, be it known unto thee, O king, that we will not serve thy gods, nor worship the golden image which thou hast set up." (Dan. 3:17–18)

Philosophy and Faith

God replied, "First tell them that I am He Who is, that they may learn the difference between what is and what is not, and also the further lesson that no name at all can properly be used of Me, to Whom alone existence belongs."

Philo Judaeus, *On the Life of Moses* (1.75)

Philo was an Alexandrian Jew learned in Greek philosophy, particularly Platonism. He's defending his Jewish faith *not in opposition* to the Greek use of reason, but in concord with it, seeing it as fulfilling the Greek quest to know the ultimate reality. Here he sees and elaborates upon the proposition that eluded the grasp of Plato and Aristotle. God is not merely supreme among beings; he *is Being*.

Or Jonah, unlikely and unwilling prophet, finally doing his job, preaching impending doom to the heathen Ninevites, who repent, from their king down to the meanest hired hand. Of those lowly people, as foolish in matters of good and evil as their own beasts are, the Lord has care: "And should not I spare Nineveh, that great city, wherein are more than sixscore thousand persons that cannot discern between their right hand and their left hand, and also much cattle?" (Jon. 4:11).

A thousand years are as a day

"Salvation is of the Jews," said Jesus to the Samarian woman at the well (Jn. 4:22), revealing in a play on his name his mission to all mankind (Hebrew *yeshu'ah* = salvation), and identifying that mission as fulfilling the role of the Jews in the history of man. I have said that we would never expect such a role to be played by so lowly a people, we who are impressed by raw power. More than that. The deep assumption lying within Christ's words is that there is such a thing as salvation, meaning that God is the Lord of time, who works within time, but is not bound to time. It is He, not blind fate, who writes the narrative of the world, and of each man's life, and of the glory to come.

This salvation is not the same as what other theological systems offer; and the difference is crucial for understanding the West. Let's see why by comparing it with a few of the contemporary competitors.

I am a world-weary Roman citizen living in Greece in the second century AD. I might assuage my fear of death by turning to one of the renowned *mystery religions*—for instance, that of Demeter at Eleusis.[4] The idea behind a mystery religion, as also behind the Gnostic heresy (a New Age cult of old), is that you can wangle immortality by becoming a member of a cabal.[5] If you follow certain rules (sometimes requiring ritual sex with priestesses, or beatings), then you can advance in the mysteries, gaining more and more "knowledge" hidden from the fools outside. Even the noblest of pagan moral philosophies, for instance the Stoicism of the gruff slave Epictetus, or the world-denial of the Buddha, promise enlightenment only to those who undergo the spiritual regimen. The rest of the world is left to its folly.

In other words, "salvation," such as it is, is available to this person or that, but is never meant to reach everyone. Epictetus, an immensely appealing teacher, does preach the brotherhood of man, but when it comes to that movement of the heart out towards the unenlightened, the best he offers is a little patient instruction and pity; the worst, indifference:

> What then, ought we to publish these things to all men? No, but we ought to accommodate ourselves to the ignorant [Greek *tois idiotois,* literally, those fools wrapped up in themselves] and to say: "This man recommends to me that which he thinks good for himself. I excuse him." (*Discourses*, 1.29)

In the Old Testament, by contrast, we have vigorous prayers for victory over Israel's hated enemies, alongside mystical visions of the coming together of all the nations at God's holy mountain: "I will also give thee for a light to the Gentiles, that thou mayest be my salvation unto the ends of the earth" (Is. 49:6). Nor is there a hint that some people, for instance women and children, cannot scale the heights of salvation. Everyone, after all, is poor before the Lord. Hence the West's fascination with the weak who prove strong, with the least who overcome the mighty: Joan of Arc, the barefoot soldiers at Valley Forge, the little boy commenting on the nakedness of the emperor, the child with the crutch and iron brace whose goodness batters the heart of a miser named Scrooge, working man Rocky Balboa's fight against the Champ. The Jews have graven for us the templates of our moral imaginations.

The salvation on offer from the pagans is also strangely detached from time. Stoicism, with all its noble insistence upon duty and resignation, never shows us where that duty takes the world. If you are intelligent and severe enough, you can be as wise as the Stoic emperor Marcus Aurelius, beholding the vain spectacle of human life before him, not moved to love it, nor to envy it, but to do right by it, no matter what others do or say. But to what end? The Stoics believed in a providential Mind governing all things, but if that Mind had a goal for the world, man could never know what it was.

But God's promises, in the Old and New Testaments, stretch not only to the future but to the consummation of the world. That world is *going somewhere.* All nations shall worship the Lord, says Isaiah, prophesying the peaceable kingdom of the Messiah to come, and "the wolf also shall dwell with the lamb, and the leopard shall lie down with the kid" (Is. 11:6). In those days, says Jeremiah, God will replace our hearts of stone with hearts of flesh: "I will put my law in their inward hearts; and will be their God, and they shall be my people" (Jer. 31:33). An army will arise from the dry bones of the dead in the Valley of Jehosophat (Ez. 37). "Behold," says the One seated upon the throne, "I make all things new" (Rev. 21:5).

Yet although time is an instrument of God's plan, He forbids the Hebrews to observe "times and seasons" (Lev. 19:26), or to worship the zodiac, as their weather-predicting Chaldean neighbors did (cf. 2 K. 21:3–5). God is not a deity confined to the cyclical patterns of nature. He is not the Phoenician Thammuz, slain every fall only to be reborn for his beloved Astarte in the spring.[6] And precisely because God is not a nature God, he is not a God bound to time. Other gods may be established elsewhere to justify how we came to be where we are, and where we (that is, we the powerful) are going to stay. Legends of Romulus, apotheosized after his death, "justify" Roman preeminence, and legends of Osiris "justify" the hegemony of the Pharaohs, but never do they imply that the whole people, indeed the whole world, is going somewhere, is going to be redeemed. All the development happens in the legendary past, and ends with the powers that be. But in Israel, the development is mainly in the future, and is a threat to the powers that be.

The typical human view of history was that it is cyclical, or static. It has no arrow to it, no goal. The Scriptures change all that. It is indeed one of the defining features of the Western mind, this notion that we are on a journey, all of us, to a place that is sweeter and happier than what we know now. Even people who have lost their faith in God retain, sentimentally, the notion that man's history is not cyclical, not static, not random, but a real story, with meaningful events, great discoveries, influential minds, and "salvation" in some secular Land of Rest to come.

It's the old Jewish faith in a God who molds man's history, but without God, and without the hope to "dwell in the house of the LORD for ever" (Ps. 23:6). So feminism is supposedly an advance in human relations, a wash of secular grace along our path to the peace of being neuter. Or the religion of environmentalism comes as a chic hobo Christianity, with Earth as mother, consumers as sinners, global warming as hell, and recycling or organic farming or mass sterilization as the Savior who will lead us all to harmony on earth. Marxism is incomprehensible without the view of time and history revealed in Scripture. Even Darwin, under the influence of this vision of things that unfold to their appointed fulfillment, slid from talking about how species developed to the vaster and less clearly established "evolution"—a word he did not at first like and seldom used, as it suggested the unwrapping of a finished state that had lain hidden long before.

Jesus of Nazareth, King of the Jews

Let me be frank. I'm a Roman Catholic, and I believe that Jesus Christ was the promised Messiah, the Son of God.

But as far as the history of Western civilization is concerned, my belief is neither here nor there. Nor is that of an atheist, a Buddhist, or anybody else. The fact is that a Jewish carpenter named Jesus, who came from

Nazareth and preached for a few years before he was crucified by the Roman authorities, is the most influential man in the history of the world.

I know I must derogate from my faith, to talk about Christ as I would talk about Cicero or Pericles. There's no help for it, though; we must examine what Jesus has meant for all men, even those who do not believe.

Most important: Jesus sums up in his person and his preaching one universal yet often latent feature of the Old Testament and the history of the Jews. That is the primacy of love. When the scribe asks which is the greatest of the commandments, Jesus appeals not to the requirements of the natural law as codified in the Decalogue, but to the heart of the matter: "Thou shalt love the Lord thy God with all thy heart, and with all thy soul, and with all thy mind, and with all thy strength: this is the first commandment. And the second is like, namely this, Thou shalt love thy neighbor as thyself" (Mk. 12:30-31). For "on these two commandments hang all the law and the prophets" (Matt. 22:40).

It isn't an isolated episode. One day Jesus is dining at the house of Simon, a leading Pharisee and therefore learned in the law of Moses. A woman suddenly enters with an alabaster box of ointment. She anoints Jesus' head, and then falls to his feet to wash them with her tears and dry them with her hair. The scene would be scandalous even for us today, who manage to be licentious and self-righteous at the same time. Simon and his friends think that Jesus can be no prophet, or he would know what kind of sinful woman, possibly a whore, knelt at his feet. But Jesus shows his oneness with the Father, the God of Love, precisely by knowing full well

Make a Feminist Cringe

PIG

"Your wife will be like a fruitful vine within your house; your sons will be like olive shoots round your table."

Psalm 128:3

what kind of woman she is, and what kinds of men have condemned her in their hearts. He turns to Simon:

> "Seest thou this woman? I entered into thine house, thou gavest me no water for my feet: but she hath washed my feet with tears, and wiped them with the hairs of her head.
>
> "Thou gavest me no kiss: but this woman since the time I came in hath not ceased to kiss my feet.
>
> "My head with oil thou didst not anoint: but this woman hath anointed my feet with ointment.
>
> "Wherefore I say unto thee, Her sins, which are many, are forgiven; for she loved much." (Lk. 7:44–47)

A Book You're Not Supposed to Read

The Bible

"This is my commandment," He says to his apostles on the eve of his arrest and death, "That ye love one another, as I have loved you," meaning by love no mere sentiment, but the gift of self, for "greater love hath no man than this, that a man lay down his life for his friends" (Jn. 15:12–13). Hirelings work for their own advantage, and will abandon the sheep when the wolves come, but "I am the good shepherd," says Jesus, and "the good shepherd giveth his life for the sheep" (Jn. 10:11–12). That should help us understand how revolutionary is the love he demands of his followers. When, after the resurrection, Jesus turns to Simon Peter, the man who had denied him three times, and asks, three times, "Simon, son of Jonas, lovest thou me?" (Jn. 21:16), Peter knows he is being asked not about liking or compatibility of temperament, but about the most profound act of giving that a man can make, a love unto death. "Lord," says Peter, "thou knowest all things; thou knowest that I love thee." Whereupon Jesus commands him, "Feed my sheep," and foretells Peter's crucifixion, the death he would endure for the sheep, to glorify God (21:17–19).

Consider what *love* means, for the pagan cultures of that day, and for our pagan culture now. The materialist poet Lucretius (99–55 BC) describes it as a hunger, usually for something vain; not simply the nude body of the beloved, but a delusive image of that body. Nor are lovers satisfied when they have done the deed, for

> . . . the same madness returns, and the fury too:
> They long to attain they don't know what, and can't
> Find any trick to master this disease. (*On the Nature of Things,*
> 4.1108–10)

Cato the Elder, the stern moralist of the last days of the Roman republic, scoffed at a young man in love, advising him to go to the whorehouse instead. Knock one nail out with another, said Cato.[7]

Plato is the great philosopher of love; but for him too love is essentially *eros*, a hunger for what one does not have. It is exuberant and rich, born of Plenty, but also needy and beggarly, born of Poverty (*Symposium,* 203b–c). I'm not saying that Romans and Greeks did not love. They loved their children (those whom they did not expose at infancy). The usually self-important Cicero was crushed by the death of his beloved fourteen-year-old daughter Tullia.[8] If popular poetry and epitaphs and letters are evidence, they loved their spouses, too. Friendship was highly esteemed, a stronger part of a man's emotional and civic life than it is now: we can hardly imagine a scene like the gathering of friends about the bed of Socrates on the day of his death, with a young man named Plato so moved by it that it became the pivotal moment in his life. But there was no identification of God with love. The idea that God *could love* would suggest that He needed something. Therefore there was only a dim notion that the love we are called to show—feelings here are beside the point—must apply to all men, everywhere. Jesus, as the King of the Jews, revolutionized what the very idea of loving must mean.

How so? A Zeus might "love," might be overcome with sexual desire; but Plato derides these stories as unworthy of a god (*Republic* 3.390b–c). Then if God essentially loves, it cannot be like Zeus' lust for Hera, or the craving that Lucretius suspects will ruin your life. Love is what God *does*: He creates, He gives bountifully, He is of infinite patience, He redeems, He empties Himself and puts Himself at his enemies' service: "For God so loved the world, that he gave his only begotten Son, that whosoever believeth in him should not perish, but have everlasting life" (Jn. 3:16). Then if we would love God we must love those whom God loves. We cannot retreat into the cell of a mystery cult, ignoring our grumbling neighbors. To be like God is, more than anything else, to love as God loves. So Jesus instructs his followers in that most realistic prayer of love for God and man: "Forgive us our sins; for we also forgive every one that is indebted to us"

Individual Dignity Comes from God

Deism, or the Principles of Natural Worship, are onely the faint remnants or dying flames of reveal'd Religion in the posterity of *Noah*…Our Modern Philosophers, nay and some of our Philosophising Divines have too much exalted the faculties of our Souls, when they have maintain'd that by their force, mankind has been able to find out that there is one Supream Agent or Intellectual Being which we call God.

From **John Dryden**, Preface to "Religio Laici"

Dryden turns instead, in humility, to divine Revelation and the teachings of the Church, handed down through the centuries (he would convert to Roman Catholicism three years later, in 1685). He may be wrong about the weakness of human reason, but he is surely right about Deism, which was no great intellectual discovery, but a pale and incoherent shadow of Christianity. Much the same sort of specter haunts the politically correct, who airily talk about "rights," without troubling to note that their belief in the dignity of each human person—if they still do believe in that dignity—derives its life from Judaism and Christianity.

(Lk. 11:1). For the first time in the history of the world, God is proclaimed as love, to be loved, and to be loved also by loving others.

So important is the distinction that the writers of the New Testament cannot use the Greek word *eros* to describe this love. They use *agape*: and reveal a most fruitful field for western thought and art. If *eros* and *agape* are not the same, and if true love makes the soul most like the loving God, what place does *eros* assume in a good life? How can that desire be well-directed? It is the subject of Dante's *La Vita Nuova,* Petrarch's *Canzoniere,* the sonnet sequences of Spenser, Sidney, and Shakespeare, Titian's *Sacred and Profane Love,* Caravaggio's *Mary Magdalene,* Fielding's *Tom Jones,* Graham Greene's *The End of the Affair,* and Evelyn Waugh's *Brideshead Revisited.* It's impossible to imagine Western artistic and intellectual development *without* the problem of the right ordering of human loves.

There's more. It is not just that *agape* is different from and nobler than *eros*. It embraces *eros*, perfects it, and still inverts what most people think love must be. Consider the act that, for Christians, consummates Jesus' life of love: his willing death upon the ignominious cross. Saint Paul sings about it:

> Let this mind be in you, which was also in Christ Jesus:
>
> Who, being in the form of God, thought it not robbery to be equal with God:
>
> But made himself of no reputation, and took upon him the form of a servant, and was made in the likeness of men:
>
> And being found in fashion as a man, he humbled himself, and became obedient unto death, even the death of the Cross. (Phil. 2:5–8)

Love, then, does not grasp, but flings away. If in man love is needy, what it most needs is to be absolutely poor, absolutely *for* the beloved. Then only do we begin to live abundantly. That is the meaning of the true

Christian life: "Whosoever will save his life shall lose it; but whosoever shall lose his life for my sake and the gospel's, the same shall save it" (Mk. 8:35).

The West will be infected by this high vision of love, which links utter divinity with utter humility. If only the infection were ten times as virulent! But even in the best of times it is a hard lesson to learn, and most times are not great. Still, consider to what it leads: look at the new heroes of the West. We have a Saint Francis of Assisi who becomes the father of an army of barefoot friars preaching and living among the poor. He does it not by empowering himself, but by flinging power and luxury and privilege away, literally stripping his clothes off in the piazza of Assisi, disowning his merchant father before the father can disown him. Or we have a Father Damien lying about his health so that he can wangle a one-way passage to the leper colony at Molokai, a place of physical and moral squalor, where he will bring the gospel, and spiritual hope, and medicine and food. There he will die of the very disease to which he had ministered.

Or consider even the heroes of our popular art. In *The Man Who Shot Liberty Valance,* the bravest man is the sharpshooting John Wayne, but not because he can kill at fifty paces. It is because, in his submission to the good of the woman he loves, he gives her up, without a word of reproach, to a lesser man who did not shoot the gunfighter, but who accepts the reputation for having shot him and parlays it into a career as a senator and a builder of his western state. At the opening of the movie, Wayne's character is lying in a bare pine box, without so much as a pair of boots, and with no one to mourn his passing but a loyal Negro servant and one or two old friends. A Christ, taken down from the Cross.

We understand such love now, or we think we do. Whatever we believe, we must come to terms with that love, as little sense as it makes to all who prattle about power and the fulfillment of desire.

The peace of God that passeth understanding

Do not suppose that this vision of love leaves the West dour and self-abnegating. The puritan we will always have among us; and if you want the essential killjoy of our day, he will be easy to find in the garb of a secular spy, afraid that someone somewhere might be singing a hymn. Jesus did not say, after all, that we must lose our lives. He said that we will gain life by that loss, gain true life by the giving: "I am come that they might have life, and that they might have it more abundantly" (Jn. 10:10). The message of the Scriptures blows the lid off the universe: we are not cramped by a blind Fate, not hemmed in by the determinism of matter, not forced to walk the endless toils of human sin and sorrow.

"Be of good cheer," Jesus says at the Last Supper, "I have overcome the world" (Jn. 16:33). It is impossible to underestimate the force of this declaration, which is in accord with God's saving acts throughout Jewish history. The prophets all testify to this high hope. It is not a world that seeks our destruction, but a world created and sustained and to be redeemed by God, who desires not slaves but sons (cf. Gal. 4:7), and who has made us "a little lower than the angels" (Ps. 8:5). That confidence in a fundamentally good world governed by a God of love means that we can stride forth in time, knowing that the end is not dissolution. It has given man hope, and that hope has allowed him both to wonder, and to achieve wonders.

No man is an Oedipus now. No man is accursed. The blood on our hands may be washed clean; the scandal of our sins may be turned to rejoicing. Such reversals too are at the heart of the western imagination. For Saint Paul was a persecutor of the Church, standing by while the innocent were murdered, yet he was caught by the Lord, and came to preach of the peace that passes understanding. No peoples are accursed or beneath our notice. All boundaries of race and culture have been overleapt: so Boniface ventures among the tree-worshipping Germans, to hew down their totem and show them rather the true tree of life, the Cross, the tree of love. He brought thousands to the faith, and laid down his life as a martyr along the Rhine. Even the southern slaveholders, bowing to the better angels of their nature, had to preach the gospel to their slaves, and had to concede that in Christ there was neither slave nor free. It was that gospel above all that inspired the black man with a view of his own dignity, and of the prospect of liberty.

The West then considers the world—thanks to the Jews, and to the person of Christ, and to the preaching of his church—to be comic, not tragic, possessed of limitless possibilities. Dante ends each of the great divisions of his *Divine Comedy* with the word "stars," not because he was so naïve as to think that man would dwell upon those points of light, but because the stars are the clearest emblem of human destination, in the loving providence of God. Not Olympus, not Rome, not an estate in California, but *somewhere else*, a place which is beyond all human reckoning and is therefore most fit for man. It is a credit to this Christian vision that even when the West goes terribly wrong, it only substitutes an invented Christ for the true, an imagined realm of eternal love and truth and beauty for the life of God, which is heaven. So did the Marxists, longing for the dictatorship of the proletariat. So do the feminists, longing for an impossible androgyny. So do our militant atheists, dreaming of a ghoulish trans-human world of man-machine hybrids, everlasting.

They cannot escape the shadow of the Cross.

Chapter Four

THE EARLY CHURCH: CHARITY
AND TOLERANCE ARE BORN

Your name is Dionysius. You're a well-off youth in Athens, a city that long ago governed itself, but then fell to the imperial bureaucrats of Philip of Macedon, and now suffers the tax collectors and proconsuls of Rome. Your language boasts the finest poetry known to man, but that too was composed a long time ago. The epic poets have given way to editors and scholars, a sure sign of cultural decay. Your writers now have neither the mind nor the heart for such soaring flights of fancy. They cannot sustain the necessary reverence. They write witty drinking songs, or finely crafted epitaphs, or small bursts of creative obscenity:

> Euagoras is made of brass;
> he doesn't need disguises:
> he does them with no change of shape,
> both sexes and all sizes.
> (Antipater of Thessalonika, 48 BC–32 AD)[1]

Olympus is a cold and empty mountain peak. You can tell a farmer from one of your friends in the city by whether he can say, "Zeus, father of gods and men" without a smirk. You suspect that there may be gods, but they never turned themselves into bulls or swans to ravish pretty girls, or

Guess What?

- Europe's glories were created by the church.

- Christianity brought to the world the virtues of tolerance and charity.

- Christianity would have perished if the heresies had not been stamped out.

97

boys. You're fascinated and appalled by some of the strange airs blowing from the east. You know a lad who follows the Great Mother goddess. It was no surprise. He hung around the gymnasion, naked with all the other boys, but not to hurl the javelin—*that* sport is not taken so seriously anymore. Then one night he went to the woods with the worshippers of the Mother for a drunken orgy, and came back bleeding between the legs. No need for him to worry about marriage now.[2]

Your philosophies, too, are shrunken. No one since Plato and Aristotle has attempted to incorporate into a coherent system all the questions, moral and cosmological and theological and political, that man can ask. They have snatched at shreds and patches. Maybe when the memory of a free city finally faded, the heart went out of your wise men, too. They advise their disciples, in a sad and kindly way, what to do with the diminished thing called life. Some follow Epicurus, and shirk civic involvement altogether, living for the modest pleasures of mind and body. They buy a house in the countryside, read a little, eat and drink temperately, avoid marriage and the irritation of childrearing, and have pleasant conversations about the meaninglessness of the world, the negligence of the gods, and the inevitability of death. Others, believing that Epicurus did not draw the full conclusion from his materialism and agnosticism, laugh at such temperance. Better to follow Aristippus, and cram as much debauchery as possible into these short days, till death do swallow us up. A nobler group, the Stoics, recommend courageous resignation to fate, which they call providence, although it is impersonal and inflexible: "We must make the best of those things that are in our power, and take the rest as nature gives it" (Epictetus, *Discourses*, 1.1).

The Academy founded by Plato still exists. Its adherents have turned the restless questioning of Socrates in upon itself. Socrates once sought truth, showing the smug that they didn't know what they were saying. Now he ends the search before it begins, insisting that he himself doesn't know what he is saying. Platonism, that potent force against the drag of materialism, has degenerated into the witticisms of the skeptic. Thus Archesilaus, asked whether he knew anything for certain, replied that he wasn't sure (Cicero, *Academici* 1.45). Some manners may be growing gentler as convictions fade—slaves are better treated—but it is hollow. The best of your moralists to come, a Tacitus or a Juvenal, will inveigh against the degeneracy, but will have nothing to offer as an alternative but a sentimental glance at the pieties of forefathers long forgotten.

You literally have *nothing to do.* Your whole civilization, Greek and Roman, seems perched at the pinnacle of its grandeur, yet from now till its fall in the West in 476, it will produce no great new ideas. Its art will be derivative, copying the works of old, or monstrous, turning emperors into colossi. It bustles with merchandise, and is dead.

So you, Dionysius, accompany your friends one day to the Hill of Mars, on the Athenian Acropolis, to listen to the day's run of madmen, "for all the Athenians and strangers which were there spent their time in nothing else, but either to tell, or to hear some new thing" (Acts 17:21). No quest for truth, but a listless search for novelty, to rouse the sluggish mind. Today's speaker is but a small swarthy man, a tentmaker with a wheezy voice.

You don't know it, but here, now, a new world overcomes the old. For that man, Paul or Saul or something, uses the shards of your culture to reveal what fulfills it and conquers it at once. He was on the road to the Acropolis, he says, looking at the temples, when

> I found an altar with this inscription: TO THE UNKNOWN
> GOD. Whom therefore ye ignorantly worship, him declare I
> unto you.
>
> God that made the world and all things therein, seeing that
> he is Lord of heaven and earth, dwelleth not in temples made
> with hands;

> Neither is worshipped with men's hands, as though he
> needed any thing, seeing he giveth to all life, and breath, and
> all things;
>
> And hath made of one blood all nations of men for to dwell
> on all the face of the earth, and hath determined the times
> before appointed, and the bounds of their habitation;
>
> That they should seek the LORD, if haply they might feel
> after him, and find him, though he be not far from every one
> of us;
>
> For in him we live, and move, and have our being; as cer-
> tain also of your own poets have said, 'For we are also his off-
> spring.'" (Acts 17:23–28)

Now this is something. The man knows Greek poetry, and sees in it a glimmer of the truth he preaches. The man lives in the empire, yet asserts that in the beginning, before all empires, God had made "of one blood" all nations. The man feels the fluttering pulse of pagan religion: he preaches what the heart had longed for but could never hope, that God might "be not far from every one of us."

Then he delivers the blow from which the world has not recovered:

> [God] hath appointed a day, in the which he will judge the
> world in righteousness by that man whom he hath ordained;
> whereof he hath given assurance unto all men, *in that he hath*
> *raised him from the dead.* (17:31; emphasis mine)

"But the dead don't rise again!" the audience scoffs. Precisely, replies the speaker. "And the flesh?" they laugh. "The soul perhaps, but the flesh?"

They leave for food and drink. You, Dionysius, stay to hear more. You will one day be honored as Saint Dionysius. A nation called France, named after the Franks stirring beyond the Alps and the Rhine, will con-fuse you with another Dionysius and revere you as their patron, Saint

Denis. Then a brilliant abbot will build a chapel in your honor, to flood the hearts of the worshipers with light.

You might, in your old age, have said that you too were raised from the dead on that day. So were Greece and Rome. It was a miracle, and all the more wondrous, in that it took centuries to accomplish.

How Christianity saved the West

God made the victory possible; so a Christian will say. But the Jewish Scriptures had been preparing for it all along. Typical is what Isaiah says of the glory of Zion: "And the Gentiles shall come to thy light, and kings to the brightness of thy rising" (Is. 60:3). Granted, the Law is rooted in the traditions of the Jews, their feasts, their dressings for the altar, and their regulations regarding purity. Yet there is in the Old Testament a wild crosscurrent threatening to burst the bonds of culture and spill out among

The Strength and Manliness of the Early Church

"I write to the Churches, and impress on them all, that I shall willingly die for God, unless you hinder me. I beseech of you not to show an unseasonable good-will towards me. Suffer me to become food for the wild beasts, through whose instrumentality it will be granted me to attain to God. I am the wheat of God, and let me be ground by the teeth of the wild beasts, that I may be found the pure bread of Christ. Rather entice the wild beasts, that they may become my tomb, and may leave nothing of my body; so that when I have fallen asleep [in death], I may be no trouble to any one. Then shall I truly be a disciple of Christ, when the world shall not see so much as my body. Entreat Christ for me, that by these instruments I may be found a sacrifice [to God]."

St. Ignatius of Antioch, from his letter to the Romans (4:6)

The early Christian martyrs are a fine contradiction to the modern notion that Christianity and moral conviction are reserved for effeminate men and hysterical women.

all peoples, making them *all* sons of Abraham. The mysterious Melchizedek, king of Salem, is a priest of the Lord, but he is not among Abraham's people (Gen. 14:17–20). Job the just sufferer dwells in Ur of the Chaldees. Many were the lepers in the days of Elisha the prophet, says Jesus, but only Naaman the Syrian did he heal (cf. 2 K. 5).

So far from being embedded in any one culture, God seems, if you'll forgive the jest, to shake free of it. He commands the Jews to burn holocausts, and then says through Isaiah that he has no delight in holocausts, but only in the sacrifice of a humble heart. He commands the males to be circumcised, then says through Jeremiah that such circumcision in itself has no significance. He requires the circumcision of the heart. He does *not* command the building of the great Temple of Solomon, the center of Jewish worship (whose master-builder comes from Phoenicia; cf. 2 Chr. 2:13). Centuries after the Babylonians have destroyed that Temple and the Jews under Zerubbabel have rebuilt it (Ezr. 3), Jesus would say, referring to himself as the true holy of holies, "Destroy this temple, and in three days I will raise it up" (Jn. 2:19). In his resurrection and in the preaching of his church, he carries the Temple everywhere. All nations shall come to Jerusalem, says the prophet, bringing "gold and incense; and they shall shew forth the praises of the Lord" (Is. 60:6). But Jerusalem too goes forth to all the nations, "for out of Zion shall go forth the law, and the word of the LORD from Jerusalem" (Is. 2:3).

In other words, there is in the Old Testament a seed of the mad notion that the Jews are the Chosen People not for themselves, but for everyone else. There can be only two ways for such a thing to be true. One, as in Islam, is to believe that the whole world will eventually accept circumcision and the laws of kosher and the passover meal and the Holy of Holies. That is, the religion is inextricable from the state and culture, and dominates the world by obliterating its human variety. That is the way of the world. Its inclination, as the last miserable century testifies, is to unite by reduction, to turn men into a manageable and homogeneous mass. It is political correctness on a global scale. Something of this falsely conservative tendency confronted the first generation of Christians. Must Gentile converts keep the dietary restrictions of the Jewish law? Must they keep the rules of ritual purity? Must the males be circumcised?

The answer of the Church, as reported by Luke in Acts and by Paul himself, is *no*. It is a stunning answer. Converts to Judaism, after all, signaled their conversion precisely by their adherence to the Jewish law. But Jesus proclaimed himself as the fulfillment of the Law, by his sacrificial death on the Cross, and his resurrection. Baptism replaces circumcision now and forever, by the commandment of the Lord (Matt. 28:19–20). That is not simply the substitution of one ritual for another, but a re-centering of law and worship upon the person of Jesus Christ. In baptism, the believer is united to Christ's death, that he may also rise with him again. It is the prime act of faith, transcending time and place and culture:

> Wherefore the law was our schoolmaster *to bring us* unto Christ, that we might be justified by faith.
>
> But after that faith is come, we are no longer under a schoolmaster.
>
> For ye are all the children of God by faith in Christ Jesus.
>
> For as many of you as have been baptized into Christ have put on Christ.
>
> There is neither Jew nor Greek, there is neither bond nor free, there is neither male nor female: for ye are all one in Christ Jesus.
>
> And if ye be Christ's, then are ye Abraham's seed, and heirs according to the promise.
>
> (Gal. 3:24–29)

There we have it, the second way. It had never before been imagined. It is broached by Paul, and would be made manifest in the experience of Christian evangelists over the centuries. It is to believe that each culture might be blessed by the Jews in its own way, becoming more truly itself in the bargain. It unites as it distinguishes—for Paul does *not* say what liberal Christians want him to say, that there will be only trivial differences between Greek and Jew, bond and free, man and woman. He means that in the baptism of Christ there is not one sacrament for a Greek and another for a Jew, one for a man and another for a woman. They are *one,* even as the distinct members of a body are one (cf. 1 Cor. 12:20). What worldly honor the Greek attached to his being Greek, is of no consequence in the baptism of Christ. What spiritual preference the Jewish man attached to his being Jewish and a man, is of no consequence in the baptism of Christ. That insight lay at the heart of the Christian mission to Greece and Rome and, eventually, the rest of the world.

Here we see a truth that the Left in America and Europe today find laughable. They ignore it at their peril. Their "tolerance" is based liter-

Christianity's Crime against the State: Mercy

Volusianus raised the objection that the preaching and teaching of Christ was in no way compatible with the duties and rights of citizens; for, to quote an instance frequently alleged, among its precepts there is found: "Do not repay injury with injury."...Now, it seems clear that such moral norms could not be put into practice without bringing ruin to a country...Would anyone, thenceforth, refuse to punish according to the laws of war the devastation of a Roman province?

Etienne Gilson, introduction to Augustine's *City of God*

The Christian Marcellinus, who begs Augustine to respond to these charges, confesses that "it is manifest that very great calamities have befallen the country under the government of emperors practising, for the most part, the Christian religion." He is referring principally to the weakling Honorius. We commonly hear that Christianity is aggressive and imperialist, but for most of its history, its detractors have decried it as otherworldly and passive. Can't win.

ally on emptiness: we tolerate because we are indifferent, because objective goodness and truth do not exist. Then the State enforces its will anyway. But the forbearance of a Christian is based upon the belief that all good things, including noble traditions and cultures, can be raised up and redeemed in Christ.

This openness is at the heart of Christ's preaching and life. When he departed from his disciples at Bethany, he instructed them to "teach all nations, baptizing them in the name of the Father, and of the Son, and of the Holy Ghost" (Matt. 28:19). He said nothing about making them all Greek, Roman, or Hebrew. This promised King of the Jews, after all, was no overlord with marauding armies. He arrived in Jerusalem not on a chariot but on a donkey, with some fishermen in tow. Many of his Jewish countrymen hoped he would help them throw off the yoke of their Roman overlords, and many others hoped he would try to do that and fail, so they might seek occasion against him.

But Jesus was set to break the yoke of a more sulfurous tyrant than the one in Rome. So when they asked him whether it was lawful to pay taxes to Caesar, he replied, "Render therefore unto Caesar the things which are Caesar's; and unto God the things that are God's," affirming a certain autonomy for temporal government, and making any genuine theocracy a violation of his teaching (Matt. 22:21). Note the irony here. The Left cries "Theocracy!" whenever men of faith have anything to say about how we are to live together. They thus hobble the Christian soldier, heap gold upon Caesar, and leave us vulnerable to the real theocrats amassing their forces, the armies of Mohammed.

Instead of enhancing the Jewish hopes for political independence, Jesus consistently appealed to the time before the Jews were a people at all. When he was asked when a man might lawfully divorce his wife (a hot topic at the time), Jesus cites the authority *behind* Moses, the lawgiver and the greatest of the prophets. Moses, he says, granted the people a concession for divorce, because of the hardness of their hearts,

> But from the beginning of the creation God made them male and female.
>
> For this cause shall a man leave his father and mother, and cleave to his wife;
>
> And they twain shall be one flesh: so then they are no more twain, but one flesh.
>
> What therefore God hath joined together, let not man put asunder. (Mk. 10:6–9)

Those who heard him understood his radical claim. "Verily, verily, I say unto you, Before Abraham was, *I AM*," said he (Jn. 8:58), uttering as his own the name of God that could only be spoken once a year, by the chief priest, in the Holy of Holies, within the Temple. He is Himself the Temple, then, and the Chief Priest, as He is one with the Father to whom He prays, for "when ye have lifted up the Son of man, then shall ye know that I am *he,* and that I do nothing of myself; but as my Father hath taught me, I speak these things" (Jn. 8:28).

Christianity brings equality and tolerance

Watch the eyes of a liberal when you tell him this: Christianity brought to the world our modern notion of "equality" (though in a wiser form than what is preached today).

Sometimes in the history of man one idea, well expressed and preached by people afire with zeal, makes all the difference. Consider the ringing cry, a garbled echo of Moses and Jesus and Paul, "All men are created equal." The affirmation that man is saved by Christ, in Christ, is such an idea. For most pagans, this made no sense. You were created chosen or not. For an atheist this makes no sense. In our material selves (our atoms, our genes, our muscles) we evidently are all different from birth. But Christianity affirms that in our dignity before the Lord, we are equal.

That faith is meant to leaven one's life; and in this way the new Christians are at one with their elder brothers, the Jews. But it is not a set of cultural rules. It is a relationship to the person of Christ, adaptable to all cultures, at all times, everywhere. It could be Jewish or Armenian, Ethiopian or Persian, Greek or Roman; and soon after Paul it would be all these. We now preach "tolerance," by which, as I've suggested, we mean two contradictory things: a refusal to distinguish between true and false and good and evil, and a supine submission to the politically correct rules of an intelligentsia. It is intolerance, with hair spray and a smile.

The first Christians, who endured periods of persecution and long ages of contempt, set upon by spies after their property or emperors after their blood, learned tolerance by living it. They dwelt among people who traded in slaves, exposed babies on the hillsides, seduced young boys, and made homicide into daily entertainment in the arena. And they brought them to the faith without making them a whit the less Roman or Greek, rather returning them to the noblest virtues of their own traditions.

For Christianity, rightly understood, fairly invents the virtue of tolerance, precisely because, as Saint Paul says, the Lord wants sons, not slaves. You could get along in the Roman Empire if you submitted to worshiping Rome and the Emperor. It didn't matter what you really thought, so long as you made that public act of submission. If you stand before a witness in Saudi Arabia and say, "There is no God but Allah, and Mohammed is his prophet," no one will probe too deeply into the corners of your heart. What lies there is of no consequence, so long as you go on to obey the law of the prophet. You are a submitter, a Muslim.

It's the same with contemporary political correctness. If you nod as someone says, "Women can make effective soldiers, just as men," it doesn't matter whether you know that your nephew riding the bench for his junior high football team could put a hurt on the typical Private Benjamin. What matters is your outward submission.

But you cannot be compelled to accept Christ, because that acceptance is an act of your will, an act of faith, hope, and love. Christians could not compel conversions any more than they could compel love. The notion makes no sense, and that is why they very rarely even made the mistaken attempt. They *evangelized:* literally, they brought the good news that man was not given up to sin and suffering and death.

The State, that pagan god

In part the Christians did this without any grand plan. They wanted to live their ordinary lives among their countrymen, in peace. But they had a problem. Their private meetings to celebrate the Eucharist and to hear the word of God were suspected. Roman emperors were always wary of "secret" groups, and for good reason, given the life expectancy of those who were elevated to that honor.

But long before the imperial chaos of the third century, the Christians were accused of heinous practices. They were thought to murder children and eat their flesh; that was an obvious pagan garbling of the Christian meal, when the faithful would partake of the Body and Blood of Christ.[3] So Pliny the Younger, an official of the generally wise emperor Trajan (98–117), writes to Rome to ask what to do about these pestilent people who will not worship the pagan gods or sacrifice to an image of the emperor. Pliny's tribute is all the more impressive in that he intends it as criticism:

> Those who deny that they are or ever have been Christian I have thought well to dismiss, so long as they would invoke our gods as I dictated the formula, and pray to your image, which I would have commanded to be brought in along with the statues of the gods, would pray with offerings of incense and wine, and then curse Christ—none of which things a true

Christian can ever be compelled to do, as I have been told. (*Letters*, 10.96)

Pliny cannot understand such "pertinacity," and believes it should be punished. Hubert Poteat observes tartly, "We may be reasonably sure that very few Romans, if threatened with the alternative of death, would have hesitated a moment to deny the whole Capitoline hierarchy"—the whole panoply of official gods, including those scarred, bloated, disease-raddled gods known as emperors.[4]

The Romans had long respected the integrity and ferocity of Jewish devotion to their sole God, though many thought it narrow-minded, even atheistic. But by the time the Christians came on the scene, the Roman

Love God, or Hate the World

We may chart the degeneration of the Christian belief in the goodness of the created world thus:

- The world is beautiful, because it was created by God (Augustine, Aquinas, Francis).
- The world is beautiful, and it happens to have been created by a God (the Deist Voltaire).
- The world is beautiful, but it was not created by God (the early Darwin).
- The world is not beautiful, and it was not created by God (the later Darwin).
- Because the world is not beautiful, it was not created by God (Richard Dawkins).

But the world is beautiful. Not only that, but intelligible, too, even that part of the world inhabited by slovenly modern atheists.

pantheon had been absorbed by the State. You could believe in any god you pleased, so long as you also bowed to the State gods. You could say, with a wink, "Ah yes, Jupiter, ravisher of women, a figment of rude imaginations," so long as you took part in the devotions to the Capitoline protector. The gods might or might not be real, but the State certainly was. So the Romans, who had breached the last-resort Jewish fortress of Masada in 73, were not going to encourage another outbreak of religion, which was then, as now, the single greatest threat to the omnipotence of the State.

That's how we should understand Roman persecutions of the Christians. They weren't a battle between Jupiter and Jehovah, but between two visions of the world. It was an episode in the constant battle, as Augustine put it later, between The City of Man, characterized by empire and lust for domination, and The City of God, characterized by *caritas*, selfless love, with plenty who thought they belonged to one army actually fighting for the other.[5]

What else can explain the persecutions, not characteristic of Roman governance? Not crimes. The Christians are agreeable citizens, Justin Martyr pleads to the good emperor Antoninus Pius.[6] They don't get drunk in public, they don't rob, they are forbidden to lie, they don't take vengeance against their enemies, they don't divorce a wife to steal their neighbor's. Nor do they expose their children to die. So Clement of Alexandria inveighs against that form of birth control for Roman matrons who prefer pets to babies: "They do not receive the orphan child; but they expose children that are born at home, and take up the young of birds, and prefer irrational to rational creatures" (*Paedogogus*, 3.4).

But the Christians threaten the self-conception of the Empire. They were dangerous not because they were disobedient, but because the God they obeyed, while commanding them to obey legitimate state authority, could brook no rival. The State could be *under* God, but it could not be *beside* God. The Romans, having lost a vital faith in the gods, turned to the State instead, and were in danger of losing both God and State. The Christians, with their vital faith in God, remained in the State that hated them, and saved it from its delusions. The pagans testify to the influence the Christians wielded by being good, far more than great or high. The Emperor Julian (r. 361–363), called the Apostate for his reversion to pagan Stoicism, in urging his fellow pagans to help him revive the glory of old Rome, complains that the Christians not only cared for one another when they were sick or poor but they also did a better job caring for the pagans than the pagans themselves did.[7]

If the Romans were suspicious of the Christians, the Christians too were divided on what to make of Roman ways. Many saw no reason to withdraw from Roman civic life. At the time of Marcus Aurelius, the philosopher and emperor who permitted a terrible persecution of Christians—wherein Saint Justin earned his honorific title as Martyr— many of the soldiers in the Roman legions were Christian. The African theologian Tertullian (c. 160–235) relates an account, probably ficti- tious, of a letter in which Marcus himself "testifies that the great drought in Germany was broken by rain obtained through the prayers of Christians, who, as it chanced, were among his soldiers" (*Apology,* 5.6). The point is not whether the miracle happened, but that it was uncontroversial for Tertullian to remark that Christians served in the Roman armies. The Christian loved his country too, and would fight to defend it against invaders.

But many Christians saw wisdom in isolation. The intellectuals divided according to whether they thought pagan learning was worth- while, or ought to be rejected altogether. Tertullian, in his fiery way, flung the most famous cry of scorn:

> What indeed has Athens to do with Jerusalem? What concord
> is there between the Academy and the Church? what between
> heretics and Christians? (*Against the Heresies,* ch. 7)

Faith and Reason

PIG

If the fathers thought of revealed truth as the more certain knowledge, the early Christian father, and [the Jewish philosopher] Philo before him, often made the important supplementary assumption that there is really only one truth, and properly conducted philosophy or human reason will also arrive at that truth.

Marshall Clagett,
Greek Science in Antiquity

Or will arrive at as much of the truth as it can, given the limits of reason and the matter under investigation. Clagett is not sympathetic to Christian theology, but he is an honest historian. Such confidence in reason will allow for the "virility of the Hellenistic tradition in the thirteenth century in mathematics, mechanics, and other subjects" (168). The Greek spirit of brave inquiry, central to the West's intellectual heritage, was *more* characteristic of the University of Paris in the days of Thomas Aquinas and Bonaventure than it is now, anywhere in America.

Saint Jerome, translator of the Latin or "Vulgate" Bible, was a classically trained writer and rhetorician. Perhaps he had a bad conscience about it, because he dreamed one night that Christ appeared to him to ask, sternly, "Are you a Ciceronian, or are you a Christian?"[8]

But Jerome continued to write in Ciceronian prose. And most Christians decided to take what the pagan culture offered, on the principle that God grants to all peoples some knowledge of the truth, as incomplete as that knowledge must be, and as distorted by bad customs and error. In this regard they did not break with the Scriptures or with Jewish practice. For Jews dwelling in Alexandria and elsewhere in the Greek-speaking world had, in the two centuries before Christ, become familiar with Greek philosophy, and used its terms, and sometimes its ideas, to illuminate their sacred writings. The Book of Wisdom (c. 150 BC), though profoundly Hebrew in its conception of a personal God who makes covenants with a chosen people, is indebted to Platonic and Pythagorean philosophy, even as it boldly claims to correct that philosophy, particularly by founding wisdom in a relationship with its Giver:

> For both we and our words are in
> his hand,

as are all understanding and skill in crafts.

For it is he who gave me unerring knowledge of what exists,

to know the structure of the world and the activity of the elements;

the beginning and end and middle of times,

the alternations of the solstices and the changes of the seasons,

the cycles of the year and the constellations of the stars,

the natures of animals and the tempers of wild beasts,

the powers of spirits and the reasonings of men. (Wis. 7:16–20)

The apostle John, writing from the Greek city of Ephesus, follows the same strategy. His gospel is an answer both to Jewish commitment to the Law of Moses and to the Greek search for the fundamental order of the cosmos. The Stoics had called that order the *logos,* meaning "structure" or "logic" or "word." John seems to agree with them: and then stuns them by declaring not simply that the logos underlay the world, but that *through it the world was made,* and that (most unbecoming of a Greek principle) it entered the world in the flesh: "And the *Word* was made flesh, and dwelt among us, (and we beheld his glory, the glory as of the only begotten of the Father,) full of grace and truth" (Jn. 1:14).

It is the same confidence and judicious generosity that moved Augustine to see in Platonism a preparation for the New Testament. In the Platonists, he says, "I read, not indeed in these words but much the same thought, enforced by many varied arguments, that 'In the beginning was the Word, and the Word was with God, and the Word was God'" (*Confessions*, 7.9; citing John 1:1). Much else he found there, and yet much he did not find, particularly regarding the salvation of sinners. Augustine, like Jerome, could acknowledge the greatness of the pagan philosophers, and, like Jerome, was ready to affirm that greatness is perhaps not the finest thing in the world: "For 'you have hidden these things from the wise, and have revealed them to little ones,' so that they who labor and are burdened might come to him and he would refresh them. For he is meek and humble of heart, and he guides the meek in judgment." (cf. Matt. 11:29–30)

So the Christian thinkers neither rejected the pagan philosophers nor accepted them simply. They engaged them, and breathed life back into them. For, except for the half-mystical development of Neoplatonism, pagan philosophy was as stale and old as pagan religion. If Jerusalem could get along without Athens, Athens could no longer get along without Jerusalem. Philosophy derived the powerful understanding of God not simply as supreme among beings, but as *the Being* whose essence it is to exist; or what "person" means; or the role of free will in the choice between good and evil. The results far extended philosophy's reach. Augustine, for one, is our first great examiner of the nature of time. He is our first philosopher of history. He affirms a distinction between two kinds of love, in the Platonist fashion, but with Christian meanings attached to them: lust and charity. That distinction will remain fruitful in philosophy and art for over a thousand years. You cannot understand Chaucer or Dante or Shakespeare without it.

A few Christian writers, revering the old philosophy, tried to preserve it in its own right. Here the politically correct historian will scoff, noting that in 529 the eastern emperor Justinian shut down the old Platonic Academy. But if that school had burned to the ground three hundred years before, Western civilization would not have been the worse. The school had long been committed to a sterile skepticism, and produced no work of note. Besides, we are the last people who should complain about discarding ancient curricula. We cannot manage to preserve the teaching of grammar, let alone the metaphysical flights of Plato.

So then, after the fall of Rome in the West in 476, the most learned man of his age, Boethius, deeply influenced by the Platonists and the Stoics, by the writings of Augustine and other Church fathers, did all he could to preserve and develop the ancient philosophy. It was already difficult to procure Greek texts in the West, given the political upheavals, so he translated into Latin several of Aristotle's works on logic and linguistics. He attempted to show a deep harmony between Plato and Aristotle. He wrote a treatise on music, inspired by Pythagoras, that became the standard textbook until the eighteenth century. And as he awaited a horrible execution for a trumped-up charge of treason (the ruling Goths feared that a patriotic old Roman might betray them to the Emperor in the East), he wrote his masterpiece, *The Consolation of Philosophy*. For the next thousand years, only the Bible was translated more often. In it, this orthodox Christian scholar employs Platonic dialogue, with classical poetry, to prove that the wicked do not prosper, and that the just cannot be harmed by the evil that men do to them. It is steeped in the lessons of the Book of Job and the Gospel of John, but it does not cite Scripture. By then, it did not need to.

How Christians elevated culture

What did the Christians cherish from the pagan traditions, and what did they change?

They raised the status of women.

It's dogma in our public schools today that women in ancient times were oppressed, because women had no voting rights, women had not the same opportunities as men, and so forth. You will be mocked if you deny that this spells oppression. If you're a college professor and you deny it, get ready for the stake.

But the charges are anachronistic and chauvinist. People who make them never imagine what it was like for people of another culture to put food on the table, a roof over their heads, and clothes on their backs, never mind bearing enough children to keep the population stable. The Romans in general treated their wives with esteem. The matron of the house had better be consulted along with the important males if the paterfamilias was going to make a decision. Still, the Christians preached that there was no separate baptism for men and women. All were one in Christ. If Christ was Himself the Holy of Holies, then that inner sanctum was thrown open for all. Jesus had been seen on Easter first by women, then by his apostles. The Gnostic heretics, who disdained the body, have Jesus saying that one could not be blessed unless one were made male; Christians condemned that nonsense. They did not expose baby girls (or boys, either). They did not divorce their wives. They shunned sexual practices that put them and their spouses at risk. They honored women who defied emperors, centurions and soldiers to witness to the faith. In his *Confessions,* Saint Augustine wrote the first tribute in history to an ordinary woman, his mother Monica, without whose love and faithful prayer he would never have known the love of God. (9.8–13)

Even so, early Christians were sexist because they, like everybody else who has walked the earth until now, did not treat women as indistinguishable from men. That indifference is our politically correct ideal, though it's hard to name a time and place wherein women would not have decried such treatment as insulting.

They palliated pagan cruelties.

Christians did not take part in the blood sports of the arena. That does not mean that all of them kept away from the stands; but the Christian attitude toward the gladiatorial combats is well captured by, again, the irrepressible Tertullian:

> And are we to wait now for a scriptural condemnation of the
> amphitheatre? If we can plead that cruelty is allowed us, if
> impiety, if brute savagery, by all means let us go to the
> amphitheatre. (*De Spectaculis*)

Those games were as popular then as football in America is now, or soccer in Europe; but Christ's injunction to love one's enemy would eventually put to death the sport of death.

Christians were forbidden to help riddle the whores with diseases. We can't attribute moral degeneracy to the whole Roman empire; but the most populous cities really were sinkholes of depravity, if we can trust pagan and Christian testimony. Here's Clement of Alexandria again, describing how low the debauchery descended:

> Such are the trophies of your social licentiousness which are
> exhibited: the evidence of these deeds are the prostitutes. Alas
> for such wickedness!...For fathers, unmindful of children of
> theirs that have been exposed, often without their knowledge,
> have intercourse with a son that has debauched himself, and
> daughters that are prostitutes. (*Paedogogus*, 3.3)

Again, we should not expect that Christians all lived up to their ideals, any more than we live up to ours. But it's one thing to violate a law, and another to deny that the law exists.

Christians softened the institution of slavery, as common then as the service industry is now. The teachings of Jesus made it clear that it was the position of the master, not that of the slave, that placed one's salvation in jeopardy. Some Christians sold themselves into slavery to ransom a Christian brother. As the years went on, under the influence first of Stoicism and then of Christianity, laws condemning the maltreatment of slaves become common.

Contrary to what our Bible-despisers say, the Scriptures do not support slavery. They take it for granted as a social institution. How else might a poor man without land keep himself and his family alive? If a man had nothing, he at least had his back and his hands. It is not as if he could work for a day, or would even want to work for a day, and then go home, when most often there was no home to return to, or when he could have a better meal and something like a bed in the master's house. But the whole thrust of the Scriptures is towards freedom and away from bondage—unless it is the "bondage" of love. Jesus warns his followers that if they would be great in the Kingdom of Heaven they must be slaves to everyone else.

They thrust a dagger into the heart of the State-worship.

Their failure to worship the Emperor angered a Roman like Diocletian not because he thought he was a god. Diocletian knew it was all nonsense. It angered him because they struck against the sanctity of the State he was struggling to hold together. Hence his notorious persecutions, perpetrated, as persecutions usually are, for reasons of State. But in a few decades, Constantine legalized the religion, and then Theodosius made it the official religion of the empire. That was not the same as Statist idolatry.

One example will show why not. The emperor Theodosius, a valiant soldier and a defender of the orthodox faith, attacked Arian Goths in Thessalonika and massacred them. For his pains, his bishop, Ambrose of Milan (the man who later baptized Augustine) threatened to excommunicate him unless he did immediate penance for his great evil.[10] Diocletian, for political purposes, had demanded to be called *Dominus et Deus*, "Lord and God." But Theodosius had to suffer the rebuke of a mere bishop. More than a rebuke: he had placed his immortal soul in danger. For the Emperor, though he is the legitimate ruler, is but one Christian like another, and all are servants of the one and only Lord and God.

They took up the burden of civic responsibility.

People trained on Hollywood epics may think that everyone in the Roman Empire wore flowing white tunics and relaxed at the baths and ate figs from silver platters. But as we have seen, the population of the Empire stalled in the third century, and the economy stalled with it. That brought de-urbanization, as did the shortsighted increase in taxes. Meanwhile, the Empire had spread its legions as thinly as possible along the thousands of miles of borderland to protect its citizens from barbarian invasions. Rarely were emperors to be found in Rome. The great city became a backwater. Constantinople was the thriving capital in the East. Milan, closer to the vulnerable passes over the Alps, became more important in the West, as did the Adriatic port of Ravenna. But with food supplies dwindling, more and more people abandoned the cities generally, nor was it lucrative for the remaining magistrates to do the work.

"Wives, Be Subject to Your Husbands"

Have you ever been at a wedding and watched a guest wince, gape, or maybe just giggle when the lector reads the words Saint Paul wrote the Ephesians: "Wives, be subject to your own husbands"?

Not only is this beautiful passage from Paul's letter politically incorrect because it assigns gender roles and eschews modern notions of equality, but its deeper meaning is even more subversive to today's mores. Read the whole passage:

> [B]e subject to one another in the fear of Christ.
> Wives, be subject to your own husbands, as to the Lord. For the husband is the head of the wife, as Christ also is the head of the church, He Himself being the Savior of the body. But as the church is subject to Christ, so also the wives ought to be to their husbands in everything.
> Husbands, love your wives, just as Christ also loved the church and gave Himself up for her....

Marriage becomes not an institution for mutual gratification, but for mutual humbling. Given today's gospels of "empowerment" and self-esteem, this universal call to servitude is pretty startling.

Here's where Christian deacons, priests, and bishops came in. The Christians had developed networks of care for their sick, their widows, and their orphans. Moreover, a priest or a bishop did not have a family to support (celibacy among the clergy had become the norm in the East, and almost universal in the West), so they became natural choices to assume the places vacated by the old senatorial families. It was the persecutor Diocletian, and no Christian bishop, who first called sectors of the Empire "dioceses," but it wasn't long before bishops were in charge of those dioceses, for practical reasons—as, for instance, to see that grain shipments came in to feed the poor. When Augustine traveled to Milan, then the hub of government in Italy, the man in charge was not the Emperor, who had to be on the move with his army, but the bishop, Ambrose. He was the primary man responsible for preserving law and order and promoting the common good. Two centuries later, after Rome had shrunk from a city of nearly two million to a town of forty thousand, in ruins, the people chose as their bishop a humble monk who had long served their practical needs as an able administrator. His name was Gregory, and when he first heard they might choose him, he fled—for how could such as he be a worthy successor of Saint Peter?

Yet the people persuaded him to return. History knows him as Pope Gregory I, one of the wisest and holiest men to assume the chair—and, after all, a true Roman.

They ennobled manual labor.

Unlike us, now. It is one of the purposes of the college degree, to safeguard the holder from a sore back and calluses. But the Christians could not look down upon the kind of labor that their Savior did, for Jesus was a carpenter. And Peter was a fisherman, and Paul a tent-maker.

We should not underestimate this acceptance of hard physical labor. It may be that Christianity is truly healthy only where this principle is affirmed, and that its denial is a symptom of a sickly faith, as among the

French aristocrats in the eighteenth century, or the overschooled in ours. The principle long predates the Protestant Reformation. The craftsmen who built the medieval cathedrals often memorialized their trades in wood or glass or stone upon the very walls. But the Church was reviving a Roman ideal that had fallen into the yellow leaf. The Romans were fond of looking back upon the modest-living gentlemen farmers who had been the backbone of the Republic. By the second century of the Empire, many city people found themselves yearning for the peace and health of a farm. But it had been a long time since men with any money stooped their shoulders. A rich man might own a farm, but slaves dragged the plow.

Now, as I've said, a slave economy is a stagnant economy. The Romans were terrific engineers, as we see from their aqueducts and sewers and basilicas and roads. Were it not for slavery, they might have had an industrial revolution. By the time the Germans and the Huns had invaded, political and economic conditions made that impossible. But the Christian re-valuation of work would eventually build the continent anew.

They "baptized" the paterfamilias.

One of the great unheralded events in history occurred in the early sixth century, when a monk named Benedict of Nursia was asked to write a rule governing life in the monastery at Monte Cassino. Benedict aimed to provide a Roman orderliness and moderation, unlke the spiritual athleticism of the East, with its daring flights of physical deprivation and marathon prayer. In the East, you might find a Saint Daniel the Stylite, sitting atop a pillar for years in swelter and storm, praying for the people and doing penance.[11] But Saint Benedict's genius was Roman; his instincts favored the stable and conservative.

He gave the West a blueprint for orderly life under hard conditions. Imagine twenty or thirty men in their prime, sworn to remain in one place, to observe an orderly round of prayer, reflection, labor, and rest, and to obey their *paterfamilias*, the abbot (from Hebrew *abba*, "father") who stands for them in the place of Christ. Imagine that they see their work as a form of praise and prayer. What can such men not do? They cleared the water-logged land of Germany, all swamp and dark forest, and brought forth grain for bread and beer, and grapes for wine. They brought their learning to far Ireland and England and Scandinavia. They copied manuscripts (work more laborious than that of the plowman, without the benefit of muscles stretching in the open air) and embellished them with decorations fanciful and bright. Their monasteries became a network of economic hot spots, sharing their learning and their technological improvements.

They elevated the "barbarian" cultures from which they came.

The monks were not colonizers in any sane sense of the word. They entered a land, found what was good in it, attempted to preserve it and

The Poor Will Always Be with You

Everything around Him participates in His poverty;—His parents, who scarcely possess a few coarse garments to clothe Him with; the poor shepherds, who at the voice of the angels leave their flocks to come and adore Him.

   Consider that this wretchedness of the Son of God was not necessary and compulsory, like the poor in the world; it is free and of His own choice. Conceive a high idea of this poverty, which appeared so precious to our Lord, that to espouse it He quitted heaven and His glory.

Saint Ignatius of Loyola, *Spiritual Exercises*, "The Poverty of the Birth of Jesus Christ"

Here we have the truly Christian championing of poverty. It does not pass over the wretchedness of those who suffer hunger and thirst and nakedness; the Jesuits were tireless advocates for the poor. But it exalts poverty to its true spiritual grandeur; we are to possess things, says Saint Paul, as if we possessed none. That is incomprehensible to the materialist mind, that sees human poverty only as an evil and only to be overcome by money—other people's money.

bring it into harmony with the faith, and gave to the people their inherited gifts of Roman and Christian civilization. So the monks gave the Irish their first alphabet. English, Gothic, and Icelandic are all first written by monks. Did they then eradicate the native oral poetry? Far from it. The genius who composed *Beowulf* was almost certainly a Christian monk, writing for his beloved Saxons soon after the dawn of the faith in England, cherishing the memories of the old sagas, but seeing in them a heroism that without Christ was incomplete.

Let me illustrate the point with a famous account from the Venerable Bede's *Ecclesiastical History of the English People*.[12] Bede, writing from the Irish-founded monastery at Jarrow, recalls an incident one or two generations before, when one night the cattlemen, laymen working at the monastery, were sitting round a table drinking beer. As was the custom, they passed a harp from man to man as they drank. When it came to you, you were supposed to sing one of the old pagan heroic songs, the grand deeds of a Sigemund or a Beowulf. But one fellow at the beer feast was embarrassed and used an excuse to leave, going to the cattle shed to tend the stock for the night. When he fell asleep, an angel of the Lord appeared to him in a dream and called to him, "Caedmon! Sing me something!"

"I don't know anything to sing," replied the herdsman. "That's why I left the feast, because I can't sing."

"Nevertheless, you can sing."

"What shall I sing?" said Caedmon.

"Sing me the First-Making," said the angel. At which point Caedmon burst into a hymn glorifying God the Father who established the heavens and the earth:

> Now let us laud   the Lord of heaven's realm,
> the Measurer's might   and his mind-plan,
> work of the Glory-Father   as every wondrous thing,
> Chieftain eternal,   he established from of old.

> He first shaped,   for the sons of earth,
>
> the high roof of heaven,   holy Creator;
>
> the middle-yard   mankind's Lord,
>
> Chieftain eternal,   adorned after that,
>
> made the earth for men,   the Master almighty.

This charming hymn he composed was in the heroic meter of the old sagas, using the same heroic language. When Caedmon awoke, he told his bailiff about it, who brought him to the abbess, and she, wise woman, instructed the monks who could read to tell him a story out of the Scriptures, to see what he would do with it. He returned the next day with a heroic narrative poem. "It is a gift from God," she concluded. So Caedmon was brought into the monastery, not to learn Latin, but to compose song after song in Anglo-Saxon. It is an astonishing instance of the fusion of two cultures, and because of it we have the glories of Old English poetry.

"What does Ingeld have to do with Christ?" asked the learned Alcuin at the court of Charlemagne, one of the bright spots in the centuries of social confusion after the breakup of the Western empire.[13] Alcuin was annoyed that his monks were entertaining themselves with tales, passed down by song over centuries, of the feats of the pagan Germanic heroes. He was, of course, echoing Tertullian's rhetorical question from long before. But the answer would come from the experience of missionaries, and from the artists who saw in the old ways a foreshadowing of the Christian revelation. What did Ingeld have to do with Christ? According to the author of *Beowulf,* a great deal indeed.

The truth about heretics

If you study the heresies condemned by the early Church, you'll find excellent ammunition against the accusations of the smug atheist. First, many anti-Christians believe that their opponents actually accept some of the harsher, world-loathing heresies. Alternatively, they condemn Christians for being closed-minded, authoritarian, and, yes, intolerant; while *they* have the privilege of condemning all to themselves. It does not occur to them, or they don't care, that a faith without definition is like a body without skin. A cursory study of heresies will reveal the folly of these positions.

True, the Church fathers spent much time debating, not always coolly, who Jesus was, what was the nature of his relationship with the Father, what was to be understood by the Holy Spirit, what was the true Church, which books were inspired by God, and how man is to be saved.

But before the reader shakes his head with a superior air (easy to do, when the debate is far away and he is ignorant of what is at stake), let's enumerate a few of the heresies.[14] Some people believed that a true Christian must be a martyr of blood, so they sought violent death, sometimes by provoking their oppressors. Some, tainted by the body-hatred of certain Eastern cults and religions, believed that Jesus did not have a genuine body (because matter is intrinsically evil), and that to be saved we must cleanse away this corporal scurf, by fasting and abstaining from sex. Or, as a more convenient alternative, one might gleefully indulge in orgies, since, after all, only the soul counts for anything.

Some believed that the God worshipped by the Jews was evil, superseded by the God of love whom Jesus called Father. Some believed that Jesus was not the Son of God, but a creature, "adopted" by the Father for his obedience. Some believed that Jesus never died, and that it was only a specter that the Romans nailed to the Cross. Some believed that one could earn one's way into paradise by energetic good works, as if man needed no savior at all.

Set aside the question of whether Christian orthodoxy presents the truth about God and Christ and man's destiny. The controversies, which lasted several centuries, were no waste of time. Their resolution redounded to the cultural benefit of the West. Why?

Again, the pagan religions had nowhere to go. No educated man really believed in the Homeric gods, and as for neoplatonic mysticism, with its melange of obscure terms, airy abstractions, and magic, even the educated would find it nearly impossible to understand, let alone be guided by it from day to day. It was the superstitious and fidgety who sought out the mystery cults, with their secret knowledge and their orgies of initiation. That was a cultural dead end, and several of the heresies would have sent Christian worship along the same short unproductive road.

Most notorious was the body-reviling Gnostic heresy which, to listen to the ill-informed critics of Christianity in our schools, you would think was Christian dogma. Had the Gnostics won the day, Christians would have retreated from the world. Why bother plowing fields and copying books and repairing the aqueducts, when this world is all an illusion, and the only real knowledge is whispered from one secret master to another?

The danger (speaking culturally, not theologically) of other heresies was more subtle. The most popular heresy, Arianism, maintained that Christ was a creature, though exactly what kind of creature the Arians did not make clear. Here is Saint Jerome, discussing the verbal sleight-of-hand used by Arian-leaning bishops of the fourth century:

> Eminent Christian bishops of course, began to wave their palms, and to say they had not denied that He was a creature, but that He was like other creatures. At that moment the term *Ousia* [meaning "being" or "substance," as in the creedal statement that Christ is consubstantial with the Father] was abolished: the Nicene Faith stood condemned by acclamation. The whole world groaned, and was astonished to find itself Arian.
> (*Dialogue against the Luciferians*)

Had the Arian heresy triumphed, I would not now be writing a *Politically Incorrect Guide™ to Western Civilization,* because the Christian faith would have fizzled out, along with the Greco-Roman world it in part preserved. The reason is hard for us to see, because we do not appreciate the cultural revolution ready to explode from the declaration, God is Love.

If Arius was correct, then Jesus was only a creature, albeit the highest. Then God can be said to love, but He cannot said to *be Love*. He is not in his own right a relationship of love among three Persons. He retreats into transcendence: he does not really enter the world to dwell among us. In that case he either becomes the inscrutable and irrational Allah of the Muslims, a universal sultan, or he vanishes into an abstraction, a Neoplatonic Being, impersonal and unapproachable. Christian worship either way loses its bridge between earth and heaven. Its commandments harden into the dictates of a despot, or decay into a moral philosophy, like Stoicism, benevolent enough, but in most men too weak to withstand the furies of the heart. It is the path Unitarianism took in nineteenth century America, from a dilute Christianity at the Harvard of John Quincy Adams, to a vague theism with an overlay of Christian moral teaching at the Harvard of his grandson Henry Adams, to the cultural nonentity it is now, a hobby for atheists or pantheists who like hymns and incense.

In one fashion or another, the heresies flatten Jesus, mostly to deny his humanity, as unworthy of him, and sometimes to deny his divinity. Here I am not arguing theologically but culturally. Christianity survives— nay, it *exists*—only where Jesus is affirmed as both God and Man.

That matters. Recall that the Jews and the Greeks had much to say about the natural law, what C. S. Lewis called "The Tao," a set

A Book You're Not Supposed to Read

The Great Heresies by Hilaire Belloc; Rockford, IL: Tan Books and Publishers, 1991.

Belloc is always worth reading, enjoyable and perceptive, but this treatment of heresies—from the earliest Arian heresy, to the catastrophic heresy of Islam, to the seemingly benign, but mortally harmful intellectual heresies of the Modern Age—is a grand and sweeping treatment and condemnation of all things contrary to the true, the good, and the beautiful. As such, it is sure to offend many—a sure sign that it's right on target.

of principles that are not the *result* of moral inquiry, but its foundation, self-evident to all men who are not corrupted.[15] You do not steal. You love your family. You sacrifice for your country. You take care of the infirm. But, as well-attested as these principles are everywhere, they are also violated everywhere, and their connection with man's destiny and his being is not clear. With the Jews that connection is clear, since the laws are given by God himself. But the Jews are in part constricted by culture. The prophets do *preach* that the law will be given to all nations, and, as I've written, the Jews were chosen to carry that law. Yet Rome and Greece and Germany and Ireland could only become Jewish, so to speak, by becoming Christian. And then men saw not only that Christ came into the world, but that the very meaning of this world is stamped with Him, redeemer and creator both. For the world too is loved, and made new.

The Good News brings charity

To the ends of the earth, then, came the word, brought by saints, marauders, plowmen, tyrants, ordinary people, that each human being possesses a measureless dignity, by virtue of his having been created and redeemed by a God of love; not by a philosophical idea, and not by a god bound to a mountainside or river. The Greeks had the wisdom to end slavery, but why lose the temporary economic advantage? The Jews understood why, but lacked the power. The Jews who are called Christians, after a long struggle, did put an end to it; too long a struggle, but triumphant at last. If we believe that it befits a man to enter a burning building to save someone else's child, it is because we hear the words ringing in our ears still, "Inasmuch as ye have done *it* unto one of the least of these my brethren, ye have done *it* unto me" (Matt. 25:40).

It may offend secularists and those prudes who think that religion ought to be kept behind closed doors, but charity and concern for the poor are integral to our culture today *because* of Christianity. If we build hospitals for the destitute beyond our own lands, with no desire for personal or national profit, and risking life and limb to do it, it is because we retain a trace, a cultural memory of the voyages of Saint Paul, of Boniface martyred by the Germans, of Cyril and Methodius trekking north among the Slavs, of Patrick driving the snakes from Ireland, of Gregory the Great seeing blond slaves in the marketplace and, hearing that they were called "Angli," replying, "*Non Angli sed angeli*," "not Angles but angels," and sending missionaries among them, to give them the best he had to give.[16]

That is only one benefit, and not the most important, which the priests and bishops at those early councils conferred upon us, ensuring that Christianity would survive.

Though it is not polite to say so, still it cries out for notice. Hindus do not send holy men into foreign lands to feed the hungry and house the naked; they will not do so for the pariahs in their own land. Buddhists, practicing benevolent detachment from the world, do not do so. Muslims, who conquer by force, and who reject natural law on the grounds that it "fetters" Allah, are required to take care of their own, but they ignore everyone else.[17] All cults of ancestor worship, like Shinto, are too firmly fixed upon the local and the familial to care for people far away. The Jews and Christians would care, because of the God they worship: and they did. If the world speaks of human rights now, and the dignity of the poor, it is because the world has heard of Moses and the prophets—and, summing them up in himself, Christ. Men have come at last neither to love the world nor to despise it simply, but to love its goodness, not as a final end, but as a manifestation of the goodness that is eternal.

Chapter Five

THE HIGH MIDDLE AGES: THE BRIGHT AGES

We all know what the Middle Ages were like. My freshmen know. They've learned it from the infallible authority known as High School Platitudes.

First, the Middle Ages were dark. People lived in squalor. Beset by terrible fears, they burned kindly old ladies peddling herbal remedies, calling them witches. They made no progress in the natural sciences. They knew nothing of the world beyond their time and place, and had no desire to know. Their studies were narrow and dogmatic, and the few great minds of their era plied their intelligence to discover how many angels could dance on the head of a pin. Life was so miserable that most people, especially the dirt-peasant majority, lived only for the next world, placing all their hope in a heaven beyond the stars.

Let's set the record straight. From 962 (the crowning of Otto the Great as Holy Roman Emperor) to 1321 (the death of Dante), Europe enjoyed one of the most magnificent flourishings of culture the world has seen. In some ways it was the most magnificent. And this was not *despite* the fact that the daily tolling of the church bells provided the rhythm of men's lives, but *because* of it. Because the people believed they lived in a *comic* world, that is a world redeemed from sin, wherein the Savior had triumphed over darkness and death, they could love that world aright. They were pilgrims at heart, who yet passionately loved their native

Guess What?

✦ Medieval Europe's creativity and vitality makes our age look sluggish and drab.

✦ The Middle Ages was the true era of love.

✦ A warming climate—much warmer than today—was good for culture.

lands, their town walls, their hillsides, their many colorful festivals, their local food and drink. They enjoyed the freedom of hope. They were not pressed to death with the urgency to create a heaven upon earth, a longing that ends in despair, or the gulag.

You won't hear this tale on television or in school. A powerful Church should be a regular monster, destroying intellectual endeavor and enforcing dreariness upon art—long before academe made artistic dreariness a mark of sophistication. Forswearing instant gratification (not that everyone in the Middle Ages did forswear it) should produce a continent of mopes, or seething villains, or something miserable which Americans with their dropout factories and nearly three million incarcerated men know nothing of. Besides, because we all believe in inevitable social progress, everything must have been terrible in the past, at least compared to today. Why, I feel myself progressing morally with every tick of the clock; don't you? Mainly, the Middle Ages must have been bad because they were *middle*.

Any close study will disabuse us of this PC bigotry.

Islam vs. civilization

Before I discuss what this flourishing brought us, I'd like to note that the real question is not *why* it happened, but why it didn't happen *sooner*. It might have, were it not for three things over which the Christians in the West had little or no influence.

The first of these were the invasions of the old empire by Germans and Slavs and others. Some had already been converted to a form of Christianity (the Goths were Arians), and were attracted by the high culture of the Roman cities in Gaul and Italy and Greece. Some, like the Huns, were spurred by the love of marauding. Still others, like the Vandals (whence we derive our word for people who smash things for fun and profit), blazed across the continent, yet eventually settled down to stable kingdoms under law.

These incursions—lasting many centuries, until Otto the Great thwarted the Magyars in 954, and until those seacoast and river pillagers the Vikings were brought to the Christian faith—made trade difficult and costly. Economies shriveled; coinage vanished; people had to live on what they got from the land. With a poor climate and empty purses, that was often little enough. Peasants were reduced to serfdom, trading their labor and freedom for whatever poor protection the local lord could provide. Worse still for the culture, the chaos and the danger of the seaways severed the Greek East from the Latin West, and so vast tracts of Greek philosophy, science, and literature were lost.

The chaos might have been overcome from the East, had the empire in Byzantium been strong and outward-looking. It was not. It too was pressed by Eastern tribes, but, more important, it had to resist the second factor, jihadist Islam. Recall that in the days of Augustine, around 400 AD, all of Africa north of the Sahara, including the Nile Valley from the

Marx Misreads the Middle Ages

The PC myths about the Middle Ages are passed down to us, in part, from Karl Marx.

> The history of all hitherto existing society is the history of class struggles.
> Freeman and slave, patrician and plebeian, lord and serf, guild-master and journeyman, in a word, oppressor and oppressed, stood in constant opposition to one another.

Karl Marx, *The Communist Manifesto* (79)

No, they didn't. Take the medieval journeyman. He benefited from training he had received as an apprentice, and when he produced a work of sufficiently impressive quality—literally, a master-piece—he too would become a full member of a guild. In fact, the guild system is exactly what Marx's contemporary, Pope Leo XIII, a great opponent of socialism, recommended for the workingman, whom Marx held in scorn.

sea to the heart of the Sudan, was Greco-Roman in culture, and mainly Christian in faith. Augustine was an African, and died as bishop of Hippo Regius, in what is now Tunisia. Tertullian was an African. Anthony, the hermit whose example over the 108 years of his life spurred a tremendous movement of desert piety, lived in Egypt. Alexandria was the scholarly capital of the world. The wildfire of Mohammed swept it away, and an ancient civilization, extending from Spain to Persia, was no more.

So the Byzantine Empire never had the power to return Greek learning to the West and unite the lands under one law. It had enough to do at home. It did have moments of glory, winning time for itself and the West, as when Leo the Isaurian crushed the Muslim navy in 717 with ballistics and a naphthaline concoction known as "Greek fire." But for the most part, the West was on its own.

Warmer is better—someone tell Al Gore

The third factor is a subtle one. We hear a lot about global warming these days, and since I'm no geologist I won't venture an opinion, except to say that in history the great threat to man has not been warming but cooling. It's obvious why. If you shorten the growing season by a few weeks and make the summer highs a little cooler, you remove millions of acres of land from the plow. You put stubby grass and mosses where cattle used to graze on the savannah; and you turn into savannah what used to be prime land for growing cereal grains.

The cooling helps explain the barbarian invasions: they and their cattle were cold and hungry. And, as I've noted, one winter they had a Rhine River frozen solid, so they could cross where they pleased, and the Roman legions, already stretched thin, could do nothing about it.

Cooling weather causes the occasional failed harvest. But if harvests are only fair, any outright failures will deplete your stores of grain. People grow sickly. Life expectancy drops. Population shrinks. The cities—

dependent upon storeable grain—empty. Town life withers away. People cannot afford the division of labor that allows for scholars, accountants, merchants, sculptors, actors, whatever. Back to the land they go: for man needs bread.

But when one or two of these factors had disappeared or been overcome, Europe was ready for its grand resurgence. Consider its cultural advantages. Christianity had scrubbed away most of the late Greco-Roman prejudice against manual labor. Recall Benedict and his monastic rule. Monks, whatever their background, worked the land. They cleared the thick, damp German forests of trees and stumps. They drained the marshes. They dug wells, built granaries, planted vineyards, and communicated technological innovations among themselves, in a network extending across Europe.

The monks retained a healthy respect for hierarchy and law. Imagine what it might be like to build an economic hot spot where nothing but black firs and mosquitoes had been, *without* a clear and effective chain of command. At the same time, they inherited the Christian revelation that Christ came for all men, not only for the rulers. Their model of hierarchy and equality, or equality expressed by obedience and Christ-like service, exerted a powerful influence upon the villages that grew up around the monasteries, and then upon medieval life generally. For Christ Himself was obedient, even unto death upon a cross, and therefore, says Paul, every knee shall bend to Him, in heaven, on earth, and under the earth. So despite wickedness and selfishness, which we will always have with us, the people of the Middle Ages knew that the soul of a peasant was no less worth saving than was the soul of a duke. That meant that, as harsh as serfdom could be, the continent could never quite slide back into slavery. The irrepressible movement in the Middle Ages is towards freedom.

Then, around 1000, the weather warmed up,[1] and the Vikings began to settle down to civilized life. What happened afterwards does not disappoint.

Ruggedly alive

We probably wouldn't enjoy living in a medieval town. We'd have animals everywhere, chickens, pigs, goats, dogs, cows, and all that they eat, and all that what they eat becomes. Not until the nineteenth century did Europeans build sewer systems to match those of ancient Rome. People were crowded within the town walls, many of them living in houses with packed earth floors, and rushes laid upon them to catch droppings from the table and from other places. People ate with their fingers, though the food was saucy and spicy. Chaucer gently satirizes his Prioress in *The Canterbury Tales* by praising her daintiness at table: she never let the grease fall on her lap. If you caught a disease, you couldn't expect much from a medieval physician, particularly in northern Europe. People lost most of their teeth (from eating a lot of starchy food; meat was for the rich, and for holidays), so you might find them chew-

A Medieval Feminist

Had all the world no other authority,
Experience is quite enough for me
To speak of all the woe that marriage brings. ("The Wife of Bath's Prologue," 1–3)

The Wife of Bath has sure had that experience. She's been widowed five times, driving at least four of her beloved husbands to their graves. Her garrulous prologue and tale are racy flings of ignorance, misinterpretation, excuse-making, and unwitting self-revelation. Feminist critics hail her as a heroine for woman's expressive freedom. Chaucer shows us otherwise: the Wife of Bath is a loud, sexy, silly woman who is rapidly reaching the age when she'll have to go begging to find anyone to warm the bed with her. And unless she repents of her ways, she may one day get more heat than she's bargained for.

ing licorice before a tryst to hide their bad breath, as Chaucer's Absolom does in "The Miller's Tale."

But one thing it was impossible to be, if the art of the time is any indication: you couldn't be lonely. Granted, it's hard to base an argument upon an omission, but the lack of any mention of loneliness in medieval literature really is striking. You were busy. You worked alongside your fellow villagers. You slept three or four in a bed. You might belong to a guild. You stood alongside everyone else as you crowded the church for celebration.

Your life was also not drab. For the first time since the heyday of the Roman empire, people of the West, if they were not as poor as church-mice, enjoyed bright clothing, spices from the East, sweet wine from the Mediterranean (Chaucer's Pardoner is a connoisseur of the heady port wines from Spain), not to mention music and dancing and folk poetry ranging from the delicate and genteel to the coarse and randy. So we have songs of awakening love in the springtime, for the Lord of Easter:

> When I see the blossoms spring,
> And I hear the small birds sing,
> A sweet love-longing
> Pierces all my heart.

> And we have merry peddlers eyeing the girls and crowing up
> their finest jewels:
> I have a pocket for the nonce,

> And in it are two precious stones:
> Damsel, if you had tried them once,
> You'd be right ready to go with me![2]

We would shy away from the Middle Ages not because of its drabness, but because its vitality would fray our weak nerves. We'd have to rub our eyes to get used to the light.

The Bright Ages: Life in the cathedrals

Where shall we look first for this light? Why not in those stone symphonies, the Gothic cathedrals?

Let's be clear about this. The men of the Middle Ages did not build their cathedrals to be squat, dark, ghoulish structures manifesting their fear and ignorance. We have to scrub from the church walls the smoke of the later Industrial Revolution, and from our minds the smoke of Victorian Draculas. Nor had they progressed as far as modern man, who aspires to work in a steel cage or a cardboard box. No, the medieval master builders wanted light, because their faith taught them to want it, for "the light shineth in darkness; and the darkness comprehended it not" (Jn. 1:5).

That association of divinity with light was as old as Genesis. The first creature God made was not mud, not a habitation for himself, not a consort to rut with, but *light.* Christ, too, in John's gospel, is called the light that comes into the world, and his disciples are to let their light shine before men. The Church fathers, taking their cue from Scripture and from Plato, saw light as the noblest thing in creation: not simply the brilliant light of sun and moon and stars, but the light of the intellect, whose first and final dwelling place is the mind of God. The contemplative Syriac monk who called himself Dionysius (naming himself after the man Saint Paul had converted on the Athenian mount) developed a grand theology of light, and the thinkers and the artists of the Middle Ages paid heed.[3]

One man who took it to heart was a powerful abbot in Paris, named Suger. He wanted to help unite the squabbling dukedoms of France under the authority of the anointed king; and to that end he would build a chapel worthy of the patron saint of France, Saint Denis, or Saint Dionysius. What better way than to take the architectural innovations of the last two centuries—vaulted ceilings, pointed arches—and put them together to pour light into a sanctuary such as no one had seen before? That would fashion a gem for the king's capital and would honor God—for "God is light" (1 Jn. 1:5).

They did not have reinforced steel then, or fiberglass, or super-light mixtures of concrete. The problem for Suger, and for builders generally over the next two or three centuries, was how to build high, span broad interior spaces, and remove stone from walls and replace it with glass, without having the roof cave in or the walls buckle.

Here we discover ingenious engineering solutions, both practical and beautiful. No doubt you've seen some of them. There are the flying buttresses, spindles of stone thrust out from the exterior walls like the spokes of a wheel, "nailed" in place by decorative caps of statuary. Or the rope-like interior ribs of marble, perfectly hewn, often alternating white and green or white and pink or white and gray, reaching up along pillars to the roof in slender curves, the blocks not mortared but set in place by the magic of balance and gravity. Or the lacework of stone tracery, setting off the windows stained in deep blue and red and green and gold—rose windows of mathematical complexity, a kaleidoscopic glance into paradise.

But more interesting than *how* these masons, carpenters, smiths, and glaziers built what I believe are the most splendid architectural works to grace the earth, is *why* they built them so. Let the Abbot speak for himself, in the verses he engraved upon the doors of Saint Denis:

> All you who seek to honor these doors,
> Marvel not at the gold and expense but at the craftsmanship of
> the work.
> The noble work is bright, but, being nobly bright, the work
> Should brighten the minds, allowing them to travel through
> the lights
> To the true light, where Christ is the true door.
> The golden door defines how it is immanent in these things.
> The dull mind rises to the truth through material things,
> And is resurrected from its former submersion when the light
> is seen.[4]

Here, from the pen of the man who more than any other deserves the honor of having invented the Gothic style, we find the medieval reveling in both the bright and beautiful things of the world, and the infinitely brighter and more beautiful things of heaven. The beauty of the world is not rejected but ordered towards the beauty of heaven. Deep calls unto deep, and light unto light.

That is the theological meaning of color: the one inaccessible light of God, made manifest, incarnate, in the objects of our sight. So the stained glass windows are meant to reveal a trace of that luminous feast in paradise. Here Dante describes it:

> [Then] a new power of vision burst aflame—
>> nor is there light too radiant and pristine
>> for sight so strong. And I beheld a stream,
> A river of flashing light that flowed between
>> two shores the spring had touched with wondrous hues,
>> dappled with glimmerings of a golden sheen.
> And from that river living glints arose
>> to settle on the banks with stippling blooms
>> like rubies in a rounding ring of gold. (*Paradiso* 30.58–66)

But these glories were confined to the church, yes? Or to precious manuscripts touched with indigo and emerald and scarlet? What of the common life of the people?

Forget that the church was the heart of that common life, and that the people dwelt in the shadow and the reflected gleam of these places of beauty. Neglect to imagine what it was to "own," with the rest of your townsmen, a structure that pierced the skies with its grandeur, yet that also welcomed you in; and that stood an eloquent witness when you were born, when you married, when you had children, and when you died. What is still astonishing, what we find hard to fathom now, is that those common people were the ones *who built the churches.* We're not talking about huge indistinguishable blocks of stone hauled up the side of a pyramid by sledge and slave to commemorate a dead pharaoh. We're not talking even about the Athenian Parthenon, with master sculptors hammering at the pediment and frieze, while slaves haul the stone from the quarry and dress it.

We are talking about free men, troops of them moving from place to place, paid pretty well, masters of their crafts, with local laborers for the less skilled work. We don't know the names of most of these, and that too is telling. For the work is not designed and mandated by potentates far away. It is true folk art, maybe the most muscular and bodacious folk art the world has known.

The whole of a Gothic cathedral, wrote John Ruskin, is scrawled over with the spirit of playfulness.[5] Maybe over here a gangly boy named Wat, not yet a master, chisels the leer of a dragon whose mouth will gush rainwater and keep the roof from leaking. Over there a carpenter works at a coffered wooden ceiling, gouging out for decoration—and for affirming the goodness of all God's creatures—the flowers and animals of his native

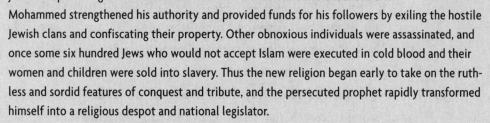

The Religion of Peace

At Medina, Mohammed and his fellow refugees found it difficult to earn a living and soon resorted to plundering caravans for a livelihood, a practice which they justified upon the ground that the merchants were idolaters and unbelievers.... Mohammed strengthened his authority and provided funds for his followers by exiling the hostile Jewish clans and confiscating their property. Other obnoxious individuals were assassinated, and once some six hundred Jews who would not accept Islam were executed in cold blood and their women and children were sold into slavery. Thus the new religion began early to take on the ruthless and sordid features of conquest and tribute, and the persecuted prophet rapidly transformed himself into a religious despot and national legislator.

Lynn Thorndike, *The History of Medieval Europe*

land. If he's an Italian, look for lemons and pinecones. Back toward the sanctuary a priest may be asking the glaziers for a rose window in the east based on the number eight, since the eighth day is Easter, the day beyond all days, the day of resurrection. The townsfolk, who have contributed much to the building, will also gain from it. People will come to see the church, and people need food and drink and lodging. For the church is also an expression of town pride and love, and if it takes fifty or sixty years to build (or more) the people bequeath the project to their children. It is their great artistic and economic triumph.

Did the Church usurp that energy? It was the faith that brought that energy into being.

Drama's rebirth: Another fruit of Christianity

Let's take one example of this vibrant life. For civic creativity and whole-hearted bustle, let alone the transcendent *meaning* of it, I know of nothing we Americans enjoy, with our mass entertainment, mass government, and withered neighborhoods, that can compare.

Imagine that for several weeks every spring, the guildsmen in your town are in high gear. The carpenters are nailing together floats, to roll them in a pageant from church to church. The weavers are mending colorful costumes, some a suspiciously fiery red, with horns and spiky tail. The ironmongers are hammering a special gate with a hair-trigger that will spring it open at the right touch. The priests and clerks are rummaging up old scripts and trying them out on the "actors," one of whom is that fat blustery neighbor of yours, playing Herod.

Everyone is waiting for the great three-day feast of Corpus Christi, beginning on the Thursday after Trinity Sunday. On those three days, amid sacred processions and boisterous children and women hawking fruit, you and your townsmen will put on a cycle of plays spanning all of time, from the Creation of Man through the Redemption to the Final

Judgment. These plays will be composed with homespun rhyming and tags of Latin scripture, yet with an imaginative power which you will find quite natural, seeing the end of man even in the beginning, and the revelation of Christ even in the curse that God pronounced upon the snake in the garden.[6]

Imagine that these cycles of plays show up not here and there, but from Portugal to Germany, from England to Italy. Then you will understand why in the Middle Ages, after a thousand years of dormancy, drama was reborn. This was no accident. The people intuited that the Christian faith is intensely dramatic, with all kinds of wondrous surprises. So in the famous *Second Shepherds' Play* at Wakefield, the lowly shepherds (after a lot of medieval shenanigans, including tossing the villain in a blanket, and forgiving him at last) find the Christ Child, the creator of the world, in a manger. There they give him three humble gifts: a bob of cherries, a bird, and something else you will find in no manger scene now:

> Hail, hold forth thy hand small;
> I bring thee but a ball:
> Have thou and play withal,
> And go to the tennis.

Cherries, a bird, and a tennis ball? Don't dismiss it as earthy clowning, for even earthy clowning, in medieval art and culture, is touched by the clowning of God. These gifts are the hayseed way of symbolizing the red blood Christ will shed (blood that is as fruitful as spring), his rising again, and his ruling the globe. In that same village—for generations!—the people will behold one of their neighbors playing Jesus, standing before Hell's gates, defying a buffoonishly impotent "Sir Satan," bursting the bars open with a command that recalls Moses when he delivered the Jews from their bondage in Egypt: "Open up, and let my people pass!"[7]

Was This a Good Thing?

The standard account holds that the Middle Ages were a period of technological stagnation. Real historians of the era shred that notion. For one thing, modern industry was launched:

> The great expansion of the use of watermills and windmills that took place during the later Middle Ages, in association with the growth of manufacturing, brought in an essentially new stage in mechanical technique. From this period must be dated that increasing mechanization of life and industry, based on the ever-increasing exploitation of new forms of mechanical power, which characterizes modern civilisation.
>
> **A. J. Crombie**, *Medieval and Early Modern Science, Vol. 1*

It was rollicking stuff, comic and solemn and colorful and reverent all at once, simple enough for any child to understand, yet steeped in rich and subtle theology. Do not judge it by our standards of mass entertainment. The people produced it, the people enjoyed it, the people remembered it, and handed it on, for centuries. Shakespeare saw such plays when he was a boy, *350 years after the tradition began.* It is quite true, and accepted (though often ignored) by Renaissance scholars, that without this dramatic revival, there would have been no Shakespeare.[8]

PC myth: The Middle Ages were the Dark Ages

Whence, then, comes the nonsensical charge that in the Middle Ages, the commoners lived lives of unutterable dreariness, while churchmen and warriors (often illiterate warriors) lorded it over them? In a typical medieval town—I am not talking about serfs in the backcountry of eastern Europe—there was more real equality of life, less of a gap between rich and poor, less of a division between one man's life and another, than there would be in the West until the American pioneers were made equal by a forbidding land, no money, and hard work.

It wasn't that life was easy. Life for most people has never been easy, until fairly recently. Nor should we think that the warrior aristocracies throughout Europe were all enjoying fine poetry and intellectual discourse. In many places they were simply marauders. But the leaven of Christian teaching, that all men are precious in the sight of God, was working its way up to the kings. So we have the pious king, Saint Louis IX of France, stationing himself under an oak tree in Paris to adjudicate cases brought by artisans and shopkeepers and plowmen. Louis was an able politician, but more than that, he was a true Christian king. Our heads of state would do well to heed the advice he left to his son and heir. Note, for instance, his preference for the poor, but also his politically incorrect acknowledgment that sometimes the rich too are in the right:

> Dear son, if you come to the throne, strive to have that which befits a king, that is to say, that in justice and rectitude you hold yourself steadfast and loyal toward your subjects and your vassals, without turning either to the right or to the left, but always straight, whatever may happen. And if a poor man has a quarrel with a rich man, sustain the poor rather than the rich, until the truth is made clear, and when you know the truth, do justice to them.[9]

Indeed, commoners frequently allied themselves with their king, against their common rivals, the noblemen. On this too Saint Louis gives his son advice:

> Preserve [your towns and cities] in the estate and the liberty in which your predecessors kept them, redress it, and if there be anything to amend, amend and preserve their favor and their love. For it is by the strength and the riches of your good cities and your good towns that the native and the foreigner, especially your peers and your barons, are deterred from doing ill to you. I well remember that Paris and the good towns of my kingdom aided me against the barons, when I was newly crowned.

Kings granted charters to individual towns or guilds, guaranteeing them wide freedom in business affairs, in return for a modest tax revenue. On the whole it worked quite well. English wool traders sent raw fleece to the free towns in Flanders, where the fullers and weavers wove it into cloth and sent it along to the town-republics in northern Italy and Tuscany.

There, for instance in Florence, the cloth would be dyed, and sent further east, to Venice and her trading ships, or overland to Constantinople and beyond. Cloth and other goods would be traded for spices, gold, herbal drugs, and so forth, with the encouragement of local rulers, but managed through private banking houses. A merchant might need "factors" or agents in several far-flung cities, Antwerp, Genoa, Hamburg, Constantinople, to whom he would write letters asking for credit. Thus we see in medieval Europe the beginnings of capitalism and home rule: of local independence and productive (in Italy often bloodily productive) economic rivalry.

Finally, there's the favorite slur against the Middle Ages, which has the added virtues of being a handy metaphor for anti-communism and persecution of women: witch-hunts and witch-burning. Witches were a real preoccupation of the Middle Ages, right? Not really. Probably more people have been shot in American shopping malls and high schools than were executed for witchcraft in all of Europe from 1000–1300. The real hunts for witches began only after the bouts of mass hysteria in the wake of the Black Plague, which struck Europe in 1348 and flared up every twenty years or so until the nineteenth century.[10]

The most famous witch trials, of course, were conducted in 1700 by post-Reformation, post-Renaissance Puritans in Massachusetts, after demonology had become a "science." Racialism would soon follow in the wake of the Enlightenment. The Middle Ages were ignorant of *these* sciences, I admit. Still, the Middle Ages serve as the politically correct hitching post for any unsavory episodes in Western history.

When love and nature were richer

By now the reader should see that to call the people of the Middle Ages "otherworldly" is as accurate as to say that their lives were drab and ignorant and miserable. We need to draw distinctions here.

In the darker corners of ancient Greek religion, which was about as sunny as paganism can be, there still lurked a fear of the tremendous forces of nature, and an urge, with sacrificial blood or ritual orgies, to placate them or to try to wrest them to one's will. Hence would you see young maidens, at a feast for the wine-god Dionysus, carrying a huge wooden phallus in ritual procession.[11] But Christianity drove out those gods and, as Chesterton puts it, made it possible for people once again to revel in nature with a free conscience.[12] Long before the Renaissance, we witness a flourishing of art and literature that pays loving attention to the beauty of the natural world, *even when it is God and not that earthly beauty* that is the object of the artist's ultimate desire.

We have Saint Francis of Assisi, that barefoot fellow, "Frenchy," as we might call him by name, stripping himself of the fancy clothes his

Church and State

The divine right of the anointed king was counterbalanced throughout the greater part of the Middle Ages by its conditional and revocable character; and this was not a mere concession to theological theory; it was enforced by the very real authority of the Church.

Christopher Dawson, *Religion and the Rise of Western Culture*

Else why do you think that statists such as Stalin took such risks in persecuting the Church? No despot, whether one man or a legislature or nine Nazgul perched on a judicial bench, wants his right to be "conditional and revocable."

merchant-father provided for him, but in his burlap not stripping off his love for the fancy creatures of God's world. So he sings in his famous hymn:

> Praised be You, my Lord, through Brother Fire,
> through whom you light the night,
> and he is beautiful and playful and robust and strong. (*Canticle of Brother Sun,* 17–19)

That love is sweetly captured in Giotto's painting of Francis preaching to the birds, with a fellow friar nearby raising his hands in surprise and incomprehension, or in the amiable story of how Francis persuaded one Brother Wolf to stop harassing the good people of Gubbio, promising him a daily meal if he would leave them in peace.[13]

Francis was not alone in this regard. Only someone who reveled in the humble and the earthy could give us Dante's delicate description of a mother bird waiting for the dawn, so that she might fly from the nest to feed her chicks (*Paradiso* 23.1–9), or Chaucer's portrait of the luscious pin-up wench Alison, who tweezed her eyebrows that were "arched and black as any sloe" ("The Miller's Tale," 3246), or these lines steeped in the sweat and grime of a good deer hunt, written by a great anonymous poet:

> Ah they brayed and they bled and died by the banks,
> while the racing dogs ran right on their tails,
> hunters with high horns hastening after,
> with a cry so clear it could shatter the cliffs! (*Sir Gawain and the Green Knight,* 1163–66)

Or we may see their taste for color, for the winsomeness of sky and leaf and flower, in the illuminated pages of the Duc de Berry's *Tres Riches Heures.* My favorite page celebrates a truly Merry Christmas, with the work of that blessed time—feasting—rambunctiously going on, dogs and all, under the quiet order of the stars.

And those stars are filled with meaning. They are not random points of light in the sky, the debris of an old and meaningless explosion. They are signs in the book of God. Nature is all the greater in that it beckons beyond itself. If you take nature's beauty to be final—if, like the old man in Chaucer's "Merchant's Tale," you marry a frisky girl because a wife is a man's sport and earthly paradise (1332), and that is all—you will be cruelly disappointed. "All flesh is grass," says the prophet (Is. 40:6), and the people of the Middle Ages were quick to acknowledge that judgment. Where are the snows of yesteryear?" asks the affable rake Francois Villon, considering the beauty of ladies unremembered.[14]

The ruling wisdom had it that all this wealth of beauty—the leaping of Brother Fire, or the gleaming smile of a little girl as she meets her father beside a stream whose bed is encrusted with jewels (*Pearl*)—is meant to lead man to contemplate its Creator, whose beauty does not fade. Naturally, people do not contemplate God all the time, and the medieval authors will cheerfully recount their rascality, as when a friar seduces a dimwitted lady by dressing himself up as the angel Gabriel (Boccaccio, *Decameron* 4.2). Still the ideal is present and powerful. It beats warmly at the heart of the greatest thinkers and artists. Let's take the greatest of those in turn: Dante and his theological master, Thomas Aquinas.

I was nine years old, says Dante, "when there appeared before my eyes the now glorious lady of my mind, who was called Beatrice," that is, the woman who blesses, "even by those who did not know what her name was" (*The New Life,* II). From this chance encounter springs, in the transforming imagination of the poet, the allegory of love to which he devoted his poetic career. As he tells it, he fell in love with Beatrice, or rather this love overtook him, changing him from within. That is what happens when one encounters and submits to divine beauty,

> . . . for where she goes
> Love drives a killing frost into vile hearts

> that freezes and destroys what they are thinking;
>
> should such a one insist on looking at her,
>
> he is changed to something noble or he dies. (*The New Life,*
> XIX)

Now of course a young man in love is prey to self-pity, and the callow Dante was no exception, as he relates to us his youthful infatuation. But after Beatrice dies young, and Dante has been jolted from his ensuing spiritual dullness by a vision of glory, he resolves to do for her what had never been done in honor of any woman before. The result will be the poem we call *The Divine Comedy*—wherein that earthly woman named Beatrice Portinari, whom Dante beheld and loved, will lead the poet's vision to heaven and to the face of God. Nor is that simply a subject for a fascinating poem. Dante is quite serious about it; the hope enlists all the ardor of his mind and heart. For even after he writes his incomparable tribute, he says, he shall yearn for more:

> And then may it please the One who is the Lord of gracious-
> ness that my soul ascend to behold the glory of its lady, that is,
> of that blessed Beatrice, who in glory contemplates the coun-
> tenance of the One *qui est per omnia secula benedictus* [who
> is for all generations blessed]. (*The New Life,* XLII)

Perhaps the reader is not interested in learning how a young love led to the wonder of *The Divine Comedy*. That would not surprise me. We find it hard to imagine how loving a pretty but otherwise seemingly ordinary woman can open the soul up to the vistas of paradise. That, too, without one's ever having been granted a kiss. But that is the point. We cannot imagine it, not because the medievals lived in some gauzy daydream of another world, but because we do not feel as intensely as they the beauty of this or any world, "beauty" having been demoted to a matter of taste, as of crackers or postcards. Our teachers preach it as dogma. No doubt we *experience* beauty subjectively—I happen to find the polyphonic music of Palestrina wondrously complex and lovely, while your heart may rather be touched by the brooding fury of Beethoven. But to say, flatly, that the beauty of their works does not itself really exist has consequences. Cold and ugly modern art and atonal concerts are bad enough, but worse than those is the assertion that there is no real order in things; all is random and without purpose. And how can anyone fall in love with the random and purposeless?

But medieval man's faith in an ultimate and immutable beauty whetted the appetite. So for three centuries, almost everything that people write or preach or sing has to do with love, with passionate love. Dante is at the peak of a long tradition. "Now one who asks for a kiss," writes the austere monk Saint Bernard of Clairvaux, "is in love. It is not for liberty that she asks, nor for an award, not for an inheritance nor even knowledge, but for a kiss . . . With a spontaneous outburst from the abundance of her heart, direct even to the point of boldness, she says, 'Let him kiss me with the kiss of his mouth'."[15] Bernard is talking about the faithful soul, longing for God. If such longings are hard for the modern heart to bear, we can turn to William of Aquitaine, the first great troubadour of Provence. In one song he

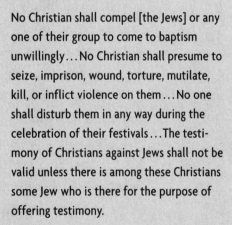

Jews in the Middle Ages

Pope Gregory X in 1272 issued a papal bull regarding protections for Jewish people:

> No Christian shall compel [the Jews] or any one of their group to come to baptism unwillingly . . . No Christian shall presume to seize, imprison, wound, torture, mutilate, kill, or inflict violence on them . . . No one shall disturb them in any way during the celebration of their festivals . . . The testimony of Christians against Jews shall not be valid unless there is among these Christians some Jew who is there for the purpose of offering testimony.

And the protections continue, by order of the Pope, repeating similar proclamations by his predecessors, particularly Gregory the Great. We forget how difficult it was to ensure that secular officials thousands of miles away obeyed such orders as these, in the days before instant communication. If you were Jewish in western Europe, the closer you were to Rome, the safer you were.

pretends to be deaf and dumb so he can enjoy bedding down with two ladies at once. They give him a surefire test: they drag a big red cat down the side of his naked body, to make him cry out. When he still makes no sound, they let him have his way with them, maybe more than he'd wanted, for eight whole days. "No, no!" he moans at the end of the poem, "I cannot tell the vexation, it hurt so bad!" He is not, ahem, talking about the scratches he got from the cat.[16]

The trick of it was, in art and in life, to find the harmony between earthly beauty and heavenly beauty, to fall so deeply in love that no earthly creature could finally satisfy the longing, although love could and did lead you along the way to that satisfaction. Or it could lead you astray from it, if you indulged a sinful love.

So Lancelot, after years of betraying his friend and king by sleeping with the gentle (and treacherous) Queen Guinevere, must turn from that love, if he would do right by himself, his king, his queen, and God. If he did not love the queen as his idol, he would have no problem setting her aside; and if he did not long for God, he *would not* set her aside. It is precisely the strong passion that we admire, and that we in our art cannot find the strength to celebrate. At the moment of his repentance Lancelot wept "as bitterly as if had seen the object of his dearest love lying dead before him, and with the desperation of a man at his wit's end for grief" (*The Quest of the Holy Grail*).

That struggle between what we ought to love best and what we do love instead provides the medieval poet with terrifically fruitful ground to work. Should Isolde give way to her love for the handsome and courtly Tristan, even though she is married to his uncle, King Mark of Cornwall? Or is sexual desire too powerful to resist? Is that what the poet Beroul means when he has her drink the potion that turns her heart toward the young man? If love brings joy and life, why is it self-destructive?[17]

Why does Chretien de Troyes have Lancelot cross a twenty foot long sword-bridge set on edge, maiming his bare hands and feet and knees, to save Guinevere, held in custody in a castle on the other side, kidnapped by a man who "loves" her as unreasonably as Lancelot does?[18] Or, if you are an aristocratic lady at the court of Eleanor of Aquitaine, do you follow the advice of her chaplain Andrew, who says that Love demands that the beloved deny nothing to the lover? Or is the good priest winking at "courtly" amours, slyly revealing them for the follies they are?[19]

The point is that in medieval song and poetry and art we are never far from the passions, but also never far from that divine Love that Dante says is his sole inspiration:

> I'm one who takes the pen
> when Love breathes wisdom into me, and go
> finding the signs for what he speaks within. (*Purgatory,*
> 24.52–54)

Then the artists could not take the passions for granted. "God is Love," says Saint John (1 Jn. 4:8), and "God is not the author of confusion," says Saint Paul (1 Cor. 14:33). So then if love brings confusion, as anyone with eyes open can see, we must distinguish between love and love, between passions that are licit and illicit, passions rightly ordered and disordered. In other words, precisely because they took the passion so seriously, medieval thinkers searched for a way to see how true human love springs from the love that comes from God and is God. Consideration of love brings us inevitably to theology.

PC trope: Dancing angels and pinheads

Here we must debunk another charge against medieval thinkers: that they were divorced from the world, wasting centuries arguing about metaphysical trivia. Set aside for the moment whether, during their two hundred years of brightest glory, their metaphysical debates were in fact trivial. Were they divorced from the world?

Certainly there were mystics, as there are today (and as there will be in any age) whose imaginations soared into realms where only a contemplative can go. Richard of Saint Victor was one. He described, with painstaking attention to the progress of actual people on their spiritual journeys, how we climb, step by step, from contemplation of the material creatures around us to loving union with their Creator.[20] Saint Bonaventure called such an ascent the mind's journey *into* God, and he too insisted that the soul must begin by reading the Book of Nature, written by the hand of God.[21]

If such language seems quaint, we should note that it is anchored in physical things that we can see and touch, here and now. No medieval thinker could say, with the Gnostic heretics of the first two centuries after Christ, or some German idealists after the Enlightenment, that this world is an evil illusion, a mere husk. The Incarnation of Christ—the *enfleshing*—forbids it. Christ was wrapped in swaddling clothes and laid in a manger. His mother nursed him at the breast. He worked with his carpenter father at the plane and the lathe. For the first time in Christian history, Christmas, the day that most powerfully celebrates the fleshliness of the Savior, assumes its place, second only to Easter, at the heart of the Christian calendar. It is from the Middle Ages that we derive our first Christmas carols. It is Francis of Assisi, that earthy beggar and mystic, who constructs the first Christmas creche.

Then the things about us are blessed, as the Incarnation shows. It follows that we should pay them heed. Saint Albert the Great taught his students to do just that. Albert was by avocation a biologist, gathering and classifying examples of flora and fauna, and compiling accounts of creatures he saw, creatures described in books, and creatures reported by travelers (who do engage in exaggeration).[22] In the same mind, Albert welcomed into his school the close study of Aristotle. Muslim philosophers in Spain and North Africa had long been fascinated by Aristotle's works, and had been attempting, without much success, to reconcile his metaphysical deductions with the Koran. So the works of the man whom the medieval schoolmen came to honor as simply The Philosopher had been reintroduced into the West via translations and commentaries from the Arabic, particularly those of Averroes, whom they honored as The Commentator.

What was important about this? Aristotle insisted, against Plato, that everything we know, we learn first from the senses. Now, many medieval thinkers hedged, believing that our finest way of knowing is by direct intuition of the truth, an illumination by God. But many agreed with The Philosopher, as did the great student of Albert, Thomas Aquinas.

In his *Summa Theologiae* (*The Encyclopedia of Theological Questions* is a fair translation), Thomas aligns himself with one side of this vigorous debate, and insists that all of our knowledge, including our knowledge of God, comes to us first through the senses. That does not mean we are limited to knowing only what we can sense, he says, since the existence and operation of a cause we cannot sense can be inferred from its effects.[23] Thomas, I'd like to assert, is not less of a rationalist and an

The Dark Ages?

Comparing medieval civic life to that of today's atomistic, isolated, air-conditioned, commercialized suburban America, it's hard to use the slur "Dark Ages" against medieval Europe:

> Men, women, and children in medieval towns did not, like the denizens of the crowded slums in some modern cities, go from one end of the year to the other with scarcely a glimpse of nature or a moment under the open sky. Medieval towns were much more careful of the public health than used to be supposed. Many of them had municipal physicians; hospitals and public baths were common; such occupations as butchers were under strict hygienic regulation.
>
> **Lynn Thorndike**, *The History of Medieval Europe* (338)

empiricist than a modern scientist would be, but *more.* He allows reason a broad scope. He encourages us to see everything about us (including human passions), and draw rational conclusions from them, rather than limiting our attention only to those things we can place on the scales or measure with a ruler. Thomas combines the most precise metaphysical acuity with common sense, and in this regard he is both the best and the most typical of the medieval thinkers.

Let's see how this reasoning, both practical and metaphysical, works in practice. Consider the question, "Is it ever morally justified to swerve from the letter of the civil law?"[24] Thomas understands that, in answering this question, reason must begin with the everyday objects around us, and the situations in which we may find ourselves. That is where reason *begins.* But, since reason is a far more powerful tool than modern man believes, that is not where it ends. So if a man in fury wants you to return the sword he lent you, even though the law says you must return it, you can justly refuse. That's because laws are created for the general case, and cannot foresee every event in which they might be used for harm. You must use prudence to apply the law to the circumstances. We of course agree with Aquinas here; it's an easy case.

Yet there *are moral absolutes,* as patently offensive as that would be today, and these too are discoverable by reason. "Is it ever justified to tell a lie?" Thomas asks. Here, unlike the case of the man who wants to keep the sword from his hot-tempered friend, we are dealing with the very nature of man. We see that a dog, for example, wants food and water and a place to rest, but man is not satisfied only with these things. Man possesses an intellect. He hungers to know the truth, and his principal means of learning and teaching is language. To say what you know is not true, then, is to strike at the heart of who we are: "For since words are natural signs of the intellect, it is unnatural and uncalled for to use words to signify what is not in your mind. That is why [Aristotle] says that *the lie is in itself crooked and to be avoided, while the truth is good and to be praised"* (*Summa Theol.* 2.2.110.3). Here we see Aristotle taken seriously—not simply as an ancient thinker whose thoughts should be dissected, diagrammed, and analyzed—but as a philosopher whose conclusions about right and wrong, articulated in a most judgmental and politically incorrect way ("in itself crooked" vs. "good and to be praised"), ought to guide our actions.

While clear and absolute in his moral teachings, St. Thomas was not at all simplistic, regardless of what our more ethically-creative peers might say. One can, for instance, refrain from revealing the truth to wicked men, or refrain from speaking at all. The good sisters in *The Sound of Music* were shrewd Thomists, not lying to the Nazis pursuing the Von Trapp family, but neither telling them where they were, and managing to remove their car's distributor cap to boot. It is a sign of our intellectual confusion that we can no longer fathom the difference between law and prudence; we sin with abandon, but will set a murderer free over a legal stutter.

But that flatfooted, earthbound, commonsense observation, that man alone among beasts hungers to know, leads Thomas to potent conclusions. For there is no other creature whose principal faculties are in vain. The dog has teeth, and there are deer for his prey. Man has a mind, and there are things around him to know, but these things by themselves fail to satisfy. I see a crystal, and I experience real pleasure in beholding it, testing it for hardness, chiseling it apart, learning why, chemically, it has its pale violet color. But if I investigated a million such, I would be no wiser about who I am than before. I want not only to know, but to know the highest things.

And in fact, Thomas affirms, we can know much about those highest things without the revelation of God.[25] We see a table, a stream, a stalk of corn, and know, by experience, that none of these things need have been. They are contingent. If the carpenter had not worked the wood, there would be no table. If the earth had not had a sufficient mass, there would have been no atmosphere to hold the vapor for rain to fill the stream. If the seed had not fallen to the earth, there would have sprung no corn. We can regard the whole world as a great collection of such things, no one of which need have been, though each of which, once it exists, is bound by the necessities governing it, as a droplet in the desert must evaporate. Then the collection itself, because it is only a collection, need not have been. But the world—the *cosmos*—exists: we see it. Therefore there must be, Thomas concludes, something whose existence is not contingent, but necessary in itself, "not possessing the cause of its necessity from somewhere else, but the cause of the necessity of other things" (*Summa Theol.* 1.2.3).

The attention to the question of God, then, is not browbeaten into the heads of docile scholars. It springs from the observable nature of man as a knowing creature, and from the observable order *and insufficiency* of the world. If we limit reason to detecting the hairs on a pussy willow preserved in a lump of coal, as fascinating as that may be, we will never accost those questions of greatest importance, as "What is this world for?" and "What is it good for me to be?" and "Where did I come from, and where am I going?" Perhaps, if medieval men had plied their minds to study hydraulics and optics and agriculture (and some of them did, preparing the way for the explosion of natural science in the Renaissance) then people would have had superior wells, and eyeglasses, and white bread. But Aquinas and Bonaventure, for all their stark differences on the question of how we know things, agreed that man, by that nature of his that we can see before our eyes, needs far more than wells and eyeglasses and white bread. The low bar set by our secular materialistic culture today makes it hard to comprehend, but maybe modern conveniences and healthy bodies are badly purchased at the price of modern vices and sick souls. Medieval Europe, we may have to admit, had its greatest minds aimed in a worthier direction.

So it is not true that there were no scientists and mathematicians then. Setting aside men like the number-wizard Fibonacci, who was exactly what we would call a mathematician, the schools were bursting with people who plied their reason, beginning with observations of visible things, to grasp after the truth; and with people who, beginning with what is bodily, came to understand things that are not bodily, and to examine their necessary characteristics. These too were their scientists, these too were their mathematicians.

How many angels can dance on the head of a pin? No medieval writer ever asked such a thing. But the question, which appears to have been the invention of a smug Enlightenment satirist, could be considered no different from "how many infinitesimals can fit between any two numbers, no matter how close they are," the question that burst open Newton's imagination as he invented the calculus. Nor would it have been absurd to imagine that a being can exist without the limitation of a body. At least one such Being, Thomas showed, must necessarily exist.

Before PC: When intellectual curiosity could thrive

I have said that medieval artists and thinkers were confident that man's mind could attain certainty, even about the highest things. Some, like

Once Again: The Dark Ages?

Each commune [that is, a town with a charter of freedoms] had a seal of its own, a belfry whose bell summoned the citizens to the defense of their liberties, and a pillory and gibbet where the decrees of town justice were executed. For the [town] had its own court, made its own laws or followed its own customer, and the fines paid went into the town treasury and not into the lord's pocket.

Lynn Thorndike, *The History of Medieval Europe*

If only we enjoyed such freedom. Imagine what your schools might be like if you and your townsmen alone were responsible for what went on in them.

Thomas, had a sunny view of this capacity. Others, like Bernard, believed that our principal source of knowledge about God, other than God's revelation in Scripture, came from a mystic intuition, a gift from without. What they all had in common was that hunger, as Dante calls it, for "the bread of angels" (*Paradiso* 2.11). That confidence and that healthy appetite explain why the men of the Middle Ages invented what we still call the "university." But what we call higher education would have made the schoolmen blush. I'm not talking about the silliness of our curricula, but about how we rob reason of its function. We fear its muscles. Thomas Aquinas and his comrades had no such fear.

That timidity of ours shows up in our "universities," so called for marketing purposes, and perhaps because you can study *anything* you like there, including porn movies and other twaddle. But you can't study *everything,* because the presumption is that painting has nothing to do with dissecting a fish, which has nothing to do with reading the poetry of Robert Frost. There is nothing to unite these intellectual endeavors. What's worse, this intellectual alienation of one discipline from another falls prey to a vicious and all-pervading political orthodoxy the like of which none of the schoolmen would have countenanced. Why? If there is no universal truth accessible to reason and demanding rational argument, then partisans of one position or another fall back upon brute coercion. Feminists, for example, have long decried logic as patriarchal, and that is why they must use the machinery of power to get their way—by derailing the careers of untenured professors who disagree with them. When you can't win an argument, pull a gun. But medieval professors allowed for refreshingly free debate, even though they were discussing matters which they believed might determine not simply which candidate would teach freshman English but the ultimate bliss or damnation of millions of human souls to come.

Take Thomas's most ambitious metaphysical work, the *Summa Contra Gentiles.* He writes it to wrestle with, among others, the great Muslim philosophers Averroes and Avicenna. His approach is not that of our slovenly professoriate. He is not politically correct for his day. He never imposes dogma upon his students, ignoring evidence or arguments to the contrary. He never insinuates that Averroes believes what he does because of some social or political advantage to be gained, as if that would make any difference to the truth. He never supinely suggests that what might have been all right for Averroes was all right for him, but not for us. He has really learned a great deal from the "Gentiles," and he finds them often exactly correct. But his faith and his reason *both* lead him to conclude that they have made subtle metaphysical mistakes, and that erroneous conclusions result: for example, Averroes' argument that the world must be eternal, and that the soul of an individual human being is reabsorbed at death into an impersonal Agent Intellect that governs all things.

So Thomas pursues them with all the vigor of a passionate heart—and with all the modesty and the confidence in reason that cause you to prefer to lose an argument and learn the truth, rather than win and remain in ignorance. He will present *eighteen arguments* (2.32–34) culled from his opponents, giving them their best shot, and never tossing against them a single snide remark. He will methodically show, by reason—not by appealing to authority, or to Scripture, though he will do so to help illustrate his position—that the results do not follow from the premises, or that the premises are mistaken. Then he proceeds to give his own position, that the world was created, and to address standard objections.

In one sense it is blissfully calm, carried on at the height of intellectual abstraction: "It is therefore clear," he says, after many paragraphs of reasoning about what it means to be "before time" and the difference between asserting that "X *always* exists" and "X exists *necessarily*," "that the arguments adduced from the point of view of creatures do not oblige us to maintain that the world is eternal" (2.36). But in another sense it is the result of sweat and toil and blood-rushing competition in the arena of ideas, with Truth—not celebrity, not tenure!—as the prize. Only a lover will fight so boldly. One of my favorite anecdotes about Thomas shows this love.[26] He was sitting at table (and taking up a goodly space, as he had a healthy appetite for other foods besides the theological) along with the lords and ladies at the palace of Louis IX of France. Picture the white-clad friar lost in thought among the clatter of plates, the dogs snuffling about, the crimson gowns, the flash of ornamental swords, young people flirting and old people telling stories. Suddenly Thomas rises and bangs his fist on the table.

"*Thus* are the Manicheans refuted!" he bellows.

"Quick," says King Louis, turning to a servant, "get him a pen and paper."

Certainly, not everybody was a Brother Thomas. There's a delightful medieval picture of a scholar lecturing his students, while one lad in the back is looking out the window, and another is snoozing.[27] And a university town saw a lot of spending on groceries, clothes, and drink. Then as now, thanks be to God for the masculine invention of graffiti, students amused themselves with scurrilous verses on life at school or in the monastery. In one such poem, the abbot of the Land of Cockaygne calls his monks home from the nearby nunnery by beating the signal on the bare buttocks of one of the sisters.[28] But these same students *invented* the university. Note that well: the students invented it,

The Truth about the Crusades

The First Crusade, our students are taught, was a war of imperialist aggression. Fairness requires we read Pope Urban II's call to war:

> From the confines of Jerusalem and from the city of Constantinople a grievous report has gone forth...a race from the kingdom of the Persians, an accursed race...has violently invaded the lands of those Christians and has depopulated them by pillage and fire. They have led away a part of the captives into their own country, and a part they have killed by cruel tortures. They have either destroyed the churches of God or appropriated them for the rites of their own religion...The kingdom of the Greeks is now dismembered by them and has been deprived of territory so vast in extent that it could not be traversed in two months' time.

because they wanted to learn. Otherwise they might show up at town at great expense, to be given a full course in law or medicine or theology, only to find that the masters were unprepared, or that they would duck out on their obligations. Just as students then drank, as now, so were professors lazy then, as now. So the students formed their own guild or union—hence, "university"—to hold the masters to their word, and to standardize the curricula, so that what they learned in Paris or Cologne would hold good when they returned to London or Florence.

I'm not saying that all the students were passionately interested in their theology. Not everybody was Chaucer's Clerk, whose prize possessions were twenty books—a prodigious collection for a young man—and who prayed assiduously for the souls of the friends who financed his tuition. "Gladly would he learn and gladly teach," says Chaucer (General Prologue, 308). Many no doubt were like Alayn and John in the Reeve's Tale, who take vengeance on a cheating miller by "swiving" his daughter and his wife, all while the miller snores away in the same room. Call it the perks of Higher Education.

Still, when we survey those three centuries our impression is of stupendous cultural achievements. Magnificent churches, whose ingenuity challenges the most daring of modern architecture, and whose liveliness and beauty leave us far behind, stipple the continent. And who builds these, but teams of ordinary men? Modern music is born in the modes of Gregorian chant; one Guido of Arezzo invents Western musical notation.[29] Capitalism is born, and international banking, and credit, and modern accounting. Artisans unite in guilds to secure business for their towns, to train the young, to ensure quality work, to provide for one another in sickness, and to support their widows and orphans. The love song, which has lasted almost eight hundred years, bloomed in the racy and refined imaginations of the lute players of Provence. The university comes into being, along with its stagy oral examinations, colorful, combative, and public. No fear of competition here. Friars, not all of them looking for a pretty leg and a pleasing eye, comb the new towns and cities, preaching the Word to a gallimaufry of people, because Christ came to save everyone, not only the rich, and not only monks within their monastery walls.

Greek learning returns to the West, and at the West's insistence, as controversial as it was. Painting rediscovers the beauty of the natural world, and the human face. Christmas is exalted. Drama returns with all the sweat and humor of the common people, who are its principal performers and audience. It is the age of the mystic Bernard, and the rationalist Abelard, of barefoot Francis rebuking a wolf, and barefoot Dominic rebuking a heretic. It is the age of Dante's *Divine Comedy* and Chaucer's human comedy; an age when a Thomas Aquinas, one of the greatest minds the world has ever known, could suddenly, after a mystical experience, cease writing, claiming that in comparison with that flash of a vision all he had written was straw. Thomas did not care what name he made for himself; and so little did the great English poet who wrote *Pearl* and *Sir Gawain and the Green Knight* care, that we still do not know who he was.

Contradictions there were—because the age was alive. At the end of *The Quest of the Holy Grail,* Sir Galahad is permitted to peer into the chalice of the Holy Eucharist, where he sees "what tongue could not relate nor heart conceive," the mysteries of the Real Presence of the incarnate Christ. "I pray Thee now," says he, "that in this state Thou suffer me to pass from earthly life to life eternal." Galahad then dies, and that is how the so-called Archpoet would go, too—almost:

> If wine's for the lips of a man about to die
> Then let me go in a tavern—just the place!
> So then the angel choirs will sing for joy,
> "Lord, look upon this drinker here with grace!"[30]

Chaucer's Wife of Bath "had passed many a foreign stream" (General Prologue, 464), always on pilgrimage, to Spain, the Holy Land, anywhere, with an eye to picking up another young husband to toss her in bed. But an old man from Croatia, says Dante, will travel at peril of his life to Rome, to see the cloth with which Veronica wiped the face of Jesus, on which the Savior's image was wondrously preserved. He sits quietly in the church, amazed, saying to himself,

> "And did you look like this—was this your face,
> O Jesus Christ my Lord and very God?" (*Paradiso* 31.107–8)

Running like a river through it all is that ceaseless desire to love and to be loved, to know and to be known. For the mind and the heart, even when they bow in idolatry to a beautiful maiden or a bottle of wine, were not considered utterly separate things. They could not be utterly separate. That is because the final object of our quest to know is Love Himself:

> O Light that dwell within Thyself alone,
>   who alone know Thyself, are known, and smile
>   with Love upon the Knowing and the Known!
> (*Paradiso* 33.124–26)

Here we touch upon intellectual and amatory heights beyond which it is impossible to go, unless that Being who is the source of being should grant it. Here, in a place pointed to by all the pinnacles of medieval art and song and thought, knowing and loving merge, and we see "the Love that moves the sun and the other stars." (*Paradiso* 33.145)

Chapter Six

THE RENAISSANCE: IT'S NOT WHAT YOU THINK

The frequency of assassination, the perennial plots, the constant vicissitudes, encouraged superstition and a romantic view of Fate. Men felt themselves to be the prey of strange destinies and turned to astrologers and magicians to strengthen their hope, to check despair, and to help them meet the uncertain future with confidence. The stars were studied as intensely as diplomatic dispatches, as a guide to action; and superstitious dread threaded the daily course of men's lives. (J. H. Plumb, *The Italian Renaissance*)

Read that quote to ten college graduates, telling them only that it describes a period from the previous millennium. Then ask which. Nine will choose the Middle Ages. Yet British historian John H. Plumb, who was not friendly to the Middle Ages, is describing what life was like during the height of the Renaissance, in its epicenter in Italy, at about 1500.

You surely know the standard account of the Renaissance. Common men broke free from the tyranny of the Church, and—newly liberated—became happier and wiser. Great artists, writers, and thinkers, free to focus on something besides dusty faith, created the greatest art, philosophy, and culture Europe had ever seen. The Renaissance, in short, is

Guess What?

❦ The glories of the Renaissance were the fruits of the Middle Ages and Christian culture.

❦ Renaissance secularism is both exaggerated and given too much credit for cultural advance.

❦ The Renaissance paved the way for modern moral decay by divorcing philosophy from faith.

pitched to us as the rejection of the Middle Ages and the glorious triumph of secularism.

These formulations all serve well the purposes of today's elites. They denigrate religion, exalt modernity, and allow secularists to claim credit for a flowering of creativity. They also have the virtue of simplicity. Nonsense is simple, too.

The odd thing about the Renaissance is that you can't make a general statement about it without needing, for the sake of accuracy and intellectual honesty, to retract it or qualify it a moment later. It is an age of wild contrarieties. We celebrate the grandeur of man (but man had long been revered as made in the image of God); yet our philosophies also reduce man to a selfish and ignorant brute. We slip from the grasp of the Church; but we fall abjectly under the power of an absolute monarch like Louis XIV of France, with Thomas Hobbes' political leviathan rearing its reptilian head from the deeps. No more will parsons tell us what to do; but no more will simple Christian laborers band together in the Peace of God or the Truce of God to curb their warmongering barons.[1] Chivalry, so often only a fine cloak for mischief, is dead; and war now encompasses every class, and 20,000 ordinary citizens, including women and children, die in the siege of Magdeburg in the Thirty Years' War.

The PC myths about the Renaissance

Historians know these things, but the politically correct imagination still attributes everything wicked and backward to a "medieval" age with conveniently elastic boundaries, and everything good and "modern" to the Renaissance. We know, don't we, that the Spanish Inquisition was an arm of the oppressive medieval Church? No, it wasn't. It was requested from Rome in 1478 by Ferdinand of Spain, and was run by the State. It was designed to ferret out false converts from Judaism and Islam, but it had more to do with the creation of a Spanish state than with religion. The Spanish monarchs, having driven the last Moorish ruler out of Granada in 1492, and hankering for unity in a land that had long been a checkerboard of feuding dukedoms, ordered that Jews and Muslims leave the country or become Christian. It was almost as cruel and unjust as those systems of inhumanity dreamed up by modern man. But in the meantime, a general reform of the Spanish Church was undertaken by Queen Isabella and her confessor, Cardinal Ximenes; and the religious and nationalist conflicts that ravaged much of Europe for a hundred years found no traction in a united and reformed Spain.

Witches were a real preoccupation of the Middle Ages, right? Not really. As I've said, probably more people have been shot in American shopping malls and high schools than were executed for witchcraft in all of Europe from 1000–1300. The real hunts for witches began only after the bouts of mass hysteria in the wake of the Black Plague, which struck Europe in 1348 and flared up every twenty years or so until the nineteenth century. As for demons, none of the great medieval theologians were terribly interested in them. Dante gives them a mere supporting role, often burlesque at that, in his *Inferno*. Thomas dispenses with them in a couple of articles in his *Summa Theologica*.[2] But demons are everywhere in the Renaissance imagination, particularly in the north. The legend of Doctor Faustus, the professor who sells his soul to the devil for twenty-four years of magic tricks and voluptuous succubi, is contemporary with Martin Luther. Later in the sixteenth century comes that hotel handbook on "What to Do in Case of Witchcraft," the *Malleus Maleficarum*. One of its more delightful chapters describes how a man may bed down with a witch and later discover, to his chagrin, that he's lost his *membrum virile,* and doesn't know where to find it (downright Victorian, one might charge).[3] Then comes a book that influenced Shakespeare's *Macbeth* and *King Lear*: the *Demonologie* of King James VI of Scotland, later James I of England and

What's Love Got to Do with It?

Everything. The Renaissance is our heyday of love poetry, in all the European languages: the tradition begun and flourishing in the Middle Ages comes to full flower.

The politically correct line on this poetry is that it "subverts" the authority of Christian moral teaching. Nonsense. It is, in the hands of the masters, a vivid and psychologically subtle and dramatically ironic portrayal of that teaching, even as it gives full play to the natural range of human emotions: love and hate, frustration and glee, jealousy and hope. It's why Edmund Spenser places the narrative of his love for his bride-to-be in the context of the true love that instructs all other loves. For his sequence of sonnets, the *Amoretti*, builds to a climax on Easter:

> Most glorious Lord of life, that on this day
> Didst make thy triumph over death and sin. (68.1–2)

Other writers will be more subtle about it. We lack the ears to hear.

the commissioner of the famous Bible. That's not to mention the Salem witch trials, conducted by learned Puritans at the turn of the enlightened 1700s.

In the Renaissance, men rose above stale authority and superstitious religious dogma, looking instead to nature and experiment to discover the laws of the physical world, yes? Actually, the ledger is not clear. Most Renaissance philosophers abandoned the Aristotelianism of the schools, which had gotten lost in a thicket of metaphysical minutiae. But they did not always take up science. The dominant philosophical outlook of the Renaissance was Neoplatonic, and gained in elegance what it lost in logical rigor. Influential writers from Marsilio Ficino in the fifteenth century to Henry More in the seventeenth believed that this world was a shadow of the immutable world of heavenly beauty, and that our contemplation ought to be channeled by earthy beauty towards that beauty above. Artists, poets, dramatists, philosophers, and even scientists were influenced by Neoplatonic mysticism, which was not conducive to making scientific hypotheses. It explains why the devout Johannes Kepler—a better astronomer, I think, than either Copernicus or Galileo—spent years trying to prove that the planetary orbits could each be inscribed in one of the five regular Platonic solids.[4] Even when he published his three laws of planetary motion, Kepler could not resist arguing that the ellipse and not the circle was the *more worthy* shape for expressing the Platonic significance of a planet.

The Renaissance lavished attention on the human body, true. Donatello sculpted the first bronze nude since classical antiquity, his famous *David*, girlish and comfortable in his skin. Leonardo drew maps of human musculature, in repose and in motion, attempting to establish the mathematical harmonies among the parts of the body. He had no formal education, but Raphael, for one, recognized the latent Platonism in his works and painted Leonardo as the heavenward-gesturing Plato in his *School of Athens*. But the Renaissance is also an age of corpses:

> What's this flesh? a little crudded milk, fantastical puff-paste: our bodies are weaker than those paper prisons boys use to keep flies in—more contemptible, since ours is to preserve earthworms. (John Webster, *The Duchess of Malfi* 4.2.124–7; 1623)

Thomas More was not the only man to keep a grinning skull at his desk as a reminder. Fashionable ladies wore rings engraved with skulls. John Donne wrote a series of meditations on a dangerous sickness he survived, and had his portrait taken wound up in a shroud. Go to the cathedral at Bern to enjoy stained glass windows of gleeful skeletons playing alongside a fat oblivious bishop or a drinker or a whoremaster. Those are Renaissance windows, post-Reformation.

Yet the Renaissance needs no cheat. It has plenty of genuine gold.

What then was this dynamic age, and what can we who gag on the oatmeal of political correctness learn from it? To answer that, I'd like to focus on three topics, each of them prime for misconception: the Glory of Man, the Resurgent Pagan, and the Collapse of Authority.

Is there a nature in this man?

"Most esteemed Fathers," writes the young polymath Giovanni Pico della Mirandola:

> I have read in the ancient writings of the Arabians that Abdala the Saracen on being asked what, on this stage, so to say, of the world, seemed to him most evocative of wonder, replied that there was nothing to be seen more marvelous than man. And that celebrated exclamation of Hermes Trismegistus, "What a great miracle is man, Asclepius," confirms this opinion. (*Oration on the Dignity of Man*)

Behold the boundless confidence of the Renaissance spirit that bursts into view here. Pico has read classical Arabic and quotes not Augustine or Thomas, but Abdala the Saracen on man's dignity. Then he quotes the mystic Thrice-Blessed Hermes, a writer in the occult mystery traditions of the third century. Pico means no disrespect to Christians. He was a good Catholic, and his *Oration* will cite, with that same wide-eyed youthfulness, Genesis, the Torah, the Psalms, the Book of Job, Saint Paul, Pseudo-Dionysius, and a passel of other Fathers of the Church. Not to mention Homer, Zoroaster, the Jewish Cabbalists, and anyone else from whom he believes wisdom is to be gleaned.

To do otherwise, "to enclose oneself within one Porch or Academy" (44), is to desire mediocrity when God has granted us the capacity to address all imaginable questions. It is also to miss real graces and glories ready to be appreciated. Among Christians, who have come late to philosophy, says Pico, "there is in John Scotus both vigor and distinction, in Thomas, solidity and sense of balance" (44), and so forth, as the youth samples them all like a connoisseur.

"So far so good," says the slack-minded professor of today, in his class on Comparative Religions, which might otherwise be called Comparative

Irrelevance. "Pico knew that it really did not make a difference what you believe." But that is to miss Pico's point altogether. We can range across all traditions and authorities, because ultimately all lead to contemplation of the One and immutable God. It is not relativism but brash confidence that God has granted to all peoples real vision of his truth and beauty. Pico did *not* say that it was ultimately irrelevant whether you were an Aristotelian or a Platonist. He said that if you examine the authors more closely, you will discover how their apparent contradictions may be reconciled. He did *not* say that Zoroaster was the equal of Moses because, as the politically correct would say, with a toss of the head, "We can't know anything about God in any case." He said that if you enter the minds of these lawgivers you will find them, in different respects, adhering to the truth.

We live in a world of multiplicity and mutability, and yet the wise behold the beauty of these many things and rise from them to the central and supreme Beauty that sustains them. It is why the eclectic Pico can in one breath recall Jacob's dream of angels ascending and descending a ladder from earth to heaven—a standard medieval image of the contemplative Christian life—and the Egyptian myth of the scattered limbs of Osiris, brought back into unity by the sun god "Phoebus," from the Greek pantheon (16–17).

What then is man, so endowed with intelligence? Pico answers with a parable. When God created the world, He endowed all other creatures with some property to define their natures. Still, He wanted a creature "which might comprehend the meaning of so vast an achievement, which might be moved with love at its beauty." But alas, God had already given away every particular place in the chain of Being. So, since this special creature, man, could have nothing properly his own, God gave him the capacity to partake of the gifts belonging to all other creatures. It would be his nature to have no nature, to ascend to the angels, or, in wickedness, to descend to the beasts:

The nature of all other creatures is defined and restricted within laws which We have laid down; you, by contrast, impeded by no such restrictions, may, by your own free will, to whose custody We have assigned you, trace for yourself the lineaments of your own nature. . . . We have made you a creature neither of heaven nor of earth, neither mortal nor immortal, in order that you may, as the free and proud shaper of your own being, fashion yourself in the form you prefer.

PC Myth: Galileo Invented Modern Science

Galileo is the stereotypical hero of "science" against the repressive forces of religion. It turns out the Church never denied Earth could move around the sun, but insisted he didn't have enough evidence to teach it as a settled fact. Albert Einstein agreed with the Church:

> It has often been maintained that Galileo became the father of modern science by replacing the speculative, deductive method with the empirical, experimental method. I believe, however, that this interpretation would not stand close scrutiny.
>
> **—Albert Einstein**, foreword to Galileo's *Dialogue Concerning the Two Chief World Systems*

Einstein acknowledges that Galileo had no proof that Earth revolved around the sun. He could not have had proof, because "a complete theory of mechanics was lacking," at least until Newton. It was his longing for such a proof which "misled him into formulating a wrong theory of the tides," a theory he never would have accepted, says Einstein, "had his temperament not got the better of him."

That trust in the infinite possibilities of man, both for good and for evil, is everywhere to be found in this time, showing up in different forms in different places. Take the work of Pico's young acquaintance, Michelangelo. In his titanic *Creation of Adam*, the first man, in classical repose, almost lassitude, awaits the spark of life communicated to him by the finger of God. It is not the clay that Michelangelo paints, but the space between God's finger and man's, a space of electric tension, to be bridged by the Almighty: "And he breathed into his nostrils the breath of life; and man became a living soul" (Gen. 2:7). It is a painting of God making a creature in His image: power, communicating power.

The same trust shows up in the poet Edmund Spenser, a staunch Protestant who one would think might be suspicious of optimism coming from Italy. But Spenser has only praise for Pico, whose ladder of contemplation he transforms into a ladder of love:

> For love is Lord of truth and loyalty,
> Lifting himself out of the lowly dust
> On golden plumes up to the purest sky. (*Hymne of Love*, 176–8)

The dour John Milton, in his blindness considering all the lovely things he can no longer see, brings his longing to a poignant and typically Renaissance climax:

> Thus with the year
> Seasons return, but not to me returns
> Day, or the sweet approach of Ev'n or Morn,
> Or sight of vernal bloom, or Summer's Rose,
> Or flocks, or herds, or human face divine.
> (*Paradise Lost*, 3.40–44)

For the face—enfolded between the words "human" and "divine"—is human because it is divine, and can reflect the divine by its intelligence and love. It is the loveliest part of the human body, which itself, in Milton,

Michelangelo, Spenser, Leonardo, and almost everyone else who wrote about it or painted it, is the most beautiful object in all of physical creation:

> Nor hath God deigned to show Himself elsewhere
> More clearly than in human forms sublime,
> Which, since they image Him, alone I love. (Michelangelo, Sonnet 56, 12–14)

None of these artists would have understood the secular aversion to seeing man as made in the image of God, and the universe, man's domain in both time and space, as the ordered and unfolding creation of God. Indeed, they well understood that if you ignore the divine, what is left of nature is cruel, and what is left of sinful man is loathsome. If the world is not oriented toward the good, and if man is but a higher brute, then, as the bloody tyrant Macbeth puts it, our life:

> . . . is a tale
> Told by an idiot, full of sound and fury,
> Signifying nothing. (*Macbeth,* V.v.26–28)

But why embrace Macbeth's madness? The artists loved the beauty of man and the world all the more, because they believed that the beauty reflected the beauty of the Maker.

If man's body is beautiful, so much the more is his intellect. Not only can it appreciate the work of the Creator, it also is endowed with the Creator's spark, and by art can work wonders beyond those of nature:

> Neither let it be deemed too saucy a comparison to balance the highest point of man's wit with the efficacy of nature, but rather give right honor to the heavenly Maker of that maker, who having made man to His own likeness, set him beyond and over all the works of that second nature, which in nothing he showeth so much as in poetry, when with the force of a

divine breath he bringeth forth things far surpassing her doings. (Philip Sidney, *Apology for Poetry*)

Are there no bounds for the intellect? Christopher Marlowe's Faustus turns to necromancy because he believes it is the one subject fit for an infinite longing to know:

But his dominion that exceeds in this,
Stretcheth as far as doth the mind of man. (*Doctor Faustus*, I.i.59–60)

Are there no bounds for man's will? Not if you want power, says Machiavelli, who recommends a bold and ruthless hand to unite Italy, "because fortune is a woman, and it is necessary, in order to keep her down, to beat her and to struggle with her. And it is seen that she more often allows herself to be taken over by men who are impetuous than by those who make cold advances" (*The Prince*, ch. 25). One may stand in alienation beyond all men, as does Shakespeare's Richard of Gloucester, who ponders how he will murder his brothers en route to grasping the crown of England:

I have no brother, I am like no brother;
And this word "love," which graybeards call divine,
Be resident in men like one another
And not in me: I am myself alone. (*3 Henry VI*, V.vi.80–83)

By now perhaps the reader senses that something is amiss. How have we slid from "I am man, I can do anything" to "I am beyond man, *I may do anything*"? There are, I think, two causes, and Renaissance writers and artists were aware of them. We are not aware of them, we who are happily sending mankind down the cloning line, reducing children to "resources" to be warehoused, altering genes, stapling breasts to men and testicles to women, and strutting about like gods while allowing ourselves to be considered no more than products of social, technological, and bureaucratic engineering, as if we were so much processed cheese. So then, let's pay attention.

The first cause can be found in Pico's narrative of the creation of Adam. The second can be found in what Pico has left out of that narrative. They are simply these. Once man accepts that he has no nature, he becomes unmoored from the rest of creation, radically alone, without any guard against committing the most unnatural of acts (as, for instance, inviting your kindly uncle and his friends to a dinner and killing them all to seize power; a naughty thing to do, says Machiavelli, but effective; *The Prince*, ch. 8). For Pico is wrong here, and the more staid philosophers of the Middle Ages were correct. Man does have a nature, glorious though it may be, and he must obey it. When he does not, he falls, sinning as Adam did. And that's the second explanation for the slide from Pico to the amoral opportunist. Man sins.

The fall of man is a small incident in Genesis that Pico, in his *Oration*, overlooks. It's a small step from claiming to transcend one's created nature to believing that all things, even good and evil, are products of one's almighty mind. So Satan wishes to persuade himself in hell:

> The mind is its own place, and in itself
> Can make a Heav'n of Hell, a Hell of Heav'n. (*Paradise Lost*, 1.254–55)

In fact this sobering revision of Renaissance confidence, verging upon Renaissance despair, Pico himself was to experience. It's politically correct to smirk at that despair, to suppose that it was a reflex of the superstition of the Church, and to deny that we, who once again propose a vision of human "nature" infinitely malleable and therefore not a nature at all, will fall into the same abyss. We will; we must. Our premises are wrong.

For Pico saw the shame of man every day of his life. He lived in Medici Florence, a city whose bankers indulged themselves in pagan luxuries, while the poor workmen struggled against plague and famine. He had too sensitive a soul and he was too honest a man to miss it. In a letter to his nephew we hear nothing about the limitless possibilities of man, but of his frailty and wickedness: "For what can we really do without the help of God? And how shall he come to help us unless we call upon Him?"[6] Pico here recommends not the life of vast speculations, but obedience to the commandments of the Lord, revealed in Scripture and in the laws of our being:

Thomas More: The Real Renaissance Martyr for Truth

Galileo was not executed for speaking truth to power, but Sir Thomas More was. His last words, spoken from the gallows, were, "The king's good servant but God's first."

> What remains to say, but that many are Christians in name, few in reality? But you, my son, seek to enter by the narrow gate, and pay no heed to what the many do, rather to the duties shown you by the natural law, by reason, by God Himself.

Pico had heard the preaching of the Dominican firebrand, Girolamo Savonarola, and had been spellbound by his denunciation of the vanity of the rich Florentines, and their hardhearted crushing of the people's liberty. The freewheeling Lorenzo de' Medici, strongman of Florence, facing a rebellious populace and the weariness of scandal, took Pico's advice and invited Savonarola to come to Florence and preach against the life he, Lorenzo, practiced. But Lorenzo soon regretted it, as Savonarola was a potent and dangerous speaker. When Savonarola decried the pagan ostentation of wealth, and the pagan spirit breathing in some of the art that graced the great halls, it was not only the dyers and fullers that heard, but the artists and poets too. Into a huge "bonfire of the vanities," built in the wide Piazza della Signoria, repentant worldlings cast their trinkets and baubles. A young painter named Botticelli cast a few of his paintings, too. Judge him not too harshly. It's easy for us to think we would like to live in a city animated by the heady spirit of paganism—so long as we are rich and well-connected. That city, Florence or Detroit, looks different from below.

By the flaring light of that bonfire we glimpse the other side of this Renaissance confidence in man. It is an honest look at man's shame, and a blunt confession that man cannot save himself. Shakespeare is seldom more eloquent than when he peers into what happens when man violates his creaturely nature. Albany inveighs against the unnatural acts of King Lear's daughters, who have exposed the old man to a pitiless storm, saying that if the heavens do not quickly curb such deeds,

> Humanity must perforce prey on itself
> Like monsters of the deep. (*King Lear*, IV.ii.48–49)

Lady Macbeth, urging her husband to the murder of his king and benefactor, would for the sake of ambition violate a woman's holiest and most natural bond:

> I have given suck, and know
> How tender 'tis to love the babe that milks me:
> I would, while it was smiling in my face,
> Have plucked my nipple from his boneless gums,
> And dashed the brains out, had I so sworn as you
> Have done to this. (*Macbeth*, I.vii.54–59)

Lear's daughters will die: Goneril will poison Regan, and will then take her own life. And Lady Macbeth, for all her bald materialist assumptions about good and evil—"A little water clears us of this deed" (II.ii.66), she says, wiping her distraught husband's hands after the murder—will be plagued with sleeplessness and guilt, beyond the cure of herb or potion. Says the doctor who witnesses her sleepwalking:

> Unnatural deeds
> Do breed unnatural troubles. Infected minds
> To their deaf pillows will discharge their secrets.
> More needs she the divine than the physician.
> God, God forgive us all! (V.i.75–79)

The Renaissance was bolder than our age in asserting man's beauty and nobility, his capacity to reason of things divine. But it was bolder too in acknowledging our depravity, in confessing the paltry return we render unto God for His gifts. Here is that Renaissance courtier, Hamlet, who knows that Denmark is rotten and that a "king of shreds and patches," his uncle Claudius, has murdered his brother to steal his crown and his queen:

> What a piece of work is a man, how noble in reason, how infinite in faculties, in form and moving how express and admirable, in action how like an angel, in apprehension how like a god: the beauty of the world, the paragon of animals; and yet to me, what is this quintessence of dust? (*Hamlet*, II.ii.310–17)

Or young Miranda, raised on an uncharted island, seeing something utterly new to her—a young man:

> I might call him
> A thing divine; for nothing natural
> I ever saw so noble. (*The Tempest*, I.ii.417–19)

She is right about that young man, as it turns out, but she has had no experience of human evil. All at once, at the end of the play, a curtain is drawn and she sees a roomful of people. Three of them tried to murder her long ago. Two of those three have been plotting another murder only a few hours since. Unaware of that sin, Miranda sees only the glory:

O wonder!

How many goodly creatures are there here!

How beauteous mankind is! O brave new world

That has such people in't! (V.i.181–4)

We would not say so. But Miranda is correct. Mankind is beauteous, or is meant to be. Her father's rejoinder does not contradict her. It is the voice of disappointment, coming to terms with sinful man as he is: "'Tis new to thee." (V.i.184)

The age that gave birth to Pico gave birth also to John Calvin. Both were Renaissance humanists, students of the philosophers, poets, and theologians of antiquity. Neither one could we now endure: Pico, because he exalts man so highly; Calvin, because he accuses man of depravity; both, because they yearn for that vision of God which our schools deride. If we want man in all his glory, we can hardly do better than Michelangelo's magnificent *David*, so naturally nude that it is impossible to imagine him clothed, with his non-classical glare of mingled trepidation, determination, and spiritual fire. Yet the same man who sculpted David, and the massive Adam of the Creation, and the nude Christ wielding his cross, painted himself in a most telling place. Look at his *Last Judgment* in the Sistine Chapel. All the saints tremble in awe before Christ the Judge. All bear some sign of their devotion or martyrdom. Bald Saint Bartholomew, who was flayed alive, holds the knife and a sagging

The Bard Speaks: Moral Relativism

"There is nothing either good or bad," Prince Hamlet says, "but thinking makes it so." Hapless high school teachers hold this up as Hamlet's philosophy: beauty, morality, and goodness are all social constructs. This reading utterly ignores the context within the play.

Hamlet is not articulating an enlightened idea; he is mocking his false friends, Rosencrantz and Guildenstern. He acknowledges that, yes, there are people for whom there is no objective good or bad: those who don't think.

skin, its face drooping in a grimace of weariness and pain. But, oddly enough, Bartholomew looks nothing like the skin he holds. That skinned face is of a heavy-jawed man with a broken nose and curly black hair. It is Michelangelo's only self-portrait. "Who shall deliver me from the body of this death?" cries Paul (Rom. 7:24), affirming the powerlessness of man, without God's grace, not only to save himself but even to do the good he sees is good and avoid the evil he sees is evil. Michelangelo paints that cry.

Honoring the past

So the Renaissance was not simply an age of glorying in man. What about resurgent paganism? What caused the tremendous and fruitful interest in pagan antiquity?

First, the cause. Remember that the scholars of the Middle Ages had long been curious about pagan philosophy and history. They were hindered by practical problems. They didn't possess the texts they needed. They didn't even know where they were, or if they still existed. Teachers of Greek were rare. But the scholars did what they could. Thomas Aquinas hired a Greek to provide him with a more accurate translation of Aristotle than the one he had been using, which had been translated into Latin from Arabic. The medieval writers are forever citing Virgil, Ovid, what Cicero they knew, what Plato they knew, Livy, Seneca, and so forth, and when they don't have the original text or a translation, they find out about it from discussions in ancient historians or critics. So Dante knows something about Homer, though he cannot have read Homer.

The Europeans were already searching for wisdom from the pagan past. They had the motive, and suddenly they were to have the means and opportunity. That's because the Byzantine Empire was fighting a last losing battle against the onslaught of the Turks. Long before the fall of

Constantinople in 1453, scholars and artists looked west for a haven, and scholars bring texts, the tools of their trade. In 1342, the Italian scholar and poet Francis Petrarch invited one Manuel Chrysoloras, an émigré from the East, to teach him ancient Greek. Chrysoloras was the first and the most famous of many men who crossed the seas into Italy, bringing with them their knowledge and their books. The trickle widened into a torrent. Scholars no longer had to rely on translations. Nor were they limited to the works known in the universities. They began to search the dusty corners of monasteries and ruins and manor houses. Every year or two brought another spectacular find, like newly discovered planets in the solar system.

All the Greek drama we still have came to the West at this time. So did almost all of the Platonic dialogues. So did Homer's *Iliad* and *Odyssey*, and almost all the rest of our corpus of Greek poetry. So did the work of the ancient historians Herodotus, Thucydides, Polybius, Sallust, Tacitus, much of Livy, and many lesser lights. Some discoveries made for intellectual drama. The cleric and book-finder Poggio Bracciolini discovered a unique manuscript of Lucretius' materialist epic *On the Nature of Things*, moldering in a monastery in Switzerland. The manuscript was priceless. Poggio set about to make a copy, but was forestalled by his friend Niccoli, who wanted to borrow it to look at it. Niccoli did, made a copy—and the original has never been seen again.[7]

Once the scholars caught fire, the artists took notice. They too hunted down books: for example, the rediscovered classic on architecture by Vitruvius. Leonardo so admired the Roman's emphasis on harmony and balance that he called his most famous sketch of human proportions, a nude self-portrait, Vitruvian Man. They also hunted down works of art. Donatello went to ancient ruins and literally dug up sculptures, to study their technique. Others, from surviving scraps of classical painting and the clean lines of classical architecture, learned the mathematics of perspective, and could suddenly achieve effects never seen before in the

West, not even in ancient Greece or Rome. Consider, for example, Andrea Mantegna's tour-de-force of foreshortening, the dramatic *Dead Christ,* the pierced soles of the Savior dominating the foreground as he lies on a slab, mourned by the holy women to his left and right.

These men who found, copied, edited, commented upon, translated, and adapted the ancient texts, and the artists who were inspired by them, are called humanists. That implies nothing about their beliefs. Nowadays, a "humanist" is someone who denies the influence of the divine upon the life of the individual or the history of man, as in the notorious twentieth century *Humanist Manifesto.* But Luther, the theologian who asserted that only the grace of God could break the bonds of man's sinful, enslaved will, was a humanist. So was his theological enemy Thomas More. More cheered the introduction of Greek studies into England, agreed with Luther on the need to reform the morals and relieve the ignorance of churchmen, and wrote the wittiest piece of fanciful political philosophy of the era, the *Utopia.*

Erasmus, translator of the Greek New Testament into Latin, and the finest scholar of his day, a friend of More, a detester of the warlike Pope Julius II, and the one man Luther wanted to join his movement, was a humanist. Erasmus affirmed the freedom of man's will, his capacity to do good, and his most common trait, folly. Calvin, who followed Luther and asserted, from Scripture, the transcendent majesty of God and his sovereign predestination of all things, including the damnation of unrepentant sinners, was a humanist. So were: the skeptic and legend debunker Lorenzo Valla (whom Luther called his favorite Italian);[8] the quack alchemist Paracelsus; the writer of obscene verses whom people simply called The One and Only Aretine; and the gentle moral philosopher Enea Silvio Piccolomini, better known as Pope Pius II.

But the humanist project then was not what it would be now. Now, we'd shrug and say, "If Machiavelli wants to study Livy and Thucydides, that's his choice, and if John Colet wants to bring the Greek Scriptures to

England, that's his choice. To each his own." The Renaissance men cared more for truth than that; they were impassioned about it. They knew well, too, what Augustine had said about taking "gold out of Egypt" (*On Christian Doctrine* 2.60): that Christians need not despise the pagan philosophers, but could be confident that there was much truth in them, though not the fullness of truth. Like the children of the Hebrews, they could bring Egyptian gold into the Promised Land.

If these scholars had shut their minds against pagan intimations of truth and beauty, there would have been no Renaissance. But had they shut their minds against the very idea of objective truth (except for that smallish portion of it that can be quantified) and beauty, as our schools teach students to do, then too there would have been no Renaissance. Livy and Seneca were wise; the Renaissance thinkers believed that, and it was for them more than a taste or an opinion. Christ was the Way, the Truth, and the Life; all of the greatest among them, with the possible exception of Machiavelli, believed that too, even when they rebelled against it. How to reconcile it all, in a coherent and glorious whole? That struggle gives us the Renaissance.

I could multiply examples of this drive to reconcile apparent contradictions, to subordinate a lower truth to a higher, to adapt pagan wisdom to Christian scriptures in surprising and revealing ways, to "baptize" *eros*, to see as manifest in our age what the pagans had glimpsed fitfully in theirs. Michelangelo covers the Sistine ceiling with imposing portraits of the Jewish prophets—and the Greek oracles! All point toward Jonah, the unwilling prophet fairly falling into the sanctuary below. Why Jonah? Because he is a foreshadowing of the resurrected Christ: "For as Jonas was three days and three nights in the whale's belly; so shall the Son of Man be three days and three nights in the heart of the earth" (Matt. 12:40). Philip Sidney pens a long romance, the *Arcadia*, examining man's fallen will, his foolish attempts to evade divine Providence, and the disorder in his loves. It is a thoroughly

Protestant work, set in pagan Greece, with characters searching for a truth that has not yet been revealed to them. It is one of the principal influences upon Shakespeare's *Winter's Tale,* whose characters go by an indiscriminate mix of Greek and Latin names, and who live in a Sicily that seems unfixed from any age, and a Bohemia with a shoreline, unfixed from any geographical place. The French poet Du Bartas, inspired by Ambrose's *Hexameron,* writes *The Divine Weeks* on God's creation of the world in seven days, and incorporates into his poetry the arguments of the ancient materialist Lucretius, on lightning and volcanoes and the wheeling of the stars.[9]

Or take this account of a renovation. Julius II, who spent more time on horseback with a spear than at a fireside with manuscripts, wanted Rome to be more than a dilapidated hole. It should be the city to which all the newly centralized European nations would look, just as all worldly wisdom must find its completion in the wisdom that transcends it, the wisdom of God's revelation as taught by the Church. That was his aim. So he needed to finish a project begun by his predecessor Nicholas: to rebuild the Basilica of Saint Peter, not least because the old basilica's walls were buckling dangerously.

Part of his scheme involved painting a small library, tucked behind the sanctuary of the Sistine Chapel. So he hired the popular young Raphael to paint the *meaning* of a library in the Vatican: that is, Raphael was to paint the Church's embrace of all truth,

PC Myth: The World Was Believed to Be Flat Before Columbus

A favorite classroom myth to aggrandize the Renaissance, deprecate the Church, and slander the Middle Ages is that before Christopher Columbus, people thought the world was flat. While almost everyone today knows this "discovery tale" is a myth, the nineteenth-century Romantics repeated it enough that it was accepted as true.

Of course, the Earth was widely held to be a sphere centuries before Columbus set sail, but who wants to credit premodern man with such insights?

from whatever source, and its ordering of the truths toward Christ. If you can understand what Raphael is doing in this room, you can guess what Milton is up to with his classical devils in *Paradise Lost*, or what Castiglione means by his Platonic ladder of love, described by a Cardinal, in *The Book of the Courtier*, or why Bernini sculpts a classical Cupid as the angel about to pierce the heart of the holy nun in his *Saint Teresa in Ecstasy*.

Consider the most famous of Raphael's paintings in the library, his *School of Athens*. You can hardly find a work that better illustrates the confidence, almost arrogance, of Renaissance man, and yet there is a profound humility to it too, a deference to the excellence of the ancients. Raphael has portrayed the men of his day as the philosophers of old, all in one place and time, even though those philosophers spanned many lands and centuries. Leonardo, as I've mentioned, serves for Plato. He's carrying his *Timaeus*, a dialogue on the creation of the world, and is gesturing upward, towards divine truth. His younger comrade and pupil, Aristotle (whose head may be that of Raphael's fellow painter Titian), gestures forward and slightly downward, towards the earth. He is carrying his *Nicomachean Ethics*, that practical guide on how to be trained in the moral virtues and live among men in the world. The rest of the scene is studded with Renaissance and classical pagan stars. The lonely and intense Michelangelo is brooding in the foreground: he is the philosopher Heraclitus, who believed that the fundamental element of the universe was fire. The bald fellow with the compasses, teaching the lads in the lower right, is the geometrician Euclid, or rather is the architect Bramante, the genius whose charge lay the rebuilding of St. Peter's. Raphael himself looks boldly out towards us, the third head from the right at the top.

Plato and Aristotle, the contemplative and the practical philosopher, sum up between them the greatest wisdom that man can attain on his own. But in the painting there's something else between them. It's hard to notice, because it's something that Raphael shows is *not* there. The *School of Athens*, with all its amazing series of arches, resembles, suspiciously, the incomplete Saint Peter's where Raphael is working, and all the classical lines of perspective merge in the center of the circle suggested by the arch above Plato and Aristotle, a space where there are the clouds and sky—nothing else. Raphael has emulated his masters here. From Michelangelo's *Creation of Adam* he has learned to suggest, by emptiness, something that transcends not only the viewer but even the wisdom of Plato and Aristotle. From Leonardo's *Last Supper* he has learned that mathematics can merge into philosophy and theology. He has seen how Leonardo funnels the lines of the architecture of the refectory at Santa Maria delle Grazie into the architectural structure of his painting, directing all perspective towards the quietly radiant center, the head of Christ.

We celebrate Plato and Aristotle. We honor them by walking in their steps. But we acknowledge that, alone, they are incomplete. All the wisdom of man is incomplete. Hence the *School of Athens* stands opposite another painting, the *Disputa*, a strange two-level work of men on earth and angels with the Trinity in heaven, and again the sky between. In this painting too Raphael has painted men of his day (including an accusatory Savonarola), now as cardinals, bishops, and popes from the early Church. But here there is something besides clouds and space in the center. Raphael directs the eye to behold what bridges the gap between earth and heaven, the worshippers below and the saints above, human theology and divine truth. Here, located against the sky, is something more than a space, a cloud, a patch of blue. It is the Eucharist, the sacrament which, as Raphael and Julius and their fellow Catholics believed, makes the glorified Christ mysteriously yet really present in the sacrifice of the Mass. In this most profound gesture of reverence, the classical Raphael and the rough-and-ready actors of the old Corpus Christi plays were at one.

Shakespeare on his knees

"That's a painter hired by a pope," you say, "but what about someone not taking his pay from the Church? How about someone working at a trade condemned from the pulpit, rubbing shoulders against whores and ruffians, and gathering crowds on the wrong side of the river?" How about Shakespeare, then?

Consider his play *Measure for Measure,* now popular in academia for its darkness, its willingness to probe the seamy underside of urban life. The Duke of Vienna, who has spoiled his people by lenience, failing to enforce laws regarding decency and morality, pretends to leave the city, giving his authority over to the puritanical Angelo, of whom it is said, according to one waggish whoremonger, "his urine is congealed ice" (III.ii.111). The Duke then assumes the disguise of a friar to keep an eye on both Angelo and Vienna. His subaltern cleans house: he shuts down the brothels and revives a dusty law that condemns fornicators to death. One young man, Claudio, betrothed but not officially married to his beloved Julietta, is condemned for making her pregnant. Claudio sends his friend the wag to beg his sister, Isabella, a novice of the severe Sisters of Saint Clare, to leave her convent and appeal to Angelo for mercy. Isabella does, in words of such hardly restrained passion that they move Angelo—but not to mercy. He requests another interview, at which he puts the moral and legal case to Isabella thus: if she will sleep with him, he will spare her brother.

The Duke, who has been playing spiritual counselor to Claudio and Julietta, arranges a subterfuge. He instructs Isabella to agree, but on condition of utter silence and darkness; and he arranges that Angelo's former betrothed, a woman named Mariana whom he jilted when she lost her dowry, should sleep with him in Isabella's place, unbeknownst to Angelo. On the next day, however, Angelo, fearing that the brother would avenge the sister's disgrace, orders that Claudio be executed anyway. The Duke, revealing himself to the jailer, forestalls the execution. Still in the guise of the friar, he instructs Isabella and Mariana to be present among the crowds later in the day, when the Duke will return to Vienna and redress complaints against his second in command.

Please forgive the summary; it is necessary, to set up one of the most theologically fascinating scenes in Shakespeare. At this point, Angelo believes that he has slept with Isabella, but that nobody else knows about it. Isabella and everyone else but the Duke and the jailer believe Claudio is dead. Angelo is, morally, guilty of rape and murder. He should suffer

Evil Popes?

Worldly, yes, in the fifteenth century. The papacy was then a prize sought by the leading families in Florence, Rome, and Milan. And the pope had either to establish the Patrimony of Peter, the lands he ruled in central Italy, as a "national" force to be reckoned with, or be steamrollered by ambitious princes on all sides.

One or two of the popes were wicked men. The worst (though he was a learned and capable administrator) was the Borgia pope, Alexander VI. Of him, Machiavelli says that he never kept a promise when it was to his advantage to break it. Yet he continued to make promises, and people fell for his charm. It was Alexander's bastard son, Cesare Borgia, whom Machiavelli had in mind as the "ideal" prince: a bloody, coldhearted, lying knave.

But soon after Luther's thundering condemnation of Roman corruption, we have popes who may have been worldly before they were elevated to the papacy, but who worked hard to reform the Catholic church (Paul III, Pius III). And after that, I'd defy the most hardened secularist to find a wicked pope from that time to the present. If only secular politicians had so clean a record.

death, for as Jesus warns, in the passage to which Shakespeare's title alludes, "With what measure ye mete, it shall be measured to you again" (Matt. 7:2). Before revealing that Claudio is still alive, the Duke sentences Angelo to death:

> The very mercy of the law cries out
> Most audible, even from his proper tongue,
> "An Angelo for Claudio, death for death!"
> Haste still pays haste, and leisure answers leisure;
> Like doth quit like, and Measure still for Measure. (V.i. 409–13)

But Mariana begs Isabella to intercede on her behalf: to kneel to save the life of the man who intended to ravish her, and who killed her brother.

Here Shakespeare has dramatized the heart of the Gospel. By the letter of the law, Claudio had to die. By the *spirit of the law,* mercy itself cries out that Angelo must die. Without Christ, without the possibility of grace, we all must die—we all must remain in our sins. As Portia puts it in *The Merchant of Venice*, "In the course of justice, none of us / Should see salvation" (IV.i. 198–99). Only when we become aware of our poverty do we cast ourselves upon the riches of divine mercy.

Essentially, Isabella here is not called on to do a good deed, for which she might praise herself afterwards. She is called on to recognize her own desperate need for salvation. She is called to become a Christian for the first time, to put to death her old adherence to rules and self-righteousness, and to come to life. That she does, with a magnificent turn of irony, using the letter of the law to blunt its edge. She points out that, in fact though not in intent, Angelo did not rape her, and Claudio's death was technically legal. In her self-sacrificing and humble plea she embodies Christ, who broke the iron bonds of the law that condemns mankind, by fulfilling its terrible judgments upon the Cross. Here mercy and justice have wedded, peace and righteousness have kissed—as we hear in the psalm for

Christmas Eve (Ps. 85:10), two days before Shakespeare and his men first performed this play, at the court of the king.

All of Shakespeare's energy, his daring portrayal of sexual license and disease, has culminated in the moment of forgiveness that lends the rest of the play its meaning. His theological insight is exactly the same as Chaucer's in The Pardoner's Tale, or the gentle unknown poet's in *Sir Gawain and the Green Knight*. It is the same as his own in *The Merchant of Venice*, *Macbeth*, *King Lear*, *Richard III*, and *The Winter's Tale*. Relying upon his strength of will, his cunning, even his righteousness, man must fall. For the letter kills, and the spirit gives life. In this, Shakespeare too, like Michelangelo and Raphael in their way, was at one with his more homely predecessors.

Where the Renaissance went wrong: Undermining authority

Then the PC dogma is a colossal exaggeration, claiming that in the Renaissance men rejected traditional authorities and set forth on their own—like bold, free-thinking, modern individualists—to discover truth, or to dispense with the quest entirely, since all is a matter of opinion. It might be as valid to say that they *multiplied* authorities. But there was certainly an intellectual upheaval whose results we are still living with, some good, some bad. First let's look at what made the upheaval possible: the printing press.

It's true that movable type was invented in China, not in the West. But the Chinese, believing their land the center of the universe, had no great use for it. Why bother doing anything except making decorative prints for the emperor, since the Order of Heaven that governs the world is unchanging in its regular cycles? Why go anywhere, when you are standing at the center? But Johann Gutenberg took the idea and invented the printing press. Soon books became, if not common, at least affordable for a well-off merchant or craftsman, and not only the duke or the bishop. Ideas could be disseminated across the continent. No printing press, no Protestant Reformation; no modern world.

Gutenberg's first printed book was a Bible. That too is significant. People who could afford a book wanted Bibles, eventually in the vernacular, since most of them would not have had enough Latin to read the Vulgate. There had been vernacular translations of Scripture before, though their influence was restricted by the fact that few people could read, even if they could afford a hand-copied book. Literacy rose, and translators—not only of the Bible—rushed in to meet the demand. The Reformers would, with some hedging, recommend that believers read the Bible for themselves, detaching them from the authority of Rome. They tried to attach them instead to the authority of the reformed theology: Calvin wrote voluminous commentaries on the Scripture, clear and commonsensical, easy for the intelligent layman to read. But the multiplicity of opinions caused some to despair of finding certitude in any one of them. Which Church is the genuine Bride of Christ?

> What! is it She, which on the other Shore
> Goes richly painted? or which, robbed and tore,
> Laments and mourns in Germany and here? (John Donne, Holy
> Sonnet XVII, 2–4)

By the time of the Puritan revolt in 1642, John Milton will write "that it is dangerous and unworthy the Gospel to hold that Church government is to be patterned by the Law" (*The Reason of Church Government,* ch. 3), condemning the established Church of England and its bishops as unscriptural. By the end of his life, still considering himself Christian, Milton will claim that "it was in God's power consistently with the perfection of his essence not to have begotten the Son" (*The Christian Doctrine,* ch. 5), reviving the old Arian heresy, and lending assistance to the anti-trinitarianism that will result in Enlightenment Deism. It is no coincidence that Milton never did join any church.

A similar splintering can be seen in philosophy. Until the Renaissance, it was taken for granted that natural philosophy, what we call science, was a part (and not the most important part) of the whole quest for *scientia,* that is, knowledge, and wisdom. When Copernicus, a Catholic priest, dedicated his work on the revolution of the heavenly bodies to Pope Paul III, he intended no rift between science and religion. There is no evidence that he disturbed anyone's faith. For one thing, the cardinal Nicholas of Cusa had already suggested that the Earth revolved about the sun, citing the ancient astronomer Aristarchus, and a disputed passage in Plato.[10] Nobody minded. It wasn't as if the Copernican system could be used for anything: its star charts were not as accurate as those drawn up according to the old Ptolemaic, earth-centered system, and it was centuries before they would surpass them. If you were navigating a ship and wanted precision, you stuck with common sense and Ptolemy.[11]

What drew people towards the Copernican system was its simplicity. It did away with most (not all!) of Ptolemy's "epicycles," little curlicue-making orbits around a point orbiting a second point orbiting a third, like wheels on wheels. Why was the simplicity appealing? Here we turn to the real revolutionary. William of Ockham, a Franciscan theologian and philosopher (c. 1285–1349)

The Bard Speaks: Human Nature

Studying the history of ideas, one is struck by how many of today's bad ideas are not new. The mutability of human nature found a champion in the storyline of *King Lear*.

"Men are as the time is," says Edmund to the captain, urging him to go hang the innocent old king and his daughter Cordelia. (v.iii.31–32) Shakespeare had no patience for people who reduced the moral law to social convention, to be discarded for advantage. Professors who teach such a thing will find themselves well portrayed in Shakespeare: as villains all.

roughly contemporary with Dante, had asserted the principle now known as Ockham's Razor. Given two explanations, the one with the fewer assumptions is to be preferred.[12] Copernicus' system required fewer assumptions. Ockham also promoted a philosophical position called *nominalism,* which applied the Razor to universal nouns such as "man" and "dog" and "horse," terms used to denote not *this man* but *man,* without individuation. Ockham denied that such terms had any meaning, except in a conventional sense. We cannot sensibly talk about man as man; we can only make loose generalizations about men, based upon our experiences with individuals. But if man as such does not exist, neither does human nature. Then moral laws cannot be based upon human nature. Instead, Ockham argued, they must be derived from the arbitrary will of God, as revealed in the Scriptures.

A Movie You're Not Supposed to Watch

A Man for All Seasons

An absolute must see. It's a brilliant portrayal of real-life faith, piety, duty, honor, and obedience. Certainly outdated, subservient virtues like these didn't exist in the freewheeling Renaissance?

Note that the Razor *proves* nothing. It's a handy intellectual device. It can advise you to make your premises few and simple, and if you're looking for a single cause of disparate phenomena (as natural scientists usually are), it may be just the thing to use. But the Razor cannot tell you why you should prefer fewer premises, or whether your premises are true, or whether the truths you discover will be vast or paltry. Applied to what used to count as science—namely, all knowledge, including that revealed by God—the Razor severs discipline from discipline. So Francis Bacon will scoff at Aristotelian metaphysics, which he has little understanding of, because it does not assist him in his quest for dominion over nature.[13] Two centuries after Bacon, when Napoleon asked the mathematician Laplace why he did not begin his *Celestial Mechanics* with a discussion of God, the man took out the Razor: "My lord, I have no need of that hypothesis."[14] Nominalism, argues Richard Weaver, was a poison leaking into the intellectual life of the West. It would alter and degrade what we mean by knowledge: not the possession or contemplation of the highest truths, but the wielding of facts in the service of power.[15]

It is historical nonsense to say that Francis Bacon invented the scientific method. Scientists had for centuries been observing nature and drawing practical conclusions from it, and scientists long after Bacon would allow unproved or unprovable assumptions about the world to color what they saw, or to determine whether they saw anything at all. What Bacon did, rather, was to restrict what we will call knowledge, and to dispense with many an old and reliable tool for gaining it. Is it then such a great surprise that our current social scientists, when they are not blinded by political correctness, will "discover" what everybody has always known—for example, that girls like dolls and boys like swords? Blind Homer could have told us that, almost three thousand years ago.

Meanwhile Europe, smitten with wanderlust since the Crusades, could not sit still at home. Vasco da Gama sailed around the Cape of Good Hope to try to win for Portugal a route to the spice-rich Indies, bypassing both the Mediterranean Sea, controlled by the Venetians, the Genovese, and the Muslims, and the overland caravan route through Muslim countries. One of his shipmates stayed behind in Africa and trekked inland to discover, near one of the sources of the Nile, a lost Nestorian Christian kingdom.[16] Columbus believed he could outflank the Italians and the Portuguese by going west across the Atlantic; and we know what happened then. Europeans were flooded with stories from strange lands: about a Pocahontas doing naked cartwheels in front of the men of Jamestown, or about the mandarin Chinese, secretive and sly, fascinated by mechanical gadgetry like European watches and clocks.

The Christian faith affirmed a common humanity, but where was that to be found, among such a welter of cultures and customs? Some writers claimed that the barbarian customs were superior to those of the "civilized" Europeans. Montaigne tried to see cannibalism in a sympathetic light.[17]

Authority? Let's not forget the nation-state, a force for political unity, but often a destroyer of tradition, and suspicious of any authority not controlled by the throne. Renaissance princes too looked back to the ancients, to revive for themselves the grandeur of Rome: states unified in religion, but far from the governance of a pope. They desired unity against the enemies outside their boundaries, but cultural uniformity within the boundaries. That unity-in-variety called Christendom dies, and all the petty and semiautonomous dukedoms and principalities die with it. The Renaissance begins the movement, still going on, to flatten the mid-level institutions that serve as a buffer between the individual and the State, and to detach the State from any theology that may curb its ambitions. Old authorities lose, and new masters win.

Take Henry VIII for example. He knew he had a slender claim to the throne. If he died without an heir, England might reel back into civil war, from which it had only recently emerged. But Henry's wife Catherine, princess of Aragon, had borne no surviving sons. He must marry again: national considerations trump theology, wedding vows, and decency. Henry appeals to the pope for an annulment. But the pope can do nothing. He is militarily weak, and Charles of Spain, Catherine's brother, is as much a nationalist as Henry, and is the strongest ally the pope has—a dangerous ally, as Rome found in 1527 when Charles' troops sacked the city. Besides, a previous pope had already granted Henry dispensation to marry Catherine, his former sister-in-law. To make matters worse, Luther had already called the pope's authority into question.

No annulment. That settled it: Henry VIII, erstwhile "Defender of the Faith" for a tract written against Luther, seized the English church. He needed money (all of the Renaissance princes did, what with the inflation caused by gold and silver brought from the Americas). So he sacked the old centers of village and rural culture, the monasteries, on pretext of reforming them. He converted the goods to cash and auctioned the estates. One of the buyers was named Washington.[18]

The local, traditional, Christian community, village and church, with its corporate life, is caught in a pincers. On one side, the new individualism: if you can afford to do it, you can read your own books, you can travel to strange places, and you can choose among a number of authorities. On the other side, the centralized nation-state. The pattern is repeated elsewhere, and the process continues to our day.

But the resistance, the human thirst for truth, and indeed for a transcendent authority to which to submit, was still strong, and proved tremendously creative. This resistance too is characteristic of the Renaissance. If one can no longer turn to the theology of Thomas Aquinas for certitude, because only churchmen study that old friar and nobody really understands him, and if the rhythms of village and church life that lend meaning to your years are drowned out by national anthems—Spenser writing *The Faerie Queene* to celebrate England as the new Rome, Camoens writing *The Lusiads* to celebrate Portugal as the new Rome,

How Disappointing: Even the Great Artists Were Christian

[Leonardo] further informed the Duke that there were still wanting to him two heads, one of which, that of the Saviour, he could not hope to find on earth, and had not yet attained the power of presenting it to himself in imagination, with all that perfection of beauty and celestial grace which appeared to him to be demanded for the due representation of the Divinity incarnate.

From **Giorgio Vasari** *Lives of the Painters* (Vol. 1, 317)

Leonardo took so long to complete *The Last Supper* not simply because he was a perfectionist—though he was. It was his faith, in him more a matter of intuition than of theological conclusion, that demanded that he strain the nerves of his intelligence and skill and vision.

Tasso writing *Jerusalem Delivered* to celebrate Rome as the new Rome—then you can look within your heart and listen to the promptings of God. Hence the Baroque paintings of Caravaggio and Rembrandt and Tintoretto, focusing on a dramatic moment in the life of *this* person, who could be *any* person, even the artist. So we have Rembrandt, painting the sadness and vanity of the hedonist's life, using his wife as a model for a barmaid, and himself as a model for the Prodigal Son, or Caravaggio, painting himself as a strangely puzzled crucifier of Saint Peter.

If this is Renaissance "individualism," it certainly does search for authority, and is remarkably ingenious about it. So Ignatius of Loyola, in his *Spiritual Exercises,* enjoins upon his Jesuit followers a strict discipline for the inner spiritual life, while they obey their superiors as privates obey their officers. Hence a directive like the following, far from the spirit of the modern age:

> To be with the Church of Jesus Christ but one mind and one spirit, we must carry our confidence in her, and our distrust of ourselves, so far as to pronounce that true which appeared to us false, if she decides that it is so; for we must believe without hesitation that the Spirit of our Lord Jesus Christ is the spirit of His spouse, and that the God who formerly gave the decalogue is the same God who now inspires and directs His Church. (*Rules of the Orthodox Faith*)

Because of that very obedience and discipline, the Jesuits quickly became the most learned men in Europe. Jesuit priests, often hated by their secular lords, would try to evangelize the world. No human culture was beneath their curiosity and their care.

Nor does the yearning for community die. We long for community separate from the state, to heal the alienated individual. John of the Cross writes his haunting poems about the soul's being wooed by God (his is the famous image of "the dark night of the soul"),[19] while serving as chaplain for a convent of Carmelite nuns in Spain. That convent includes Teresa of Avila, who reforms her order by establishing clear lines of authority and by encouraging a profound life of prayer. Her *Interior Castle*, a classic of the spiritual life, was written only at the urging of her superiors, but to the great satisfaction of her fellow sisters. The Puritans, with a very different theology from the kind that animated John and Teresa, were also moved by that same human and Christian yearning. They are called separatists, but they wanted to separate to unite. They wanted to form their own community under authority they all recognized. They could not live in England; they could not live even in Calvinist Holland. So in a ship called the *Mayflower* they sailed to America, utterly uninterested in empire, rejecting the authority of Rome, London, Wittenberg, and Geneva, yet also willing to submit to authority.

The Pilgrim Fathers, they too were Renaissance men.

Chapter 7

THE ENLIGHTENMENT: LIBERTY AND TYRANNY

Enlightenment is man's release from his self-incurred tutelage. Tutelage is man's inability to make use of his understanding without direction from another... 'Have courage to use your own reason'—that is the motto of enlightenment. (Immanuel Kant, "What is Enlightenment?")[1]

I t's telling that a modern conservative might nod in agreement with Kant here. I blame it on schooling that destroys both piety and independent thought at once.

Yet to follow Kant's prescription means social atomism, every man's mind alien from every other, with only the State remaining to enforce order. It also means, in practice, the replacement of one teacher, call it tradition, with another teacher, whether it is one's own vanity and caprice, or the ambitions of an intellectual elite. We sever ourselves from the accumulated but unproved wisdom of the past, only to submit to those few, with all their unacknowledged sins and blindness. As Edmund Burke would put it, we trade upon our own rather limited capital of experience and knowledge.[2]

The heritage of the Enlightenment is therefore profoundly ambivalent. If we credit it for the breakneck progress of the natural sciences, we may also blame it for that fog wherein we still labor, requiring that

Guess What?

✦ The rise of the State and the decline of the church caused the violence of recent centuries.

✦ America was a product of both the Enlightenment and a typically English reaction against it; its conservative revolution opened up an opportunity for genuine liberty.

✦ The wisest thinkers of the Enlightenment were the most critical of it.

all knowledge be expressible as formulae or data gathered by "experts," and ruling out ancient questions regarding the nature and the end of man.

That is ironic, since the Enlightenment was a creature begotten of the religious and political zeal of the Renaissance.

The will enslaved

What exercised Martin Luther most about the Church of his day, when the papacy lay in the grip of a few worldly Italian families, was not that bad men wore the robes of the hierarchy. Wherever there are men and robes, there are going to be some bad men wearing them. What really prompted Luther to declare, at his trial at the Diet of Worms, "Here I stand. I can do no other," was his revolt against the idea that man could attain an acceptable, bland level of "goodness," that he could buy the grace of God with a couple of well-chosen works, clearing his way to eternal bliss. Luther was rebelling against the very Enlightenment which his own break with the Church, in the sad tangle of human affairs, would help to usher in.

Luther had struggled to attain holiness as a long-fasting Augustinian monk, only to find himself plagued with failure, with what he feared was an unforgivable sin.[3] Only when he read Saint Paul's affirmation in the Epistle to the Romans that man is saved not by works—Paul had in mind especially the detailed prescriptions of the Jewish Law—but by faith, did Luther feel set free. The liberating point is that salvation cannot be earned. It is given to the faithful as a free gift by God. So when Luther heard that Dominicans were on the road in Germany, trawling for money to rebuild Saint Peter's, he was outraged. The people were being told that, if they gave a coin or two, a poor soul in Purgatory would be released from suffering;[4] or they themselves might win an indulgence in the hereafter for the sins they had confessed. The doctrine of indulgences demanded genuine penitence and a commitment to mend your life, but doctrine and practice, or even doctrine and appearance, are different things. Nor did it help that Italian hierarchs seemed to pay more attention to Cicero than to Christ; they too had caught the Renaissance fascination with man.

The Catholic Church was late in responding to the Lutheran challenge, largely because of political chaos in central and northern Italy, invaded in turn by France and Spain. Finally, at the Council of Trent (1545–1563), while condemning much of Luther's theology and ecclesiology, she declared her substantial agreement with the reformers on one point that sets both orthodox Catholic and reformed churches across a theological Grand Canyon from the easy assumptions of the modern world. For the modern world is at one with the worldly churchmen. Both believe that if there is a heaven, good people go there—"good" by the standards of the time. We are all Pelagians now.[5] God is the affable uncle in the sky, who snaps his fingers and makes things all right for us, if only we recycle, give to the United Way, pat dogs on the head, and meet standards of similar difficulty. The reformers and the Tridentine fathers both assert that without the grace of God man can do no good, and that such grace is by definition a free gift.[6]

Abolish Christianity?

It is likewise proposed as a great Advantage to the Publick, that if we once discard the System of the Gospel, all Religion will of course be banished for ever, and consequently along with it, those grievous Prejudices of Education, which under the Names of Virtue, Conscience, Honor, Justice, and the like, are so apt to disturb the Peace of human Minds.

Jonathan Swift, *An Argument Against the Abolishing of Christianity*

Not to worry, says Swift's satirical persona. Why abolish Christianity, when our modern "Methods of Education" have already seen to it that graduates possess not the least taint of those terrible virtues named above? He might have written that passage today.

The crucial difference between reformed and Catholic theology concerns the freedom of the will, and the genuine goodness of actions performed in agreement with God's grace. Trent affirms that man remains free to surrender to the grace or to reject it, and that, by grace, he can actually perform deeds that God considers worthy of merit. He can rush into the burning house to save his enemy's child. Without God's grace he would never do it; he may still choose not to do it; but he does, and it is good. The later reformers, such as Calvin, claimed that grace was irresistible. If God gives the grace, you will perform the act. It would be "good," insofar as we in the world can compare it with the wickedness of setting the fire, but it would remain infinitely far from the goodness of God, nor would it merit anything.[7]

Now this is not simply a debate about sin. It is a debate about the nature of man, and about what kind of authority men must acknowledge in their dealings with one another. The printing press allowed anyone who had the money to read the Bible for himself, thus weakening the bond between an individual and the Church. But the focus on man's fallen nature reminded everyone of the desperate need to belong to the right community of believers, for support and instruction. So a bewildering array of new churches sprang up in the sixteenth and seventeenth centuries, and a certain kind of Pelagianism crept in with them. This time it was the vague belief (taught by no reputable theologian) that if you joined the correct church, perhaps the church that most clearly affirmed that you could not earn your salvation, you would earn your salvation. Some of these breakaway communities veered into the quaint or silly or bizarre. The gentle Quakers trembled at their meetings, under the influence of the Holy Spirit. A cult under the leadership of John of Leyden seized the town of Muenster and ruled it for a year or two under communistic rules (including, their enemies said, the sharing of wives), until the nearby duke, supported by Luther, laid siege to the city and starved the people out. Adamists in seventeenth century England thought they had regained Eden already, so they walked down the streets stark naked. The Family of Love were accused of group orgies.[8]

It was a volatile time. If you were a duke with a small army, you might place yourself in the service of the church you had been persuaded was the true one. Or you might use the conflict to enlarge your lands at the expense of your neighbors. You might do some of both; such is the knot of human motives. Confusion was rife in Germany, where some local princes were eager to cast off the yoke of their Hapsburg ruler, the Holy Roman Emperor Charles V, who was also the Catholic King Charles I of Spain. But enemies of such princes might ally themselves with Charles and the Catholics. The Peace of Augsburg in 1555 only deferred the inevitable explosion. It ignored the Calvinists completely, and declared that if your prince was Lutheran, unless you wanted to sell your property and move away, you would be Lutheran too, and if your prince was Catholic, you would be Catholic. Such a "compromise" could not endure. Notice, too, how truth and conscience are subordinated to the harmony of the State.

Toss into this brew the national ambitions of England, France, Spain, and others, and you have the makings of the most brutal war that Europe had ever seen, the Thirty Years' War. You also have the makings of secessionist communities, retaining a tenuous relationship with their mother nations, or consigning them to an unredeemed world of sin and darkness. That would describe the pacifist Mennonites and the Hutterites, the Anabaptists who welcomed the Turks along the Danube, and, to a lesser extent, the Pilgrim Fathers who sailed to the New World to found a community of piety and peace.

"Enlightenment" yields tyranny

The horrors of the Thirty Years' War (and of the English Civil War that followed hard upon it) caused some European thinkers to believe that religion is essentially dangerous and divisive. Two options remained, they thought: absorb religion into the State, or dissociate religion from the State, relegating the Scriptures to individual interpretation and church membership to individual choice. The irony is that until the recent strife among Catholics and Protestants, religion had not been a motive for war among European nations, but rather had curbed the warring impulse among the nobility. Moreover, the Thirty Years' War itself was as much about competing nation-states as about competing churches; its most destructive phase came when *Catholic* France joined forces with the struggling Protestant states against their common enemy the Emperor. It would be the last religious war in Europe. It was nigh unto being the first religious war in Europe. But the "lesson" was learned.

The philosopher Thomas Hobbes, for one, claimed that the only way men might live under an uneasy truce would be for them to concede their natural "rights" to all goods. We all, he argued, have an equal claim to the plums from that tree, the iron in that hill, John's wife, or Mary's gold. Such equality breeds war. So we yield our claims up to a sovereign state—the so-called "Leviathan."

Hobbes did not argue that the Leviathan had to be ruled by a divinely anointed king. There was no divine anointing. There need not even be a king; a council might serve as well. The point is that the Leviathan's will is absolute. The unitary state is a divinity by comparison with the individual. It alone has rights. It can determine what or how much you will own. It can determine whom and how you will worship. It directs your comings and goings. It must direct them, since men are, individually, random atoms of willfulness, colliding against one another

A Book You're Not Supposed to Read

Reflections on the Revolution in France by Edmund Burke; New York: Oxford University Press USA, 1999.

The closest friend America's rebels had in England was also the most eloquent critic of the French Revolution. Arguing that order, hierarchy, and tradition ought not be lightly discarded even for high ideals such as *Liberté, Égalité, Fraternité*, this book is one of the finest articulations of conservatism, in the most meaningful sense of the word.

in a meaningless existence. There is, as the nominalists said, no such thing as "mankind" except as a convenient term, and no such thing as human nature; only individual human beings seeking pleasure and fleeing pain. Nature cannot guide us here. For the life of natural man, said Hobbes in his most famous sentence, in that ugly non-Eden before the rise of the Leviathan, is embroiled in the war of all against all. It is "solitary, poor, nasty, brutish, and short."[9]

There will be a Hobbesian streak in many of the states and revolutions to come. Louis XIV, the "Sun King" of France, rejected the quasi-atheism of the Englishman who camped out in his country during the Puritan revolt, but agreed that in his capacity as head of state the king must demand the homage of a divinity. *"L'état, c'est moi,"* said Louis, "The State, that is myself!" Louis' most eloquent critic, the saintly Bishop Bossuet, condemned the luxury of the royal court, yet also confirmed the propriety of absolute monarchy, and claimed that people had no right to rise up against the divinely anointed ruler even if he proved to be a tyrant. Their recourse was to plead, and pray.[10] The revolutionists in Paris tore down the statue of Mary in the cathedral of Notre Dame and paraded a scantily clad woman as the goddess Reason in her place. Eventually their leaders would wrest law to their will, calling it the will of the people and pronouncing it supreme. They dethroned one monarch to establish a million, dulling the blades of many an ax against the necks of their enemies. The Leviathan rears its head too in the Marxist tyranny, in the Nazi worship of the fatherland, and in the womb-to-tomb welfare state, choking the soul with its hardhearted benevolence.

The rot proceeds from the head down. In the Enlightenment, that rot came with the growing acceptance of materialism, the belief that matter alone exists; the soul, if it exists, dies with the body. The ancient materialist Lucretius enjoyed a revival; Hobbes' analysis of the condition of "natural" man is wholly Lucretian. Basically, Lucretius claims that only atoms and empty space exist, and that all the things we see are the results of random atoms, bound by physical laws, colliding without purpose. Although Isaac Newton was no materialist—he spent many years in alchemical and spiritualist "research"—still, his description of the world as made up of discrete particles was atomistic. So in "Mock On, Mock On, Voltaire, Rousseau," the poet William Blake blamed him, with some justice, for reducing the world to brute particulate matter:

> The Atoms of Democritus
> And Newton's Particles of light
> Are sands upon the Red sea shore,
> Where Israel's tents do shine so bright.[12]

Now if man is but matter, why not use him as if he were iron or clay? What sense can "good" and "evil" make in such a world? In *The Fable of the Bees*, Bernard Mandeville argued that greed and pride and gluttony were good for the hive. Private vices would result in a roaring economy and public virtues:

> Fraud, Luxury, and Pride must live;
> Whilst we the benefits receive. (415–16)

The Earl of Rochester, a sporadically brilliant drunkard and debauchee, citing poor temperate Lucretius throughout, reduces man to a speck, and scoffs at the notion that a speck could apprehend the divine. It's as absurd as to think that an ointment could make

> an Old Witch flie,
> And bear a Crippled Carcass through the Skie. (*A Satyr Against Mankind*, 86–87)

Man is ignorant, said the enlightened Helvetius, apologist for the totalitarian state. But man is made for virtue. What to do about the contradiction?

If force essentially resides in the greater number, and justice consists in the practice of actions useful to the greater number, it is evident that justice is in its own nature always armed with a power sufficient to suppress vice and place men under the necessity of being virtuous. (*On the Mind*)

Fine words, with terrible implications. When the French *philosophes* in the eighteenth century discarded the Christian belief in the fall of man, they turned, as Plato did, to *ignorance* as their explanation of evil. But if people do wicked things because they are ignorant of the Good, then we must teach them better, whether they like it or not. That need is at the heart of Plato's fanciful regime in the *Republic.* Now, Helvetius does not even believe in the Good as such. What is right, he says, is what will be materially useful to the greater number. That means that the State will define good and evil, for the purposes of a numerical majority. As for the dignity and prescriptive rights of a man or family or village, they are the flotsam of a dark age, swept away in the flood. No protection, this, against tyranny.

A Book You're Not Supposed to Read

Ideas Have Consequences by Richard Weaver; Chicago: University of Chicago Press, 1984.

A tightly argued, wide-ranging polemic against the intellectual and artistic decadence of the modern West, which Weaver sees as having sprung from one critical and avoidable mistake at the inception of the Renaissance. Knowledge was demoted from the attainment of timeless truth, to the ability to analyze particulars, in order to exert our power over nature.

What of God, who protects the widow and the orphan, who humbles the proud, and exalts the lowly? If God existed, he was a watchmaker who set the gears in motion, but had nothing *personal* to do with their operation. So said the Deists, agreeing with Lucretius that God could not be appealed to, "not won with virtuous deeds nor touched by rage" (*On the Nature of Things*, 1.49). The philosopher Baruch Spinoza talked a great deal about God, as a necessary being informing the universe. He defied his detractors who accused him of atheism. But one could as soon pray to the Spinoza's God as to a galaxy. God is not Creator but the metaphysical condition undergirding a necessary and, in the whole, perfect world: "We deny that God can omit to do what he does," Spinoza argues (*Short Treatise on God, Man, and His Well Being*, ch. 4).

Man, the Machine

Had Enlightenment authors known what their ideas would yield in the twentieth century, they likely would have recanted. Here, influential scientist Julien Offray de la Mettrie argues that natural law is a mere feeling:

> Now then how shall we define natural law? It is a feeling which teaches us what we should not do, because we would not want it done to us. Would I dare add to this common idea, that this feeling seems to me but a kind of fear or dread, as salutary to the race or to the individual?

La Mettrie assumes that because man's body is made up of the same matter as anything else, therefore man is simply a machine, and the natural law is but a wispy "feeling" he has developed over time. This feeling restrains him from hurting his enemy because he fears that he may someday be hurt in turn.

From Plato's *Republic* we descend to this—a bald assertion that our ideas of good and evil are nothing more than the working out of self-interest. But then, if you have the power, why bother about anyone else? La Mettrie believes he has reduced man to a machine; he has instead warped him into a moral monster.

Écrasez l'infâme!

That, as I've said, was one option. Consider man as stuff to be molded. Deny to God any providential care for man's end. Instead, for practical purposes, grant that care to the State (run, naturally, by intellectuals). The other option was to put religion under house arrest: to drive it back into the conscience. This healthier option granted man the dignity of a being who might pray and praise his Maker. But it made the church go begging to the State, to see in what fashion the State would suffer it to exist. Not that the established churches in England or in the Catholic countries were healthy communities. All were subject to the State's caprices: "Rulers interfered in its affairs," writes the historian Gerald Cragg, "expropriated its wealth, and altered the structure of its life."[13]

That was symptomatic of the time. Voltaire mocked the church that educated him: *"Écrasez l'infâme!"* he cried, "Tear down the horrible thing!" Yet he had something of a guilty conscience about that. When he wrote, famously, "I entirely disagree with what you say and will fight to the death for your right to say it," it was to Helvetius he was writing.[14] In other words, Voltaire did not care for the materialism that his own satires, long on style and short on philosophical depth, encouraged. The most decent character in his satire *Candide* is not Doctor Pangloss (a wicked parody of the quasi-materialist philosopher Leibniz, who argued, as did Spinoza, that the world *in toto* could not be other than it was, and as such was perfect) but a simple Anabaptist Christian, whose only creed seems to have been charity for those who suffer.

Sometimes it's hard to distinguish between the Enlightenment support for religious liberty, and the Enlightenment desire that religion should grow more modern, that is, less religious, and finally decay. Then, as now, some people supported liberty for religions primarily as a means of drawing the teeth from them all. An especially easy target was the large, lumbering Catholic Church, that purveyor of what was scornfully called "priestcraft." Then too, questions of religious liberty were embroiled in national politics. The English could not forget the attempt by the Catholic Guy Fawkes to blow up Parliament in the days of King James I (1606). So when the widower James II, a closet Catholic, made the grievous mistake of marrying an Italian duchess and begetting a male heir, the people, meaning the Parliament, had to revolt. They invited the Protestant William of Orange, son-in-law to James by his first marriage, to invade the land, oust the king, and rule in his stead. This so-called Glorious Revolution (1688), glorious because hardly a drop of blood was shed, marked the victory of Parliament in its long struggle with the throne for supremacy. From then on, the monarchs of England would lose more and more of their power, until they became what they are now, luxurious figureheads. And the law that James had passed, allowing toleration for members of all religious groups, was repealed; Catholics would wait until the early nineteenth century to enjoy voting rights in England.[15]

So religion, in Europe though not necessarily in America (and not at all in Catholic Quebec), retreats to the bedside and the hearth. Hence we see the effeminate emotionalism of eighteenth- and nineteenth-century Catholic piety, with its languishing Christ, a flimsy flower for a savior; and hence the spirited evangelical movements, with Methodism the most admirable among them, that fed the flocks, if not well-defined doctrine, at least the heart of the Gospel message as it applied to a sinner in need, often a half-literate sinner in the countryside.

Meanwhile, the newly expansive view of the State could feed from a "democratic" trough. If, as Helvetius argued, the enforcing arm of the State merely enacts the will of the people, why should the people fear? And how can people appeal beyond the people, if there is nothing higher than the State against which to judge its laws? It is a lesson that fascists, Marxists, and incautious liberals of the next two centuries would take to heart. Blood will be shed for the people, that is, for the great god of the State. The French Revolution was a clear case, but even the imperialist wars of England in the Crimea and in South Africa were spurred by the liberal "scientific" desire to siphon away to other lands the surplus population at home. The magnates of industrial Manchester, not the old lords in their manors or the enfeebled Anglican Church, provided the energy behind that desire to fight, to make all the world "democratic," English, industrial, and rubberized.[16]

How was the Enlightenment preference for democracy responsible for the bloodshed? Perhaps we need to distinguish among kinds of governments of, by, and for the people. It is not that democracy *per se* leads to tyranny, but that, as Burke observed, the "metaphysical" democratic state envisioned by the French revolutionists was already tyrannical, arrogating to itself the prescriptive rights of individuals, of villages, of groups and classes of society, and of the Church. It had already turned man into a machine or a number. At the same time, it was a kind of demolatry, to coin a term—elevating some abstract mass of the "people" into a totem for cultic worship, seeing the rule by the "people" as the natural and inevitable progression of history. Here is Burke, prompted to write by pro-revolutionary clergymen in England, who had supplanted God's providence with the "science" of progress:

> It is said, that twenty-four millions ought to prevail over two hundred thousand. True; if the constitution of a kingdom be a problem of arithmetic.

But men are not arithmetical counters. They cannot truly love their countries, Burke suggests, unless they love them simply for what they are, with all their old ways:

> You see, Sir, that in this enlightened age I am bold enough to confess, that we are generally men of untaught feelings; that instead of casting away all our old prejudices, we cherish them to a very considerable degree, and, to take more shame to ourselves, we cherish them because they are prejudices; and the

longer they have lasted, and the more generally they have prevailed, the more we cherish them.

More words we cannot stomach; but the alternative is ceaseless change, breaking the tacit bonds of duty that link past generations to our own, and:

> hazarding to leave to those who come after them a ruin instead of an habitation—and teaching these successors as little to respect their contrivances, as they had themselves respected the institutions of their forefathers.

The Pilgrim Fathers

How, then, in this political welter, and among the uncivilized natives of the New World, did the victory of the founding of America occur? Why did America, that nation with the soul of a church, avoid the bloodshed of France, the cultural stagnation of Spain, and the continued disintegration of Germany and Italy?

The politically correct tale is easily told: It was all a matter of English imperialism. The English invaded. They were bigoted and ignorant, but they had superior firepower. They spread smallpox; and that was that.

But the truth is more interesting, more human, and more important to remember now, as we yield our freedoms up to an all-swallowing State.

You're an Englishman living in the Dutch city of Leyden, long one of the hot spots of the Reformation. You don't feel at home. You stumble about in the language. The Dutch drink beer and skate on the frozen streams on the popish thing they call Christmas Day. The Calvinists baptize their children, a practice you consider unwarranted by Scripture. You have no desire to convert them to your ways. You've only moved to Holland to enjoy your own community, separate from the bad influences of the pompous Anglicans in your homeland, and free of harassment by government officials.

But you won't be staying in Holland, or returning to your native Kent. That's because your pastor, John Robinson, has conceived a grand and fearful plan. He has organized you and your brother Puritans into a joint-stock company, to cross the ocean to the New World, to farm and fish and trap, or hew lumber, or do whatever will make the company modestly profitable for the financiers on this side of the water. But you're not traveling to make money. Mainly you want to be a free community. You want to raise your families in a godly way, with no one near to corrupt them, and no bishop or lord to toss you in prison for worshipping in the wrong way.

So you set sail. Let's be clear about what this voyage was *not.* It was not undertaken to convert the natives to the gospel. Some journeys were undertaken for that, though they are not now celebrated. The young Jesuit Matteo Ricci sailed to Macao after having mastered mathematics, astronomy, and clockmaking. There he studied all he could about Mandarin Chinese and the culture of China—the writings of the wise men, the delicate etiquettes of the imperial court, the Chinese reverence for tradition and notable suspicion of outsiders. Finally, Father Ricci traveled to China, and eventually was brought in to the Forbidden

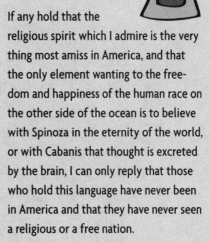

A Religious Nation

If any hold that the religious spirit which I admire is the very thing most amiss in America, and that the only element wanting to the freedom and happiness of the human race on the other side of the ocean is to believe with Spinoza in the eternity of the world, or with Cabanis that thought is excreted by the brain, I can only reply that those who hold this language have never been in America and that they have never seen a religious or a free nation.

Alexis de Tocqueville, *Democracy in America* (ch. 17, 318)

Tocqueville was a conservative liberal, that is, a tradition-minded, devout man who believed passionately in political liberty. Noting the *accidental and temporary* association of the Church with the royalists in Europe, he saw that Christian "habits of the heart" (310) protect liberty, granting spiritual force to the law, and restraining those who would overturn the social order for their own gain.

City, where he presented the emperor with an object of fascination and wonder: a clock. Ricci was honored as a Mandarin. Essentially, he became a Mandarin, so that the mandarins and the people might be won for Christ.[17]

But you know little about the natives. You've heard stories from sailors, but sailors are not the most reliable sources. You have heard of gentle and peaceful tribes, like those who met Columbus when he first struck land. You have heard of the cannibals of the Caribbean. You have probably heard of the hated Aztecs of Mexico, who exacted a tribute from the neighboring peoples: human hearts, cut hot and steaming from the bodies of young men at their chief temple to the war god Huitzilopochtli. You have no special affection for the natives you expect to meet, and no special affection for the Europeans you are about to leave.

You are also not the ambassadors of a great nation thirsty for gold. England is still relatively poor. Its forays across the ocean have been few. Long ago, Henry VII scrambled up some cash to send an Italian, John Cabot, to scout the coasts of North America. Cabot landed in Nova Scotia, and "claimed" it for England. But, though English fishermen did commence to harvesting the rich Grand Banks off Newfoundland, England had established only one colony in North America, the failed Jamestown. She could hardly afford to keep the Scots subdued, let alone natives thousands of miles away. It is true that some freebooting patriots, more pirate than patriot, had scoured the waters to pick off a Spanish ship here and there, or to set up some kind of outpost in the Americas: Francis Drake, John Hawkins, Walter Raleigh. But your leader is no Cortez with his five hundred soldiers, capitalizing upon the native hatred of the Aztecs to storm Mexico City and bring down the emperor Montezuma.[18] No government grants you money, nor will you return money to any government. It is, in more than one sense of the word, a *private enterprise*.

You are not sailors, not fishermen, not soldiers, though there are a few of each among you. You are ordinary farmers and artisans, shoemakers, coopers, blacksmiths, carpenters. Some of you have brought along wife and children. It is a new thing in the world.

William Bradford, the wise and pious first governor of Plymouth, describes in patient detail the voyage, the terrible first winter, and the perseverance of the pilgrims who survived exposure, hunger, and disease. He also gives us a close look at the establishment of an ordered community, self-governing, attempting in critical matters to harmonize the laws of man with the law of God, and in things indifferent to give men a decent measure of freedom, though not as much freedom as colonial Americans would later enjoy. Here he tells of how the few healthy persons among them, including the elder William Brewster and their military commander Myles Standish, tended to the sick in a way that would have been unheard of in the Old World, for they

> ... spared no pains night nor day, but with abundance of toil and hazard of their own health, fetched them wood, made them fires, dressed them meat, made their beds, washed their loathsome clothes, clothed and unclothed them. In a word, did all the homely and necessary offices for them which dainty and queasy stomachs cannot endure to hear named; and all this willingly and cheerfully, without any grudging in the least, showing herein their true love unto their friends and brethren. (*Of Plimoth Plantation, 1620–1647*)

So assiduous was their charity that the sailors themselves, not members of the religious community and not always kind to their passengers, were moved by it, particularly when they fell ill and the Pilgrims tended to them too. Like the pagans in the time of Julian the Apostate, those sailors looked to the faithful for assistance rather than to their own. Said one, "You, I now see, show your love like Christians indeed to one another, but we let one another lie and die like dogs" (87).

I relate the story for several reasons. First, it helps to correct the slander that the Pilgrims were foolish and violent, and the Indians, by contrast, were wise and peaceable. In fact, the Indians were no different from the Europeans or from human beings anywhere. They were prone to wickedness. At Cape Cod Bradford found a web of enmities among the Indian tribes, exacerbated by the presence of French trappers and the depredations of English slave traders. One of those traders had kidnapped Squanto—the English-speaking Indian who taught the Pilgrims how to plant corn, and whom the Pilgrims once had to restrain from stealing the fur coats from Indian women to whom they had come for trading (*Mourt's Relation*, 60). But the Christian love evident in the story of the sickness also characterized the Pilgrims' dealings with the natives. They made a compact with the chief Massasoit, stipulating fair play and mutual trust between the two peoples. The Pilgrims kept that treaty faithfully, from the time of its seal to Bradford's written account twenty-four years later. It is not remarkable, in human history, that a people should come to a land and drive out its inhabitants. What is remarkable is that, despite the hard weather, the scarcity of food, and their superior firearms, the Pilgrims did not steal from the Indians, and flogged any vagabond who tried to. Their friendship was genuine.

The second reason I mention it is to note the beginnings of a Christian commonwealth—a brotherhood of equals that yet orders itself by a hierarchy. Myles Standish, the diminutive soldier without whom the Pilgrims would not have lasted one year, is not too proud to clean the limbs of the sick, like the lowliest nurse. Yet he is their commander, too, and knows when and how to exact discipline. It is this practical piety that Bradford and his brethren tried to incorporate into the daily government of their community. And this corrects another misconception, namely that the Pilgrims lived under a communist rule. Not exactly, and never for any ideological reasons. As I've said, they had left Europe as a joint stock company, and that meant they would share the profits (they never made much) equally. But Bradford soon saw that when it came to family and community life, the model of the company was not workable. Nor was it scriptural. It smacked too much of Plato's *Republic*.

A rigorous insistence upon equality pleased nobody, motivated nobody to work hard, set the hale and industrious on a par with the weak and lazy, commandeered young men to work for other people's wives and children, reduced the aged to the indignity of youth, compelled women to cook for men who were not their husbands (which, says Bradford, they deemed "a kind of slavery"), and diminished, if it did not destroy, the natural relations that God had established among men. So Bradford and the elders parceled out equal shares of land to each family to work for themselves, and assigned each of the boys and young men (for there were many more males than females) to a family, so that none might complain of the need for another pair of shoulders and hands.

It worked, said Bradford, who understands that he is bucking a political movement of his time. His people presented communism with its best chance for success, years of effort "amongst godly and sober men"

Rousseau's Eden

From the moment one man began to stand in need of the help of another; from the moment it appeared advantageous to any one man to have enough provisions for two, equality disappeared, property was introduced, work became indispensable, and vast forests became smiling fields, which man had to water with the sweat of his brow, and where slavery and misery were soon seen to germinate and grow up with the crops.

—Jean-Jacques Rousseau, *A Discourse on the Origin of Inequality*

Rousseau's vision of the blissful life of the savage before agriculture and metallurgy owes more to the classical poets than to any observation of primitive tribes. He should have been in the company of John Smith at Jamestown or Father Marquette among the Hurons. But his vision still exerts a strange power over the politically correct. Feminists, who have over a thousand stone-age tribes to join if they please, often entertain lovely dreams about the "matriarchy" we all enjoyed before agriculture. Tell it to the aborigines.

(133). Yet their experience "may well evince the vanity of that conceit of Plato's and other ancients applauded *by some of later times*; that the taking away of property and bringing in community into a commonwealth would make them happy and flourishing; as if they were wiser than God" (emphasis mine).

What we have in Plymouth, then, and elsewhere in America, is a third way, neither the absolute State praised by Hobbes, nor the banishment of religion to the dusty corners of the soul. Here is room for individual competence and enterprise, in the service of the family, and to the benefit of the community. We have an ideal that was largely realized during Bradford's long governorship, and that remained a template for New England villages for many generations: a people united by the God they worship, who commands them to love one another.

I'm not saying that the American colonists always lived up to so high an ideal. When, in the history of man, do people live up to their ideals? But the Puritan congregation, like the monasteries of old, combined equality with the necessary hierarchies that develop among brothers who obey their acknowledged superior. Unlike the old monasteries, the congregations did so while fostering the family. Strangely enough, it was from their commitment to the local church polity that the Puritans gave us a model, not for church government, but for a secular order friendly both to family and church.

And it was, more or less, this model that colonists replicated wherever they went. In a sense it was conservative and European. It resembled the monastery far more than any Puritan would care to admit. It also resembled the chartered towns of old England. In some places, like Plymouth, to join the town was to join the church, or to put oneself partly under the direction of the elders. But if that was not to one's taste, one might settle somewhere else—Pennsylvania, for instance, where freedom of religion was guaranteed by the charter that Charles II granted to William Penn.

But even in Pennsylvania, this freedom of religion extended also to a community's vigorous practice of religion. So a Moravian settlement springs up in Bethlehem, an Amish settlement in Lancaster, and a Mennonite settlement in Germantown.

Conservative Founders?

Historians may debate whether the Founding Fathers were correct in their assessment, but they themselves believed—or at least most of them did—that in their revolt against England they were only claiming the rights of Englishmen under common law, rights recognized by long tradition. That is why the conservative Edmund Burke supported them (and why, with that same veneration for the particular pieties of a nation, he supported the Quebec Act, allowing French Catholics freedom *from* English laws regarding religion). Franklin had persuaded Burke that it was George III and his ministers who were the innovators, and Burke knew enough of the Whig party in England—mercantile, secular, and centralizing—to find the argument plausible.[19]

So when we look at the opening salvo of the Declaration of Independence, we should not be quick to assume that it sets forth an utterly new doctrine of government:

> We hold these truths to be self-evident: that all men are created equal; that they are endowed by their Creator with certain inalienable rights, and that among these are life, liberty, and the pursuit of Happiness.

What distinguishes Jefferson's assertion from the cry of *"Liberté, Égalité, Fraternité"* that echoed through the streets of revolutionary Paris? Let's answer by dispelling a few misconceptions about the Founders and their beliefs.

A Book You're Not Supposed to Read

The Scarlet Pimpernel by Baroness Emmuska Orczy; New York: Penguin, 2000.

Written as a play in 1903 (panned as too old fashioned by London's critics), it became a novel soon thereafter, and since a fine movie. The story's protagonist is the scourge of the French Revolution and the Reign of Terror, and a hero of the nobility, saving scores of them from the guillotine.

A reactionary hero defending the aristocracy? Hardly politically correct.

Error one: The Founders were Deists who believed in the cipher-god of Spinoza, or the god of the optimist Leibniz, a god that sets the celestial machinery in motion, but who cannot dwell within the heart of man.

People who say so are looking at America as if it were Europe, governed by a skeptical and cynical intelligentsia and aristocratic elite. It is not the America of the Great Awakening of 1739–1742, a movement both popular and educated, witnessing the plain eloquence of the Methodists Whitefield and John Wesley, but also the learned reformed theology of Jonathan Edwards. Setting aside natural science, there was nothing in classical learning, logic, political theory, and practical experience that the two or three most skeptical among the Founders, Benjamin Franklin and Thomas Jefferson, could have taught the likes of John Witherspoon, Samuel Adams, and Patrick Henry. Had Jefferson not become President—which is to say, had his predecessor John Adams not signed the Alien and Sedition Acts, criminalizing criticism of the fledgling government when French nationals were thought to be undermining it—we might have a very different idea of who the most important Founders were.[20]

It is true that the pamphleteer Thomas Paine, not a member of either Continental Congress, was a genuine Deist, if not an atheist outright. But that the nation was not all enamored of Paine and his equalitarian ideals is amply illustrated in a letter of John Adams. Do not call ours the Age of Reason, he says, satirizing Paine's irreverent book by that name, but rather "the Age of Paine":

> He deserves it much more than the courtesan who was conse-
> crated to represent the goddess in the temple at Paris, and
> whose name Tom has given to the age. The real intellectual fac-
> ulty has nothing to do with the age, the strumpet, or Tom.
> (Quoted in Kirk; *Selected Writings of John and John Quincy*
> *Adams*)

The evidence that even Franklin and Jefferson were not *exactly* Deists is
straightforward enough: we sometimes catch them praying. The Deist
"god" is an impersonal force. One does not appeal to an impersonal force.
Helvetius didn't; La Mettrie didn't; Paine didn't. But at one key moment
during the first Continental Congress, Franklin urged his fellows, before
they undertook any more business, to appeal to Him who directs the
course of nations, without whose assistance they could not succeed. It is
not an isolated moment of piety. Here he condoles with a woman on the
loss of a friend:

> Our friend and we are invited abroad on a party of pleasure,
> which is to last for ever. His chair was ready first, and he is
> gone before us. (Letter to Elizabeth Hubbart, February 22, 1756)

He writes the following, one month before his death:

> Here is my Creed. I believe in one God, Creator of the Universe.
> That he governs it by his Providence. That he ought to be wor-
> shipped. That the most acceptable Service we render to him is
> doing good to his other Children. That the soul of Man is immor-
> tal, and will be treated with Justice in another life respecting its
> Conduct in this. (Letter to Ezra Stiles, March 9, 1790)

It is not exactly Christian, but it is far closer to that than to the materialism of Hobbes, or to the hostile secularism of our academy today.

It is true that Jefferson cut from his New Testament all those passages wherein Jesus worked miracles.[21] True also that his friend and rival Adams slid from Calvinism to Unitarianism, and that, advising him about the establishment of the University of Virginia, he urged him to make sure that genuine divinity, of a Christian Unitarian sort, would be taught there, and not that absurd doctrine that holds that the Maker of all this splendid universe was swaddled up in flesh and lay in a manger.[22] But then, Jefferson did study this redacted "Bible" of his lovingly. He who hated the State establishment of a church—taxing men to pay the salary of a clergyman—never once protested the teaching of Scripture in local schools, built and paid for by the people of a community. Why should he have? There was, after all, an odd conservative streak in Jefferson the planter and landed gentleman, as opposed to Jefferson the political theorist and diplomat. I know plenty of churches that could use a few Deists like Jefferson.

Error two: The Founders wished to establish a purely secular state. If the term "secular" implies a public square denuded of religious discourse, or even a theory of law that is not rooted in the eternal truths of good and evil, the claim is untenable. One word in Jefferson's sentence gives it away: *Creator.*

It is not an idle word. Jefferson appeals beyond the authority of the State to the Creator of human nature and of the natural laws of good and evil. He was following a beaten path. John Locke, who wrote his treatises on government to justify the limited, constitutional monarchy established in England under William and Mary, rejects Hobbes' account of the state of nature, the war of all against all. He replaces it with something like the Genesis story of man before the Fall. The Father created man to be free and to replicate His government by paternal rule upon earth.[23] In other words, man's freedom and his rights flow from his created nature, and the natural law consists of those rules that such beings cannot break without denying that nature. Lucretius is the author whom Hobbes cites most frequently, but for Locke it is the Anglican divine and theorist of natural law, Richard Hooker. The State—the Leviathan—is no demigod. It is rather, to quote Locke, what man creates to help secure his liberty to "follow [his] own will in all things, where the rule [of law] prescribes not; and not to be subject to the inconstant, uncertain, unknown, arbitrary will of another man" (*Second Treatise on Government,* ch. 4).

I'm not arguing that Locke is wholly correct, or that the egalitarian individualism he preaches is not finally corrosive to the community. I only note that Jefferson follows Locke, not Hobbes. Jefferson sympathized with the French Revolution, undoubtedly. It was another matter on which he and Adams violently disagreed. But the Jacobin slogan lacks an appeal to the One who makes liberty, equality, and fraternity possible. Jefferson's declaration does not make that mistake.

Error three: Jefferson insists that the State cannot take away your rights by force. Well, he certainly believed it couldn't, in justice. But his sentence means something different. These rights, he says, are *unalienable.* Again he has Hobbes and the dreamers of totalitarian systems in mind. When people could no longer endure the chaos of the war of all against all, said Hobbes, they *alienated* their "rights" to everything, vesting them in the Leviathan, the State. But these rights, granted by the divine King as surely as an earthly king would grant rights to a chartered town, are ours, and not ours to hand over to any ruler or any State. We cannot sell ourselves into slavery. We cannot sign our children over as wards of the State. We cannot trade fundamental freedoms, which are ours *from the Creator,* for a pittance of health insurance. We cannot swap our right to support or criticize people running for public office for the benefit of cheaper and cleaner elections managed by the State. We can't do a hundred things we now do all the time, alienating our rights and comforting ourselves because, after all, the State will take care of them. Hobbes was more honest than we are. He wanted the Leviathan. We do too, but we pretend that we can put a ring in its nose and lead it around on a leash.

Error four: Jefferson says that each individual has the right to pursue what he thinks will make him happy. No, he says no such thing.

Jefferson was a classically educated man writing for his peers, not for *Redbook* or the *New York Times.* Those men understood that "happiness" was the aim of all the ancient moral philosophies, and of all the Christian communions. Moreover, they agreed that one of the aims of government was the promotion of the good of man, a good which was reducible neither to naked will nor to the accumulation of material goods. "All sober inquiries after truth, ancient and modern, pagan and Christian," wrote Adams, "have declared that the happiness of man, as well as his dignity, consists in virtue" (Kirk; *Selected Writings*). But man will not be virtuous by inclination. He will prefer sloth to industry, slumber to wakefulness, and pleasantries to the bracing work of liberty. Man cannot perfect himself. He needs assistance. If so, then it is not religion that needs the prop of the State, but the State that cannot long survive without religion. Madison, no friend to any established church, admitted as much.

None of these men believed that virtue was a matter of opinion—that was the rogue's way out. And they were too deeply read in scripture and in ancient moral philosophy (especially Stoicism) to believe that you could practice your virtue in privacy. Happiness requires virtue, and virtue requires a community that fosters it, wherein the virtue may be practiced. But if people are vicious, then the chaos into which they will plunge their cities will prevent even virtuous people from enjoying the full freedom of a civic life.

In other words, the pursuit of happiness *is not the pursuit of pleasure.*

America's forgotten models: Rome and Athens

The Founders had two principal models for the structure, though not necessarily the spirit, of their new republic: Rome and Athens. They borrowed something from each. What they borrowed, we have forgotten.

From Athens they retained a strong attachment to the local. There was no pan-Hellenic state before the half-barbarian Philip of Macedon created one by force. After Philip, there was no free Athens, no free Sparta, no free Corinth. Those of the Founders most committed to the rights of the individual states, especially the farmers in the South, understood the problem. They did not want to be appendages to an empire. In this sense, and maybe in this sense alone, Jefferson was *more* conservative than his Federalist opponent, Alexander Hamilton. It is to our shame that we find such loyalty to a local place hard to understand. Being *open-minded* means rising above your circumstances. Hometown pride, we sneer, is chauvinistic and narrow-minded.

But in Jefferson's time, to be a Virginian meant a great deal: Virginia had her own venerable history, her own holidays, and her own trade. Other states, for a time, had their own established churches. Kant would wince, and so would today's cosmopolitan.

Still, even the most ardent democrats understood that the example of Athens was dubious. After all, Athens fell. Its democracy lasted less than a century. It was Jefferson's more cautious democratic colleague, Madison, who noted that five thousand men, even if each were as wise as Socrates, would still be no more than a mob.[24] Democracy in its pure form tends to destroy freedom, and then it

A Fatal Flaw in America

Alexis de Tocqueville identified well a dangerous tendency of Americans:

> There is, in fact, a manly and lawful passion for equality that incites men to wish all to be powerful and honored. This passion tends to elevate the humble to the rank of the great; but there exists also in the human heart a depraved taste for equality, which impels the weak to attempt to lower the powerful to their own level and reduces men to prefer equality in slavery to inequality with freedom.

Democracy in America (ch. 3, 56)

Freedom can tolerate a good deal of pride; it can tolerate very little envy. Which passion for equality—the manly or the depraved—has predominated in our age of contempt for the genuine excellence of others?

yields to a tyrant who can settle the resulting chaos. That is what Plato said; so did the Federalist, Fisher Ames:

> Our country is too big for union, too sordid for patriotism, too democratick for liberty. What is to become of it, He who made it best knows. Its vice will govern it, by practising upon its folly. This is ordained for democracies. (Kirk; letter of Oct 26, 1803; *Works*)

So the Founders looked to Rome. Adams, theorizing about his ideal state, clearly has in mind the checks and balances provided by the Roman consuls, the tribunes of the people, the aristocratic Senate, and the popular assembly.[25] Our Senate was supposed to revive the Senate of Rome, only more committed to the welfare of all the people. Its name suggests the sort of men who would serve: *old men,* made wise by experience, and sufficiently established in life so as not to be tempted to use public power to fatten their purses. They were not elected by the people—popular appeal is *not* what you want in a Senator. They were elected by state legislatures, ensuring for the states a great measure of authority *over the federal government.*

Everywhere in our Constitution we find an attempt to combine a strong federal government, able to meet the needs of a rapidly growing nation, with a preference for the civic life of the state and the community. So the people elect representatives from what should be geographically coherent districts: a city with its outlying county, or a range of farmland, or the upland ridges. So too, by the Constitution, the people vote not for the president but for electors: and though most electors are now bound by law to follow their state's will, this hedge between the people and the presidency has had the happy result of compelling candidates to win *states.* That prevents people from the fringe from throwing American elections into confusion. If you can't win a state, you can't win anything.

Had the decadent Weimar Republic had such a system, Hitler might never have come to power.

Saving reason from itself

The founding of America was, no matter what a Frenchman might say, the most world-changing event of the century. But it also fit well with a conservative and, for the time, politically *incorrect* tradition of thought. We can call this tradition *the call for reason to return to its senses* and admit its limitations.

Suppose a philosopher were to conclude that a little child has no more rights than a chimpanzee. We might call him mad, or we might, as Princeton has done, award him an endowed chair of bioethics.[26] If we were rationalists of the eighteenth century, we'd look upon blacks or Indians as members of an inferior race, and we'd "prove" it by supposedly scientific means. We'd have charts and numbers at our call, and calipers to measure the thickness of skulls (other people's, not our own). Man has oppressed man from the Fall. But for the first time, in the Enlightenment, man summoned science to justify it. Racism properly understood begins here.[27] It begins with one function of reason, the scientific or mathematical, grown like a tumor, devouring the rest.

But the more unfashionable thinkers and writers understood, with Aristotle, that you have to match your reasoning to the subject matter. To prove Pythagoras' theorem, you use logical deduction. To discuss the structure of a just city, you call upon all your experience of human beings: you see what sort of creature man is, how he is made up of intellect and appetite, reason and will, and you legislate accordingly. You may find that a government suitable for seafarers will not work for inland farmers. That's all right, so long as each has as its goal the fulfillment of man's end: intellectual and practical virtue. It's why, said Aristotle, you can study geometry as a schoolboy, but "a young man is not a proper hearer of lectures on political science."[28] As for theology, that must require the response of our whole beings, our capacity not only to deduce but to "hear," as the Scriptures so often put it, the law and the goodness of God.

So I'd like to end this chapter with a few and woefully short glances at men who attempted to save reason from itself. First among these is the great mathematician and philosopher, Blaise Pascal (1623–1662).

When Pascal was a little boy, wrote his sister, "he played with conic sections as other children would play with toys."[29] Conic sections—shapes such as the parabola (the path of a projectile) and an ellipse (the path of a planet, Newton discovered)—marked the height of ancient mathematics; the next step would be calculus. Pascal, without a tutor, had advanced in the subject beyond the discoveries of the great Apollonius of Perga, *at age sixteen.* He is one of the fathers of projective geometry, the field that analyzes what happens to shapes when they are projected upon other shapes. By the time he was eighteen he had, from his close study of clocks, invented the world's first calculating machine. He proved that vacuums exist and that air exerts pressure. He is the first great scientist of probability: Pascal's Triangle links dice-throwing with algebra and number theory. If your Cardinals need to win eight of their

Pascal vs. the Enlightenment

If we do not know ourselves to be full of pride, ambition, lust, weakness, misery, and injustice, we are indeed blind. And if, knowing this, we do not desire deliverance, what can we say of a man…?

—Blaise Pascal, *Pensées* (450)

And maybe that is the great failing of the Enlightenment. All that blazing light struck men blind. One observable fact contradicts the premises of the Enlightenment: the heart of man.

last ten games to have a shot at the World Series, the Triangle will help you find the odds.

But, unlike those of our day who insist that all religions are the same (usually because they don't pay much attention to them), Pascal insisted upon the *limits* of reason, and upon the sovereignty of God, who might choose a shepherd without consulting the mathematician first. Pascal had an experience of the living God, which he recorded on a piece of paper and sewed into the lining of his coat, so that it would be with him always:

> FIRE: The God of Abraham, the God of Isaac, the God of Jacob—not the God of the philosophers.

"To make light of philosophy is to be a true philosopher," he said (*Pensées*, 4), distinguishing what logic can do from what it cannot do, and affirming the importance of what he called intuition. "The heart has its reasons, which reason cannot know" (277). As for the rationalist who considers himself too high and mighty for such popular things as religious faith, Pascal cuts him open with three short words: "*Skeptic, for obstinate*" (*Pensées*, 51).

Pascal reads like a *Politically Incorrect Guide*™ *to Mankind*, a great corrective to our vanity: "The Christian religion, then, teaches men these two truths; that there is a God whom men can know, and that there is a corruption in their nature which renders them unworthy of Him" (555). To ignore that corruption, man will do anything; in fact, he spends most of his life in a complicated play, pretending to care about what he does not love, all to distract himself from the loneliness of his heart, the vanity of his days, and the shortness of life.

Pascal, keenest of psychological writers, opened a way that a few would take. The direction of European culture, after Newton, lay rather in exposing the "laws" whereby we know, as if our minds were machines acted upon by machines. Eventually, as it did in the ancient world, materialism led to skepticism—other than probable knowledge about matter, could we know anything at all?

The pious Immanuel Kant, mild-mannered yet fiercely proud of his prodigious accomplishments, never traveled far beyond his native city of Koenigsberg, the capital of imperial Prussia. Yet he was typical of his age in his attempt to recast moral reasoning as a kind of mathematics, divorced from the flesh and blood of man, and from place and time. Kant had accepted the method of the skeptic English philosopher David Hume, who argued that we cannot infer an idea of "cause" from our observation of events. I see the cue ball strike the eight ball, and it moves. I associate the events in my mind, says Hume, and then add to them an extraneous conception of my own, a fiction called "cause."[30] Now if there is no such thing as cause, then many things fall into meaninglessness. Metaphysics, for one: both that of the ancient philosophers, and that of the Christian theologians, including those who, like Aquinas, used the idea of causality to prove the existence of God. But the acid corrodes further, as Kant pointed out. If we ignore Hume's challenge, scientific and mathematical reasoning too must fall. In particular, we shall have no good reason to believe in physical law, because all we ever see is that, when A has happened, B has followed.

So Kant set out to rescue both metaphysics and reason from the threat of skeptical empiricism. Kant was no materialist. He affirmed that the mind can make true and productive judgments about things apart from deductions based on sense experience. Note that well: we do not, says Kant, base our judgments about the laws of physics and mathematics upon experience, even when we happen to learn *about* such laws through experience (for example, when we see water evaporate). Hume should have not have dismissed abstract reasoning so cavalierly. Had he considered not only causality, which he wanted to attack (because he wanted to slay the dragon of theology), but mathematics, "the good company into which metaphysics would thus have been brought, would have saved it from the danger of a contemptuous ill-treatment" (*Prolegomena to Any Future Metaphysics,* ch. 4). Kant will attempt, hampered by what many believe was his inattentiveness to the subtleties of medieval thinking, to restore the idea of cause, using what he calls transcendental ideas—not thoughts so much as the structuring principles of our minds—to "destroy the rash assertions of Materialism, of Naturalism, and of Fatalism, and thus to afford scope for the moral Ideas beyond the field of speculation" (60).

Reason, then, leads Kant to affirm that objective moral good exists. Now, the method he used to determine good and evil would persuade no one but a philosopher, and would probably not move him to action, anyway. It is this, in brief:

I am a rational creature, an end in myself and no mere object. So, then, are all other rational creatures. Then I cannot use them as objects merely, without violating my nature. In particular, if I cannot "universalize" the moral rule I wish to abide by, then it is no rule at all. For instance, I want to promise my friend Stalin that I will not attack Russia if he will not attack Germany. But I do not intend to keep that promise; I hate Russia. Now, obviously, if everyone made lying promises, there would be no such things as promises, because no one would ever believe what anyone was saying. Therefore my "rule"—*I want to make a lying promise, because it would be good for me and bad for my enemy*—contradicts itself. Therefore it is no rule. It is wrong.[31]

The argument delivers a neat blow to our fashionable moral relativism. It condemns the Machiavellian notion that underlies political correctness: namely, that if x results in the political advantage of the correct people, you should do x. For if everyone behaved that way, we would be mired in chaos, and no politics worthy the name would survive. There would be no coherent *polis.*

But there is something troubling about it. When people consider good and evil, they do not think about some abstract "mankind" they have never met. They do not consider the universe. They think instead about the man next door who plays loud music, or the pretty girl across the street who dances with her curtains up. They think about flesh and blood. But the Prussian philosopher disallows that. He will even say that, to the extent that Captain Standish derived joy from tending to his sick comrades, he *was not* engaged in a genuinely moral action. Duty—a stern embrace of what you do not like—trumps the happiness of virtue. So Kant rejects the classical definition of virtue, deriving from Aristotle and given full analysis by Aquinas, who say that a good man is one who so habitually does good things that it becomes a second nature for him, and it really and rightly brings him happiness. Kant also rejects the traditional Jewish and Christian understanding of love, which is never the abstract will of a disembodied being. When Saint Francis overcame his revulsion with love and ran to embrace the leper, he wasn't thinking like an Enlightenment philosopher.

Edmund Burke, by comparison with Kant, was no philosopher at all; but his political and moral thinking was built upon the rock of piety and close observation, passionate but unsentimental observation of men such as we find them. The English politician and man of letters understood that the family and the community are the nurseries of virtue, both private and public. He also understood that what can be deduced, with mathematical logic, from clear principles is only a fraction of what man knows, and it does not include the most important things, either. Hence, like Sophocles, Virgil, and Shakespeare, Burke stressed the importance of *tradition* in moral and political thinking—not because tradition is quaint for holidays, but because it represented the hard-won wisdom of the centuries.

It may be laughable to the universalist, but Burke's sense of tradition places us firmly in the only environment wherein we can learn to be wise and good. We are "to be attached to the subdivision, to love the little platoon we belong to in society" (44), the family, the clan, the village, and hence by degrees to "proceed towards a love to our country, and to mankind. The politically correct slogan has it that we should "think globally, act locally." Burke might reply that to "think globally" is not to think at all, just as to "love mankind" is not to love at all. Learn virtue *here*. If you want to love mankind, cook a nice meal for your children. If you want to clean the world, do the dishes.

To forget tradition is to set yourself on a raging sea. Here is Burke, on what happens when thinking universally is applied locally, without consideration for history, traditions, hallowed customs, religious faith, or loyalty: "Laws overturned; tribunals subverted; industry without vigour; commerce expiring; the revenue unpaid, yet the people impoverished; a church pillaged, and a state not yet relieved; civil and military anarchy made the constitution of the kingdom" (*Reflections on the Revolution in*

Federalism—Forgotten

James Madison, in *Federalist 39*, articulated a notion of federalism that became the foundation of the new republic:

> In this relation [of the federal to the local governments], then, the proposed government cannot be deemed a *national* one; since its jurisdiction extends to certain enumerated objects only, and leaves to the several States a residuary and inviolable sovereignty over all other objects.

That was a long time ago. The federal government, like a grandmama ogre, is now pleased to dictate to the little people below how they shall raise their children, what they shall teach in school, how they shall conduct their local patriotic celebrations, and, it is to be feared, whether they shall use single-ply or double-ply paper in public restrooms. Whether such paper will be decorated with facsimiles of the Constitution has not yet been decided.

France). Those words were written in 1790, *three years before* Robespierre and the Reign of Terror. On cherishing the old, regardless of the political theorems of the day: "Is every land-mark of the country to be done away in favour of a geometrical and arithmetical constitution?" On what France lost by its proclamation of equality (which would soon end in the triumph of the tyrant Napoleon): "It is gone, that sensibility of principle, that chastity of honour, which felt a stain like a wound, which inspired courage whilst it mitigated ferocity, which ennobled whatever it touched, and under which vice itself hath lost half its evil, by losing all its grossness."

Burke's *Reflections* is a bracing guide to every foolish exaggeration of the Enlightenment, now taken up and enshrined as holy law in our social sciences, that counts voters and tabulates incomes but cannot understand the heart of man: "In the groves of *their* academy, at the end of every vista, you see nothing but the gallows. Nothing is left which engages the affections on the part of the commonwealth. On the principles of this mechanic philosophy, our institutions can never be embodied, if I may use the expression, in persons; so as to create in us love, veneration, admiration, or attachment. But that sort of reason which banishes the affections is incapable of filling their place." It banishes the affections, but not the appetite, as we now know. We moderns do not often love our country, but we do want a lot from it, in tens and twenties. The country requires the same favor from our hands—in twenties and fifties.

Rousseau and the State

Conservatives sometimes trace back to Jean-Jacques Rousseau everything that has gone wrong in our system of education. They have some justification. Rousseau did understand, against some of the French rationalists, that *feeling* was indispensable for the moral imagination. But he acknowledged no legitimate soil for the nurture of this feeling, nor could he forge a connection between feeling and reason. That is, he accepted the false severance of reason from the proper ordering of the passions. He saw that the reduced "reason" of materialists like La Mettrie was inadequate. But he could not put things together again. He is the father of educational sentimentalism, and, not accidentally, of the state adoption of the schools to ensure that students learn the "correct" sentiments. We see these offspring already in his *La Nouvelle Heloise,* wherein he shows us how to protect a child from the influence of his surroundings, namely the earthy and ordinary habits of other children, manual laborers, housewives, old ladies with strange notions of medicine, village drunks, village philosophers, and priests. It is to take a child *out of the platoon.* Naturally, since most people are not Rousseau, if their children are to have the advantage of this artificial life, the State must provide it for them. More and more, that is what the State does.

Rousseau may be too easy to caricature. He did attempt to place virtue at the heart of his theories regarding education and politics. Nor is it quite just to point out that he himself was a pretty vicious fellow, siring illegitimate children whom he neglected. But if we cross the English Channel we find a man of so powerful an intellect, and so great a heart, that his very *conversation,* recorded by his friend James Boswell, has gone to making the finest biography ever written: Doctor Johnson. He is the English Pascal.

Samuel Johnson

Largely self-taught, afflicted by neurological ailments sometimes to the point of blackest despair, Samuel Johnson fought his way from pennilessness to recognition as the greatest English man of letters of his time. To read one of his essays for *The Rambler* or *The Adventurer* is to be stunned with shame. How could one man possess so much learning, discoursing so easily about Aeschylus and Milton, without sounding like a dusty academic? How could he expect more than ten people in a London coffee house to understand what he was talking about? But he did, and more than ten did—far more.

The secret to Johnson's wisdom was not that he kept his feelings in check. Far from it. It was that his feelings were nurtured by a classical education, a deep love of England, a devotion to the Church, a personal piety that abashed his worldly friends, a calm scrutiny of mankind in all walks of life (for Johnson had spent many a night in his youth without a roof over his head), and an habitual and humble introspection. Before he saw men's hearts, he had looked into his own.

That's an operation that sentimentalists only pretend to perform. Rousseau pretended to perform it, was pleased with what he saw there, and concluded that, given the right education, man could be made perfect. Johnson performed that operation on his knees, and knew better than to believe such nonsense.

Johnson saw into things, and through them. When Boswell asked him how he would refute Bishop Berkeley's theory that all we see about us is the fabrication of the mind, that hulk of a man kicked a stone and cried out, "I refute it—THUS!" (*Life of Johnson*). It was, shall we say, a highly concentrated intellectual argument. It appealed to reason itself, past a reason that had taken leave of its senses. Or, when Boswell asked him about the freedom of the will—a question that troubled the Scotsman, as he tried to reconcile it with the predestination preached by Scottish Calvinists—Johnson replied that all theory was against it, but all experience for it.[32] That was another concentrated argument (for Johnson could write many pages elaborating upon it), based on his insight that theory comes halting behind the more complex and reli-

---

Enlightened Hobbes

"The desires, and other passions of man, are in themselves no sin. No more are the actions, that proceed from those passions."

Thomas Hobbes,
Leviathan (ch. 13, 62)

---

able, though sometimes inarticulate, intuitions of man. Asked his opinion of the American rebels, Johnson trenchantly observed that they talked a deal about freedom, but owned slaves.[33] There was a lot to that, too. Nor did Johnson blithely accept all feelings as valid. In his novel *Rasselas,* one of his characters, searching for the secret of happiness, lives for a while in a middle-class house among other girls of marrying age. Do people know their own hearts? Not according to the Princess Nekayah: "Many were in love with triflers like themselves, and many fancied that they were in love when in truth they were only idle" (ch. 25).

Johnson was never rich; but he held his head among princes. Others might theorize about equality and liberty. Johnson retained the services of Francis Barber, a black man from Jamaica, as his valet; he gave him a place to stay, paid him what he could, and educated him. When he died, Johnson bequeathed to Francis and his family a handsome sum. Johnson was a soft touch for people in suffering. He kept, at great inconvenience to himself, an old woman named Mrs. Williams in his apartment; he was careful of her welfare, though she was not always grateful for it. He married a woman much older than he was, not a "catch," yet he was devoted to her, in a simple and manly fashion. He tolerated Roman Catholicism, when the fashionable attitude toward it—then as now—was to scoff at its "superstitious" appeal to the common person. He trusted the sense of that common person. Yet no one in Europe could match his breadth of reading and his acuity of thought.

He was the most enlightened man of the Enlightenment, and nobody but some Englishmen knew it. We will not see his like again. Our schools, our legislatures, and our entertainment will see to that.

Chapter 8

THE NINETEENTH CENTURY: MAN IS A GOD; MAN IS A BEAST

What a fascinating century the nineteenth is. If the measure of a culture lies in its machines and money, not the men and their thoughts, then that century saw progress unmatched by all the centuries before. Consider what life was like at the onset:

America is a confederation of states hugging the shores of the Atlantic, wary of its old enemy England, and just as wary of its new friend France.

The streets of Paris run with blood. They call it democracy.

Italy is a checkerboard of dukedoms, most of them owing allegiance to foreign powers. The pope is the temporal ruler in the region around Rome.

Most Europeans and Americans live on or near farms.

Nails are made at the blacksmith's shop, by hand.

Mary Wollstonecraft is one of a few people to argue for the full educational and political equality of women.

The sun never sets on the British Empire, yet for most people in Europe and America such things as oranges and pineapples are still exotic, to be purchased for holidays.

If you get sick, your doctor may bleed you to drain off the excess sanguine "humour." George Washington, in 1799, fell ill of what was probably strep throat. His doctor bled him. He died.

Guess What?

- ✦ Nineteenth-century "science" spawned twentieth-century genocide.

- ✦ Romantics' worship of nature turned into a dangerous worship of man.

- ✦ Marx held the working man in scorn.

The intelligentsia believe in the perfectibility of man. This is to come about through proper education, and art.

You ride a horse to get from Philadelphia to New York. It takes two days.

People in Vienna are listening to Mozart.

At its close:

America stretches from the Florida Keys to the Bering Strait, with territories from Cuba to the Philippines. She is about to become the most powerful nation the world has seen.

France has muddled through the century, cast off her imperial government, and become a republic. Europeans more and more assume that democracy can work, and is just. The vote becomes more than a tool to secure justice; it becomes *the desired object in itself,* regardless of how it is used. Monarchs lose almost all authority.

Italy is (or pretends to be) a united nation. So are Greece, Denmark, Norway, and Sweden. Poland, carved up by Prussia and Russia, recalls her heroic past—when she alone defended Europe from the Turks—with pride and longing. We are on the brink of nationalist fervor, and horror.

New York is a city of over four million people. Farms produce more food than ever, thanks to technological innovations: the harvester, the reaper, the thresher. So people move to the cities, black with the smoke of factories and their wondrous array of electric-powered machines.

Women vote in many local and some state elections in America. The first age of feminism is in full swing. It already shows signs of enmity against the family and traditional morality, and of favoring the collective hive over local and individual liberty.

Britain is an aging tiger. Everyone's had an orange.

Louis Pasteur has revolutionized medicine, proving that disease-causing "germs" (the word means "seeds") thrive in certain conditions, and can be eliminated chemically. He establishes the connection between disease and fermentation, or the spoiling of food; it's a tremendous breakthrough for the farmer, the brewer, the vintner, the grocer, and the people who now can enjoy clean food shipped from a distance. Joseph Lister has discovered the principles of antisepsis, and European hospitals, once death traps run by the "scientists," now actually save lives.

The intelligentsia still believe in the perfectibility of man, but, ominously, it is now to come about through economic and political revolution. Marx and Engels have rewritten history to prove it. Thankfully, there are some sober exceptions to this attitude: Twain, Melville, Dostoyevsky.

You ride a train from Philadelphia to New York. It takes a couple of hours. You might even drive your automobile, powered by gasoline or steam.

People (in America anyway) are listening to Scott Joplin. In their own homes, too, on the phonograph, in a room lit by an electric bulb—until the telephone rings. Now begins the strange development, unique in the history of man, by which we conquer space and are separated from our neighbors by a vast indifference.

We think we're the first generation to feel that the world is changing fast, but the people of the nineteenth century saw it coming on. And because they hadn't jettisoned their classical and modern education (for them, "modern" meant the Renaissance and later), they had the intellectual resources to ask searching questions about it. They asked better questions about technology and its place in human life, about men and women, about the franchise, and about the dignity of work. They asked better questions about the glory and the shame of cultures from the East: India, Arabia, China, Japan. We are the inheritors of their victories. Many of these are easy enough to see: we drive in them, sleep in them, write letters with them, and talk to distant close relations on them. The troubles are harder to see, because they too are ours, and we prefer to look the other way.

The Romantics' new religion: Nature

There's an excellent scene in Samuel Johnson's *Rasselas* (1759), wherein the prince, on a quest to find the best mode of life, listens enthralled to a philosopher discoursing on living according to nature. It's the only avenue to happiness, said he, the only way to free oneself "from the delusions of hope, or importunities of desire." Throw away laws, throw away "the encumbrance of precepts, which they who utter them with so much pride and pomp do not understand." "Deviation from nature," he intones, "is deviation from happiness."

There's a lot to be asked of such a philosopher. The most obvious question is: "All right then, what should I do now? How do I live according to nature?" Rasselas asks it. The philosopher replies with breathless enthusiasm:

> To live according to nature, is to act always with due regard to
> the fitness arising from the relations and qualities of causes
> and effects; to concur with the great and unchangeable scheme
> of universal felicity; to cooperate with the general disposition
> and tendency of the present system of things. (ch. 22)

Rasselas' reaction is our own—and should be man's, too, after the heady promises of Romanticism:

> The prince soon found that this was one of the sages whom he
> should understand less as he heard him longer. He therefore
> bowed and was silent, and the philosopher, supposing him sat-
> isfied, and the rest vanquished, rose up and departed with the
> air of a man that had co-operated with the present system.

Medieval man had a home: the cosmos, circumscribed by the heaven of heavens, the realm whose only location was the mind of God. By the nineteenth century, man no longer knows that home. In a sense his world is more vast, even threatening. "The eternal silence of these infinite spaces frightens me," said Pascal (*Pensees,* 206), for now, when man looked to the sky, he saw the same world of whirling change and decay and death, writ as large as the universe, impossibly far and cold. In another sense the modern world is more cramped than the medieval world. Medieval man lived by the rhythms of salvation; his prayer on a Christmas morn made him one with Christians through all time, and with the Savior who dwelt with the Father before and beyond all time. Now nature is bigger than we had supposed, and (for a while it seemed) far more mysterious. But there is no getting *beyond* her.

The Romantic answer is to turn to Nature as a deity. Let man follow and adore her, and he will recover his place. Goethe's Faust is not a man hankering for secret methods to summon demons. Instead he longs to escape the dust-ridden study and breathe free again, to immerse his mind and heart in the beauty of earth and heaven:

> Where shall I clasp you, infinity of Nature?
> You breasts, where? You wellsprings of all life?

Darwin Lays the Groundwork for Hitler

"There is reason to believe that vaccination has preserved thousands, who from a weak constitution would formerly have succumbed to small-pox. Thus the weak members of civilized societies propagate their kind.... It is surprising how soon a want of care, or care wrongly directed, leads to the degeneration of a domestic race...."

Charles Darwin, *The Descent of Man*

Friedrich Nietzsche sounded the same tone in *Beyond Good and Evil*, lamenting how Christian charity had worked, "to preserve all that was sick and that suffered—which means, in fact and in truth, to worsen the European race." In the twentieth century, some in Europe and America would take "corrective" action on this front.

> Heaven and earth depend on you —
>
> toward you my parched soul is straining.
>
> You flow, you nourish, yet I crave in vain. (1.455–59)

On Easter morning, as the distant strains of a hymn turn him from taking deadly poison, he confesses that he cannot scale the heights of heaven, nor can he accept the simple faith of the common people, but something in the joy of the day reminds him of nature, and his childhood:

> Once the embrace of heaven's love
>
> rushed down to me in solemn Sabbath stillness;
>
> the churchbell tones were auguries
>
> and prayer was a lustful pleasure.
>
> Ineffable sweet yearning
>
> prompted me to roam through woods and fields,
>
> and through a thousand burning tears
>
> I felt my world come into being.
>
> This song proclaimed the happy games of children,
>
> unbounded rapture of a festival of Spring. (1.771–80)

It's impossible not to be drawn toward this nostalgia. It is ours still, without the joy and hope. But, historically, it is not common in literature or art, this longing for the simplicity of childhood. We see it only when people can no longer depend that the world they once knew will be anything like the world that is coming. We see it in our day, when some people do not even bother to be memorialized by a headstone.

In any case, what's born here is the *cult of the child:* not of the Christ child, or of the soul reborn as a child, but of the ordinary child as blessed because, supposedly, he comes fresh from the hand of Nature, unspoiled by the sin of his society, till the years steal upon him and take the glory away. The poetry of the early century is filled with such celebration, concealing a despair:

> The Youth, who daily farther from the east
> Must travel, still is Nature's Priest,
> And by the vision splendid
> Is on his way attended;
> At length the Man perceives it die away,
> And fade into the light of common day. (Wordsworth, *Ode:*
> *Intimations of Immortality,* 71–76)

Christians who lived on the land, for whom the rhythms of the seasons were tolled by the church bell, do not speak this way. We only begin to talk about our health when we are ill. So in the Romantic longing for Nature there is a wistfulness, a sense that she recedes beyond our reach. The poet Wordsworth, recalling a swath of daffodils on a hillside, claims that the memory of that beautiful sight will be a comfort to him, and a force for good, in the gloaming days to come:

> And then my heart with pleasure fills,
> And dances with the daffodils. ("I Wandered Lonely as a
> Cloud," 23–24)

But in other moments he suspects differently. So in the poem *Michael* the old farmer reminds his son, before he leaves to make his way in the world, of the days they enjoyed together in the peace of a simple and natural life:

> But we were playmates, Luke: among these hills,
> As well thou knowest, in us the old and young
> Have played together, nor with me didst thou
> Lack any pleasure which a boy can know. (353–56)

The boy sobs; he bids his father farewell. And goes to the city, and—it is told in five short lines—falls to dissolution and shame, never to return to his father or his youth.

A Book You're Not Supposed to Read

Rerum Novarum by Pope Leo XIII; Mahwah, NJ: Paulist Press, 1939.

Written near the end of the nineteenth century, this encyclical promotes justice among the classes, private property, and non-State-mandated charity. A critique of both capitalism and communism, it can serve as a good anecdote to the excesses of the twentieth century. So, the next time some Catholic politician tries to dodge a tough abortion question by talking about welfare in terms of "Catholic Social Teaching," hand him this encyclical to show him it's not "Catholic Socialist Teaching," at all.

The city, then, stands in this age as the locus of bustle, change, dynamism, greed, power, law, and lawlessness. And it's not the Rome that Juvenal satirized so savagely, or the Babylon that Augustine said was consumed with the lust for domination. It's *any city*, the hulking and inhuman organism that swallows human beings alive. Against the grime of London or Paris, then, "Nature" stands for a whole set of political and "theological" positions, sometimes loosely adorned with the trappings of Christianity: free love, or at least a more equal relationship between man and woman; a "genuine" life, that is, a life in touch with one's feelings; a preference for spontaneity over law, and intuition over precept; a reduction of Christ the Savior to Jesus the preacher for the poor, or Jesus the good and gentle sufferer.

Under the influence of this new "religion," primarily indulged by people who never turned a hoe or broke a horse, some great art will be produced, reminding man—who now seems to have forgotten it—that the world is full of great and beautiful things, that rocks and hills and trees can be close to the heart, and that a day in the complex peace of a lakeside can soothe the wounds of a month of the false and noisy thing we take for life. We hear the longing in Keats' finest ode:

Hedge-crickets sing; and now with treble soft,
The red-breast whistles from a garden-croft,
And gathering swallows twitter in the skies.
(*To Autumn*, 31–33)

Or, eighty years later, in the weary strains of the Irish poet Yeats, day-dreaming of giving up the mire of society and politics—to return like a prodigal son not to his Father, but to a small muddy island in a lake:

> I shall arise and go now, and go to Innisfree,
> And a small cabin build there, of clay and wattles made. ("The
> Lake Isle of Innisfree," 1–2)

So Henry David Thoreau goes out to live in the woods near Walden Pond, and has his laundry done for him by friends in town. So Walt Whitman meditates on the grass we feed with our bodies, jauntily dismissing the dread of death:

> And what do you think has become of the women and children?
> They are alive and well somewhere,
> The smallest sprout shows there really is no death. (*Song of
> Myself*, 124–126)

The elation could not last. Even in the early Romantic poets there is a tang of morbidity about it: "I have been half in love with easeful Death," writes Keats, trying to resist the melancholy by recalling the lovely song of a bird (*Ode to a Nightingale*, 52). By the time of Darwin, men will hear not the warble of a thrush but the roar of a preying lion. Nature, red in tooth and claw—that will be the heartless goddess of the age. Men will hear that a life lived according to Nature will be bloody: and some will learn that lesson well. He predates Darwin's *Origin of the Species*, but Ebenezer Scrooge speaks the gospel of that *other* Nature, not the one prettified with daffodils: "If they would rather die," he says of the poor of England, "they had better do it, and decrease the surplus population" (*A Christmas Carol*).

In America cooler heads seemed to prevail, for a time. Nathaniel Hawthorne wrote about the conflict between one's "natural" feelings and the often merciless laws of the community. Despite what sentimental teachers like to say about it now, his novel *The Scarlet Letter* emphatically *rejects* the possibility of wholesome life outside the bounds of law and common morality. That may be what the adulteress Hester thinks she wants, but the person who actually goes out and lives in the wilds among the Indians is the villain, the malignant Chillingworth. Hawthorne's friend Herman Melville wrote perhaps the last epic in the western world, an epic in mighty prose: *Moby-Dick.* In that novel, Nature is embodied in the brain and brute might of the great white whale, an offense, as Captain Ahab sees it, to order and justice and man's puny strength.

And all while this appeal to Nature rings out, man is busy, crisscrossing the continents with railroad tracks, steaming down the great rivers of America, smelting ore for the steel for the first bridge across the Mississippi, the first bridge across the Hudson, the first bridge across San Francisco Bay. Missionaries and rapacious colonialists enter the heart of Africa, whether to tame it, or to be made savage by it, is sometimes hard to tell. James Fenimore Cooper admires the Last of the Mohicans, and makes him talk like a medieval knight with an American accent.

William Morris helps to spur a cult of the medieval and chivalric, stripped of the theology that made sense of it all; it's the same William Morris who, in *News from Nowhere,* will imagine a socialist realm of lovely androgyny.[1] Owen Wister, at the end of the century, writes the story of a noble Virginian out West—just as the West emerges from nature to civilization.[2] In *A Connecticut Yankee in King Arthur's Court,* Mark Twain seems to satirize the dreamy worship of the pre-civilized, revealing those knights of old to be little more than thugs or pleasant imbeciles in armor, and their ladies, raucous, coarse, and vulgar. A Connecticut Yankee is banged on the head at the factory one day, and finds himself transported to an age of ignorance. He becomes the Boss in short order. Yet all this new Boss can bring Arthur's people is the paltry legacy of an urban life: soap, advertisements, and baseball. Those, and mass electrocution.

Nature can be honored rightly, if she is kept in her place. But that is hard to do, unless one acknowledges a God above Nature.

Worshipping man

But this worship of Nature is, for a while, a potent drug, and leads to the Romantic worship of man. It's easy enough to go from believing that, given the right social circumstances, man can be made perfect to believing that he already possesses that perfection, and all we need to do is to liberate it. In the Renaissance, Christopher Marlowe's *Doctor Faustus* dramatized the fall of a man who sold his soul to the devil so that he could become a demigod for twenty-four years. He spends most of those years dabbling in petty tricks—cheating a horse salesman, or fetching grapes out of season for a pregnant duchess. Then he sweats and frets through his last hour on earth, and the final curtain reveals his dismembered limbs and blood splashed over the walls of his study. In the Romantic age—and this heady spirit is still with us—Goethe recasts Faust as a soul struggling for the fullness of human knowledge and love.

For the poet Percy Shelley, Prometheus the rebel, not Zeus, is the bearer of truth: meaning that the divine spirit of man, inspired by universal Love, and not the God of Abraham, Isaac, and Jacob, now gives the law. Religion must break the bonds of tradition and hierarchy. Shelley's Prometheus sees a vision of Christ upon the Cross, and prays—mercifully!—that he will die:

> Fix, fix those tortured orbs in peace and death
> So thy sick throes shake not that crucifix,
> So those pale fingers play not with thy gore.
> O horrible! Thy name I will not speak,
> It hath become a curse. (*Prometheus Unbound,* 1.600–604)

Why should he not die quickly, seeing that he is no savior? Man must save himself. Or why does he need saving at all? Be true to yourself, and you cannot sin:

> Nothing, not God, is greater to one than one's self is. (Whitman, *Leaves of Grass,* 1271)

I don't mean to subject the Romantics to scorn beyond what they deserve. There is a great nobility and mystery in man, and in man as the pinnacle and purpose of the natural world. Wordsworth was not wrong to turn his attention inward and ask how nature in his rural boyhood formed the finest thing he had any direct experience of, namely his mind. For he saw mountains and rivers, "purifying thus / The elements of feeling and of thought" (*The Prelude,* 1.410–11). The problem is when we try to substitute Man for God.

It's a problem that the politically correct have not caught up with, as they continue, long after anybody has really believed in it, to press for the perfect society, the perfectly happy man, males and females perfectly the same, children perfectly wise, and old people perfectly childlike and pliable. It's enough to make one laugh as he picks his way through the ruins. People cheat, steal, brawl, and idle their hours away. Well, some people have always done things like that. Christians called it our propensity to sin. But *that* explanation won't do, if you have rejected the whole idea of sin. Then it must be that some vague thing called "society" has made us so, or our upbringing. We're *socially constructed,* that's what the politically correct social scientists tell us, generally exempting themselves from the diagnosis. All we need, then, is to rig up the right technology of government and education to fix the mistake. And who will run these vast programs? We know who. People who cheat, steal, brawl, and idle their hours away.

It's far more refreshing to encounter the worship of man in its pristine Romantic state, when it had the swagger of a soldier about it. Lord Byron set the tone for *that* Romantic ideal—the lonely breaker of all rules, seducer of women (and sometimes men), railing against stale, "respectable" religion and its God so comfortable for old ladies in charitable societies. That's a caricature of Byron, admittedly—a caricature he cultivated. The real Byron longed for some object on which to bestow his passion and his genius, and *not* the phony pieties of people who thought they could improve mankind with just the right program. So when the poets Samuel Taylor Coleridge and Robert Southey (who were intelligent enough to have known better) conceived a plan to settle in Pennsylvania and establish a society based upon the idea of human perfectibility, Byron had a hearty laugh at their expense:

> All are not moralists, like Southey, when
> He prated to the world of "Pantisocracy;"
> Or Wordsworth unexcised, unhired, who then
> Season'd his pedlar poems with democracy;
> Or Coleridge, long before his flighty pen
> Let to the Morning Post its aristocracy... (*Don Juan*, 3.93.1–6)

But give the man a chance to fight for real freedom, and the world finds Byron not writing a poem about it, or hawking himself on the political market, but in the mountains of Greece, battling the Turks. He had once

Mill the Totalitarian

I looked forward...to a future [of] convictions as to what is right and wrong, deeply engraven on the feelings by early education and general unanimity of sentiment, and so firmly grounded in reason and in the true exigencies of life, that they shall not, like all former and present creeds...require to be periodically thrown off and replaced by others.

John Stuart Mill, *Autobiography* (ch. 5)

In other words, Mill the liberal is also Mill the secret totalitarian, replacing religious faith with his own philosophy, etched into the minds of the young—who would all have to be subject to the State's training, to produce the State's and Mill's visions of the greatest good for the greatest number. Nor will the State ever succeed in this if the family remains a strong countercheck. Therefore the family must be recast; and, as always, the father's authority is the first to go.

written about what a shame it was that Greece should suffer tyranny, remembering her old victory over the Persians:

> The mountains look on Marathon—
> And Marathon looks on the sea;
> And musing there an hour alone,
> I dream'd that Greece might still be free;
> For standing on the Persians' grave,
> I could not deem myself a slave. (*Don Juan*, 2.701–706)

To Greece then he did go, and laid down his life preparing for war. To this day the Greeks honor Lord Byron as one of *their* great patriots.[3]

Byron knew, in his heart, that man was not worthy of such airy exaltation as the Romantics were prone to offer him. But events would make it clear how frail the idol was. Yes, man could steer a steamboat down the Hudson, or make ten nails in a factory in the same time that he used to make one. These brought good things under his control; people could eat better, live in warmer houses, and dress more cleanly. Yet the Industrial Revolution which lifted millions of people into what would have counted, a few generations before, as wealth and ease, also brought an inevitable dislocation. People crowded the cities for work. Slums grew everywhere. Children were herded into factories, to work at foul or dangerous jobs twelve hours a day. Man seemed at the mercy of the machine. War did not magically disappear once the telegraph had been invented. Man used it to send military instructions more readily.

The irony is that today, you will find the "progressives" railing against the Industrial Revolution, while force-feeding us all the same meal of "progress" and "revolution" that left us with colitis in the nineteenth century. This is the self-contradiction inherent in liberalism or progressivism: the brave new world you work for today becomes the accursed backwards world you will try to subvert tomorrow.

Meanwhile, in a self-abasement that continues apace, social evolutionists such as Herbert Spencer, the popularizer of Darwin, while hailing the "progress" of man from superstition to agnostic enlightenment, at the same time demoted him to the status of a greater ape.[4] A kind of genetic fallacy has bedeviled the West ever since. The new "science" of sociology, led by the aggressively atheistic Emile Durkheim, purported to see in man's moral codes the fossils of ancient and forgotten ways of life. That approach continues today. The whole question of whether stealing or adultery *is* evil is evaded. It is as if a sophomoric young man should say to the young lady he wishes to seduce, "You first came to think it was wrong because your parents taught you so when you were little, and *therefore* we may do as we please." A similar reduction of moral philosophy to psychosocial paleontology is the rule in other disciplines, too.

Men wove tales of the gods to explain what the thunder was saying—and *therefore* there is no Being whose essence it is to exist. Men invented the taboo against incest to prevent strong sons from uniting to overthrow the dictatorial father, and *therefore*—well, Freud was a moralist who understood that civilization must collapse without sexual prohibitions, but there would be others around to draw the logical conclusions.[5] Even in the nineteenth century, communities of "free love" sprouted up in Europe and America, wherein godlike and enlightened men and women would concede their natural freedoms to a socialist system, and exercise their natural rights to rut like beasts.[6] Man is a god; man is a beast. Man was everything and anything, but man.

I'd like to enumerate four responses to the disillusionment that followed.

What the Industrial Revolution wrought

One came from the Left, and is still with us. Man the beast must be dealt with *en masse,* by smart people who can maneuver him. So Marx became the father of modern propaganda: he couldn't run a business, and had no love for people who struggled to save a little capital to run one, but he did think he could touch the passions of people resentful that others enjoyed more than they did. "Workers of the world, unite!" he cried. "You have nothing to lose but your chains."[7] Not true. They had plenty to lose. They would lose their love for their native land. They would lose their childhood faith. They would lose the sense that they were men, not atoms in a great mass. They would lose the dignity of having been created by God to fill a particular place, though it might be a humble place. And they would have chains fixed to their every limb, as the following century would show. For though nobody outside of the academy preaches doctrinaire Marxism anymore, the fundamental assumptions of Marxism are still in place among the Left in the West. With one exception: Marx was a prude, and the Marxism of the Soviet Union did not smile upon sexual debauchery. The Marxism of the modern West has learned better. Tolerate—indeed, encourage—the "individualism" of lewdness, then collect the payoff in power, when people prove incapable of governing themselves.

In a sense it's unfortunate that Marx is so reviled. It's the Adolf Hitler Effect: the harm done by the man or his cause is so obvious and so overwhelming, we fail to notice the more widespread mischief done by people, sometimes well intended, sometimes not, who accept some of the same principles and put them in practice for supposedly benevolent ends. That too will be a legacy of this turn to the State, if not as object of worship, at least as a nearby Great Father, to heal our wounds and cleanse us of sin. "Father, we cannot do good," say the believers of old, "so grant us your grace." "We *can* do good," say the half-believers of the modern age, "but, Mr. President, we can't manage on our own." Such liberalism becomes an atheism without the stark courage of atheists, appealing to the needy and the meddlesome. The women's suffrage movement, whatever we may think of its justice, thus went hand in hand with the movement for Prohibition—empowering the State, and weakening the American attachment to liberty and individual responsibility.

A second response came from those admirable and sad men who lost their faith, but who did not rejoice over the loss. They felt keenly, as Marx did not, the vanity of a life wherein the imagination could not look to the heavens. Some, like Freud, tried to face up to the loss, resigning themselves to a civilization that simply was not going to fulfill the heart of man.[8] These might well have agreed with Augustine, who famously prayed to God, "Our hearts are restless, till they rest in thee" (*Confessions* 1.1), but, unlike Augustine, they could not believe in the existence of the One in whom alone man's heart could rest. More tried to substitute for faith something else. I think of the new industry of philanthropy, or the staid English respectability of those Victorians who did not exactly believe, and did not exactly disbelieve, but knew how important it was to pretend. Best among them, perhaps, was a man who knew he did not believe, and knew he was the worse for it: the poet and essayist Matthew Arnold. The Enlightenment insistence on logical deduction had killed his faith not only in God, but in all liberal political substitutes. Here he stands at an old Swiss monastery, acknowledging both losses, and sympathizing with the monks still living and praying there:

The Factories' Failure

And the great cry that rises from all our manufacturing cities, louder than their furnace blast, is all in very deed for this,—that we manufacture everything there except men; we blanch cotton, and strengthen steel, and refine sugar, and shape pottery; but to brighten, to strengthen, to refine, or to form a single living spirit, never enters into our estimate of advantages.

John Ruskin, *The Stones of Venice* (6.16)

Ruskin understood what Marx the economist did not: the measure of a nation is not its gross national product, nor the equitable distribution of material goods; the measure of a nation is the men it produces, and the goodness and beauty of the lives they lead. It is a deeply conservative insight.

> Wandering between two worlds, one dead,
>
> The other powerless to be born,
>
> With nowhere yet to rest my head,
>
> Like these, on earth I wait forlorn.
>
> Their faith, my tears, the world deride —
>
> I come to shed them at their side. (*Stanzas from the Grande Chartreuse,* 85–90)

Is there such thing as bad art?

Arnold would have loathed what has become of criticism in our day. Niggling little professors, carving out for themselves little cubicles of specialization, now teach "late nineteenth century American women's literature," or something of the sort, while possessing but a small fraction of Arnold's literary, historical, and philosophical learning, not to mention his exact taste. That would be bad enough by itself, except that we have covered over our ignorance with incomprehensible jargon. Why not, considering the theories that prevail in academe (with deconstruction the most notorious of a flea-infested lot) deny that there is objective truth to communicate, let alone objective standards of beauty to guide us in communicating it? All is political, in the Hobbesian sense of a struggle for power. Why, one "scientific" linguistic text on my shelf even denies that men naturally have deeper voices than women do. That too has been part of a dastardly patriarchal plot. The very assumption that a text can mean anything at all is, according to the anarchist of language Jacques Derrida, "theological" or "logocentric." When we reject it we free ourselves for "a world of signs which has no truth, no origin, no nostalgic guilt," no transcendent meaning, and no human purpose other than the joy of diddling about with signs that point nowhere (*L'écriture et la différence*).

But the sad wisdom of Matthew Arnold is richer than this shallow refusal to acknowledge wisdom at all. If Arnold lost his faith in God, he at least turned to a noble substitute, high culture. We will be saved, he believes, by the purifying fire of art, granting us at least the serenity of the ancient Greeks, who saw and loved the beautiful, and loved it all the more because they knew how painfully transient was the beauty of a youth or the glory of a city. Therefore they memorialized their love in song and stone, and therefore too we ought to treasure what Arnold called the touchstones of great art. The purpose of criticism, he says—as opposed to every motive now current in our academy—is "to try to know the best that is known and thought in the world, irrespectively of practice, politics, and everything of the kind; and to value knowledge and thought as they approach this best, without the intrusion of any other considerations whatever" (*The Function of Criticism at the Present Time*). The good we will gain from that? Man "may begin to remember that he has a mind."

Note that well. We are not to judge a third-rate abolitionist tract like *Uncle Tom's Cabin* as great art or deep political wisdom merely because we agree with its politics. We have a mind. We will not dignify, either, the bigotry of a Margaret Atwood, whose novel *The Handmaid's Tale* slanders Christian evangelicals with whom she clearly has never broken bread, merely because she can string a sentence or two together. We have a mind. The Left, I admit, has no monopoly on bad art. But it has a near-monopoly on the principle that there is no such thing as bad art, so long as the politics are correct. A crucifix in a pail of urine? That's deep, brother.

Arnold's ideals were honest and powerful enough to have survived, coughing and trembling, to our present day, wherein we still find, here and there, someone who believes in the old-fashioned ideals of a "liberal" education, allowing the mind to climb above the skirmishes of contemporary and provincial fads, cultural, political, and economic. But the Nazis too fancied themselves patrons of the arts, nor has good taste, as fine a thing as it is, ever restrained the malice of the heart, if occasionally it does restrain the violence of the hand. No one, I think, knew that better than Arnold himself:

> We would have inward peace,
> Yet will not look within;
> We would have misery cease,
> Yet will not cease from sin. (*Empedocles on Etna,* 232–235)

Which explains why he sees, in his funeral tribute to his kindly, liberal Christian father, the Rugby schoolmaster Thomas Arnold, a willingness and capacity to save others that he himself does not possess:

> But thou would'st not *alone*
> Be saved, my father! *alone*
> Conquer and come to thy goal,
> Leaving the rest in the wild.
> We were weary, and we
> Fearful, and we in our march
> Fain to drop down and die.
> Still thou turnedst, and still
> Beckonedst the trembler, and still
> Gavest the weary thy hand. (*Rugby Chapel,* 124–33)

But even in Arnold's day this attachment to high culture—to poetic touchstones, as Arnold called them, whence we could derive, as from the bee, sweetness and light[9]—was fading, and the liberal cult of the Bohemian artist helped it along. If you don't revere your fathers, you will not revere Virgil and Cicero. The history of schooling from his day to ours is a story of long retreat from the classics, from what is difficult and excellent, to the coarse and stupid and self-gratifying; from a lad in his garret poring over Gibbon, to romper-room textbooks that use pictures and slogans and political correctness and group projects and other blaring noise, like the magazines in a checkout line at the grocery, to elicit the planned response. A glance through the stacks of any local library will be prove it. I'll have more to say about popular culture in the next chapter, but to call our television "mediocre" is to misuse that fine word. A landfill is not mediocre.

Nietzsche: The honest atheist

A third response came from those who saw through the failure not only of the cultural ideal of Arnold, but also of the political ideals of liberal quasi-Christian reformers like Gladstone. Nietzsche and Kierkegaard come to mind. These men laugh to scorn the effeminate and bland. For those who would turn the Christian faith into a comfortable social pose, or into a set of self-pleasing activities whereby the privileged "serve" the poor and continue to make as much money as they like, Kierkegaard takes us back to the dreadful mystery of Mount Moriah, where Abraham was commanded by God to sacrifice his son Isaac, and there he went in the darkness of faith. Better that there should be no "Christians" at all, that the true faith might live again, says Kierkegaard![10]

Then there is Nietzsche, who hates what he wrongly took to be the Christian cultivation of weakness, sapping what is supposed to be the strong, free, playful, cruel self-affirmation of the masters of mankind.

Reason vs. Pride

Quarry the granite rock with razors, or moor the vessel with a thread of silk; then you may hope with such keen and delicate instruments as human knowledge and human reason to contend against those giants, the passion and the pride of man.

John Henry Newman, *The Idea of a University* (discourse 5, part 9)

Our politically correct educators, having abandoned faith, or consigned it to dusty private corners, now try to save the world, preaching "multicultural awareness" or "lifelong learning" or other such twaddle. Lash the ogre with a noodle.

For every liberal who supposes himself brave for having smiled at the quaintness of old moral precepts, Nietzsche stands ready with a challenge: to go "beyond good and evil," to leave far behind even the pretense of obeying a moral order. Nietzsche, antichristian and loather of liberalism, rises to the pitch of eloquence when describing the milk-and-water creature that his world pronounces as "good":

> The diminution and leveling of European man constitutes *our* greatest danger, for the sight of him makes us weary.—We can see nothing today that wants to grow greater, we suspect that things will continue to go down, down, to become thinner, more good-natured, more prudent, more comfortable, more mediocre, more indifferent, more Chinese, more Christian— there is no doubt that man is getting "better" all the time. (*On the Genealogy of Morals*)

But the liberal wants to have sin, without the dash of cruelty; to be a careerist, consumed with ambition, yet all for "mankind"; to enjoy the power to smother, but for the good of the soul gasping for breath. Nietzsche was honest enough to face the implications of his atheism. He saw that "tolerance" was but a ruse, to salve the timid consciences of the stale, conventional, self-satisfied liberal. A certain failed artist in Austria would see through the ruse, too, and six million Jews would die for it. The liberal prides himself on setting us all free from the God of our forefathers. He never bothers to notice the beast looking over his shoulder, waiting for him to finish clearing the area. Nietzsche at least bothered to notice.

Finally, a fourth response can be heard, disunited, but running counter to the religion of material progress, of governmental centralization, of social control, and of universal mediocrity. It stresses the dignity of a man's conscience, as with John Henry Newman,[11] or an aristocratic scorn for government in the service of gratification, as with Henry Adams.[12] It is suspicious, as was Chesterton, of both the insatiable moneymaker and the insatiable moneytaker.[13] It calls for piety, for rootedness in place and time, as did John Ruskin, who when he talked about craftsmanship was better than his sometimes socialist politics.[14] It remembers the beauty and goodness of man and woman, not indistinguishable, and not put out to the service of the state; that appreciation we find in the poetry of Coventry Patmore.[15] There are dozens to choose from, but I'll end this chapter by touching upon insights from three men of letters and one great Pope: Robert Browning, Charles Dickens, Fyodor Dostoyevsky, and Leo XIII.

Conservative champions of human dignity

At first blush it seems preposterous to consider these men together, as they appear to share so little. And a Pope, of all people? Dostoyevsky, that titanic and tortured mystic, hated the Roman Church for what he saw as its betraying true religion to political power. Murder and rape cannot move his gentle "idiot," Prince Myshkin, to passionate indignation, but the Roman Church can.[16] Dickens, too, had nothing kind to say for Rome, associating it with unnatural repression of the human spirit.[17] When Catholics complained about their treatment in his novels, he was abashed, and wrote one of his poorest works in response, *Barnaby Rudge.* In it he stands up for the civil rights of Catholics, but also continues to criticize what he saw as their nature-denying code of regulations. Browning was downright friendly to the Church, but his less perceptive readers adopted him as the apostle of Bright Vistas Ahead and Good Liberal Progress, which he was not. And as for Pope Leo, if anyone other than Catholics paid attention to his encyclicals, I cannot find a trace of it.

Yet I do place them together, because we find in each what we cannot find all at once in the Romantics or in any of the other reactions to Romanticism. These things, too, we should do well to heed. They might help us clear our systems of the politically correct dysentery. Today, they are dismissed as old-fashioned, or excoriated as hateful. Not coincidentally, they

The Last Refuge of Scoundrels?

Breathes there the man,
with soul so dead,
Who never to himself hath said,
This is my own, my native land?
Whose heart hath ne'er within him burned,
As home his footsteps he hath turned
From wandering on a foreign strand?

Sir Walter Scott, *The Lay of the Last Minstrel* (6.1–6)

Then we sure have a lot of dead souls now. Our students are *taught* to dismiss their native land, as if cynicism were some hard-won virtue. Scott loved his native Scotland, not because he believed she should be independent of England—but simply because she was Scotland.

In this, Scott rejected the Enlightenment cosmopolitan ideal laid out so simply by Thomas Paine: "My country is the world, and my religion is to do good."

are indispensible to preserving the riches we have inherited from our intellectual and spiritual ancestors. They are as follows.

An honest and unsparing look at evil.

If you want to be called a simpleton or a vicious scold, the quickest way is to acknowledge that *evil* really exists. In today's relativism, the only thing that is *wrong* is to call something else *wrong*.

But for these four men, there is no Romantic air-brushing of the wicked, a moral slouching that still infects our art. Dickens' villains destroy themselves by their cruelty. That cruelty may be hard-hearted and power-hungry, as in Ralph Nickleby, who hangs himself in despair at the end of *Nicholas Nickleby*, or silent and malevolent, as in the lawyer Mr. Tulkinghorn, caught in his own snares (*Bleak House*), or luridly affable on the surface, as in Fagin the Viper (*Oliver Twist*).

Dostoyevsky, who considered Dickens the greatest writer of his century, learned from him that anatomy of evil. Unforgettable are his mawkish, debauched Fyodor Pavlovich, who rapes a poor idiot girl and sires upon her the bastard son who would grow up to be his murderer (*The Brothers Karamazov*); or the icy intellectual anarchist Peter Verkhovensky, a prescient model for all those in the twentieth century who would kill millions in the name of secular progress (*The Devils*). So adept was

Browning at portraying the evil mind, that many critics have been taken in by it, concluding that the poet refused to pass judgment—not on a mad strangler of a woman ("Porphyria's Lover"), nor on an aristocrat who snuffs the life out of every beautiful thing he owns or marries ("My Last Duchess"), nor on a tawdry killer who had set his own wife out to a whoredom she would not endure (*The Ring and the Book*). As for Pope Leo, he never bothers to prettify with verbal talcum powder socialists and nihilists and other destroyers of the human spirit, of peaceful and independent family life, and of the highest aspirations of the heart.

A suspicion of all "systems" designed by power-seeking intellectuals.

Dickens' Mr. Gradgrind, calmly and respectably, rubs out the imaginations of the young children in his charge. "Teach these children facts, nothing but facts!" (*Hard Times*). We have inherited the system-making itch, with this difference: our students, fed the meringue of self-esteem, do not even know facts. Dostoyevsky ridicules "liberals" who believe that the right programs will make the world a paradise, and who then somehow forget to free their own serfs. Browning turns the progress-monger of his day into a shallow journalist, embarrassed when the Catholic bishop he is interviewing insists upon the small yet important truths that ordinary men can find. The journalist would place such commoners under control, but, says the wise bishop,

> Ignorance and weakness have rights too.
> There needs no crucial effort to find truth
> If here or there or anywhere about:
> We ought to turn each side, try hard and see,
> And if we can't, be glad we've earned at least
> The right, by one laborious proof the more,
> To graze in peace earth's pleasant pasturage.

> Men are not angels, neither are they brutes:
>
> Something we may see, all we cannot see. (*Bishop Blougram's Apology*, 857–65)

Here the bishop genially elucidates the old and forgotten virtue of modesty, which instructs us, even if we don't believe in the sanctity of family or common human life, to leave alone what we will probably ruin by our meddling. Applied to social questions, it is the principle of *subsidiarity,* defended by Pope Leo in one encyclical after another. It is based on a humble admission that common people may know quite a few things that are hard to articulate, and that intellectual elites and politicians know much less than they think they know, regardless of how well they can articulate it.

But that's offensive to our leaders today. *They've* graduated from college, you see. It's downright superstitious to posit a truth that a logic-chopper or a statistic-cooker has missed. And to impose limits on the power of government is to squelch progress. Where we are progressing to, the chief lemmings never say.

A confidence in the goodness of embodied being, trusting no abstract system, but this human face, this hand, this heart.

"It is better to cherish virtue and humanity," says Burke, "by leaving much to free will, even with some loss to the object, than to attempt to make men mere machines and instruments of a political benevolence. The world on the whole will gain by a liberty, without which virtue cannot exist" (*Reflections on the Revolution in France*). My four exemplars agreed: goodness and beauty spring from a care for the small and the local, and not from a fascination with grand political and social abstractions.

Dickens is savage in his satire against the liberal penchant for "helping" a faraway and disincarnate Mankind. In *Bleak House,* the tireless solicitor of charitable contributions, Mrs. Jellyby, pesters her fellow citizens to pledge money to assist the natives of Borioboola-Gha, a place as wild as its name, somewhere in the heart of Africa. What are the citizens paying for, you may ask? Why, "the general cultivation of the coffee berry—*and* the natives—and the happy settlement, on the banks of the African rivers, of our superabundant home population." It's often easier to see evil in its inception, when it slinks naked and snarling from the mind of man, than afterwards, when we've grown used to it and dressed it up in finery. In the mind of Mrs. Jellyby, the natives, whom she pretends to wish to raise to her exalted position, are objects of mass management, to be "cultivated," like coffee beans. We also see that her charity is tangled up with imperial motives. Let's make Borioboola-Gha gratefully tributary to England and her English émigrés, who will be doing all the real cultivating, both of coffee beans and of Borioboolans.

And more: the scheme will *remove a surplus.* Not only does Mrs. Jellyby want the Borioboolans to stay in Africa; she'd be happy to send extra Englishmen there, too. Dickens calls it "telescopic philanthropy." That pattern serves well for our intra-imperialists in the social service and poverty industry. Send surplus college graduates, many of them with the temperament of Mrs. Jellyby, into the Borioboolan ghettos, or rather into nice apartments not too near the ghettos, to tell the people there what social coffee beans they need and how to plant them.

What's lacking is a direct, incarnate confrontation of one human being with another. People are patronized, reduced to "cases," handled according to rule. It doesn't then matter if the procedures are a pointless lesson in Biblical brimstone, favored by some social reformers before our time, or an equally pointless lesson in how to fill out a welfare form and qualify for food stamps. The results are at best temporary, and the victims of the assistance are rendered moral children or idiots. Dickens shows us instead what is to be done, not by giving us an alternate Program, but by embodying charity in the person of his most politically incorrect heroine,

Esther Summerson. She reveals, by her diligence and patience and winsome cheer, that in its truest sense an *economy* really is the *law of the household.* Governments and philanthropists fail where Esther succeeds, because she dispenses with the telescope. She sees wickedness and despair and wretchedness for what they are.

When Esther enters a hovel of brickmakers, whose men have degraded themselves beneath the beast, she gives us no nostrums about the inherent goodness of man, nor does she preach to people who cannot yet hear the preaching. "Have I read the little book wot you left?" snorts one of them at the prim preachstress, Mrs. Pardiggle, whom Esther has been cajoled into accompanying on her "rounds." "No, I an't read the little book wot you left. There an't nobody here as knows how to read it; and if there wos, it wouldn't be suitable to me. It's a book fit for a babby, and I'm not a babby." That does not stop Mrs. Pardiggle from plying her shrewish trade, degrading the angry and violent men. But when Esther and her cousin Ada meet a woman with a little child at the moment of its death, we see what human beings can do—neither gods nor beasts, nor abstractions in a mass, nor economic counters, but human beings:

> Such compassion, such gentleness, as that with which [Ada] bent down weeping, and put her hand upon the mother's, might have softened any mother's heart that ever beat. The woman at first gazed at her in astonishment, and then burst into tears.
>
> Presently I took the light burden from her lap; did what I could to make the baby's rest the prettier and gentler; laid it on a shelf, an covered it with my own handkerchief. We tried to comfort the mother, and we whispered to her what Our Saviour said of children. She answered nothing, but sat weeping— weeping very much.

Yes, the action is small. It won't feed millions, or bring civilization to Borioboola-Gha. It does more: it revives a suffering human soul. So too

Ebenezer Scrooge, born again as a child on Christmas Day, does not shovel his amassed wealth into vast Programs, but gives a check to two men to buy "common necessaries" for the poor, and then sends a turkey to the home of his clerk, Bob Cratchit. He will need no telescope for his love. Simply seeing before him the crippled Tiny Tim will do.

Dostoyevsky portrays a similar dynamic in *The Brothers Karamazov.* The self-serving, ambitious, shallow young monk Rakitin wants to rouse a revolution against the rich not because he loves the poor, but because he envies the rich their power.[18] Replace, for our age, "Rakitin" with the name of any prominent feminist, "rich" with "men," and "poor" with women, and change the pronouns and adjectives accordingly. The liberal Miusov despises the monks in the monastery adjacent to his land and uses all the legal means he can to harass them, utterly unaware of how much material assistance and spiritual consolation they provide for the poor serfs whose cause he pretends to uphold.[19] Replace "Miusov" with the name of a contemporary city councilor or mayor, and "monastery" with "church" or "Boy Scouts."

Two Roads Diverged, and ...

The road of excess leads to the palace of wisdom.

William Blake, *The Marriage of Heaven and Hell*

There will be a pretty clear path from William Blake and the Romantics to those who preached free love in the 1960s (Herbert Marcuse, for instance, in *Eros and Culture*). If excess and gratified desire make for wisdom, the generation of Woodstock must be the wisest the world has ever seen. If they haven't produced much great art, or penetrating philosophy, or far-seeing statesmanship, well, that's no evidence against their wisdom. It's just that they have been too busy—gratifying themselves.

Still it's refreshing to hear Blake cry out *against* the safe and acceptable. We preach hedonism, but without the thrill of the bold and dangerous.

Ivan Karamazov, a young man of noble ideals and powerful intellect, sees through the phony revolutionary and the phony liberal. But he too is plagued by the telescope. He finds it easy, he says, to love humanity. It's the neighbor he can't stand—the neighbor whom Christ commanded his disciples to love, and not a disincarnate and conveniently abstract Mankind. So Ivan, picking at the sores of his soul, collects newspaper clippings describing atrocities committed against innocent children, and declares that, though he can bring himself to believe in God, he cannot believe in the world that God has made, a world in which one little girl, beaten and locked in a privy by her mother and father, would weep out her prayers to Jesus.[20] Ivan's is a powerful testimony; yet, for all that, we never see him in the company of children, though there are plenty of them nearby, suffering. That work of mercy is left to his brother, the child-like monk Alyosha, too simple to be a political climber, too honest to pretend to love where he hates, and too loving to insulate himself from the sight and smell of a drunken soldier, his angry, unpleasant, and heartbroken family, and his dying son.[21]

It is precisely Dostoyevsky's point, as against the Romantics, the liberals, and the radical revolutionaries, that one man cannot really help another unless the encounter is embodied, nearby, and grounded in a faith that breathes life into his charity and unites him, soul to soul, with his fellow creature. If Jesus is correct, then agnostic or merely material liberalism is not only wrong, it is deadeningly wrong. That is, it may be that we can love our neighbors as ourselves only by seeing both our neighbors and ourselves as loved by God, whom we adore and to whom we pray in humility. If we do not, then the neighbor at best becomes an annoyance to be dealt with humanely, and preferably not in a way that will require a mop for our floors. To put it another way: bureaucratic charity, secular and utterly impersonal, is not charity at all, but a mercenary exchange, without the honesty of street corners and lipstick.

Browning in his turn gives the lie to the adulators of classicism, from the genial Arnold to the fiery Nietzsche. He was a determinedly bumptious poet, eschewing the clean and polished line for masculine vigor; a regular right cross of a metricist. Along with that ruggedness comes a healthy respect for artistic order and the pure philosophical reason that accompanies it, and an even healthier recognition that neither can provide the fullness of knowledge or the joy we long for in life. So, for instance, in his poem "Cleon," the speaker, a Greek philosopher of the first century writing a letter in response to his philosophical king, expresses a hunger for love and truth that his own philosophy cannot satisfy:

> Indeed, to know is something, and to prove
> How all this beauty might be enjoyed, is more:
> But knowing naught, to enjoy is something too.
> Yon rower, with the moulded muscles there,
> Lowering the sail, is nearer it than I. (291–95)

The older he grows, the more he learns, and the more painfully he feels the contrast between the hunger and the few palsied days that remain to him. Cleon is, in essence, the heroic agnostic Victorian, yet the answer to his dilemma proves too lowly, too scandalously small and bodily, for him to grasp. He ends his letter to the king with an afterthought, a dismissal of one "Paulus," a "mere barbarian Jew":

> Thou wrongest our philosophy, O king,
> In stooping to inquire of such an one,
> As if his answer could impose at all!
> He writeth, doth he? well, and he may write.
> Oh, the Jew findeth scholars! certain slaves
> Who touched on this same isle, preached him and Christ;
> And (as I gathered from a bystander)
> Their doctrine could be held by no sane man. (346–53)

Browning, like Dickens and Dostoyevsky, sees what the politics of the twentieth century will deny, even as it denies also the high and somber classicism of Matthew Arnold: that a soul in love, learned or not, might be granted to see truths that the great bustlers in the world miss cleanly. For now we have populism and demagoguery, but no thriving popular culture; we have petty rules passed down from on high to lend proper hygiene to our financial and familial affairs, but neither the cleanliness of classical form nor the fire-etched plainness of the Ten Commandments. What is lost is the simply human, and, as Christians recognized, once we lose that, we lose our clearest signs of God. Says Browning's greatest heroine as she lies dying:

> Through such souls alone
> God stooping shows sufficient of His light
> For us i' the dark to rise by. And I rise. (*The Ring and the Book,*
> "Pompilia," 1826–28)

At stake in all these issues is man's ability to apprehend, even in his humble duties of work and family, what Dante had named as the power that holds all the universe in being, "the Love that moves the sun and the other stars."[22] We are playing for keeps here. The poet Shelley sang of love, but could never condescend to confine himself to a single woman. He was too idealistic for that. By the end of the century, Bertrand Russell and his fellows at university will be preaching the Higher Sodomy[23]—and why not, if our thoughts and desires are merely animal phenomena? And, if we strip away the residue of the old worldview inherited from Christendom and from classical Greece and Rome, what else did nineteenth century man have to boast of, that was not finally merely a comfort to his animal nature? Browning saw the alternatives clearly. We're either brutes in a cold, dead, meaningless universe, in which case any talk of goodness or progress or enlightenment is arrant sentimentality, or we are men made by and for Love. So he writes, in the voice of a Persian physician who has met someone with a strange medical history, a fellow named Lazarus:

> The very God! Think, Abib; does thou think?
> So, the All-Great, were the All-Loving too—
> So, through the thunder comes a human voice
> Saying, "O heart I made, a heart beats here!
> Face, my hands fashioned, see it in myself!—
> Thou hast no power nor mayst conceive of mine,
> But love I gave thee, with myself to love,
> And thou must love me who have died for thee!"
> The madman saith He said so: it is strange. ("An Epistle of
> Karshish," 304–12)

A revelation of a love that transcends the political protects man from tyranny, and it does this in a most paradoxical way. The victors in the ideological struggles of the last hundred years claim that law simply is what we make it—and whatever we want is all right, so long as we observe some ill-defined and ever-shifting "rights." That makes us at once masters and slaves to law. It also unmoors us from place and time, from any community with a beloved tradition, and, as we see in our day in the call for homosexual "marriage," from the plain realities of our own bodies.

The older view, audible in the following passage from Leo XIII, is that we cannot be slaves of the State, precisely because we are *not* gods and do not determine for ourselves

Marxism in America

Among the ten measures Marx and Engels insisted upon in *The Communist Manifesto*:

3. Abolition of all right of inheritance....
6. Centralization of the means of communication and transport in the hands of the State....
10. Free education for all children in public schools.

Three out of ten isn't bad, but even *they* didn't call for *compulsory* government education.

what good and evil mean. The State, our creation, cannot be the ultimate giver of laws, because we ourselves are not the creators of our nature:

> Of the laws enacted by men, some are concerned with what is good or bad by its very nature; and they command men to follow after what is right and to shun what is wrong, adding at the same time a suitable sanction. But such laws by no means derive their origin from civil society; because just as civil society did not create human nature, so neither can it be said to be the author of the good which is human nature, or of the evil which is contrary to it. Laws come before men live together in society, and have their origin in the natural, and consequently in the eternal, law. (*Libertas Praestantissimum,* June 20, 1888)

Notice that the Pope contradicts the notions of Hobbes, and the ambitious claims of socialists. We do not live as lawless savages and then finally unite in a contract to surrender our claims to all goods; nor do we fashion our own order, bowing to some idea of universal social progress. Wherever man is, there the laws already are, and they are the foundation of the civil order, not the other way around.

It is strange, but it's just this placement of man among eternal laws that grants him his highest dignity as *this* man or woman, in *this community,* among *these neighbors.* Marx despised the workmen of flesh and blood whom he had to mold into a revolutionary machine. His system subjected the individual to the inexorable march of economic evolution. The Pope does not consider any inexorable march of anything anywhere, except that of time, to eternity. That frees him to call things by their proper names. Theft is theft:

> The Socialists wrongly assume the right of property to be of mere human invention, repugnant to the natural equality

between men, and, preaching up the community of goods, declare that no one should endure poverty meekly, and that all may with impunity seize upon the possessions and usurp the rights of the wealthy. (*Quod apostolici muneris,* December 28, 1878)

What's wrong with taking money from people who have more than enough? Nothing, if they give it voluntarily, or if it's their reasonable contribution to the upkeep of a modest State. Much, if it is intended to efface the good of the poor man's endurance and the diligent man's labor and the rich man's generosity. For it is not the duty of some faceless generic "rich" to pretend to assist the faceless and generic "poor" by funneling cash through the works of a covetous State. It is the duty of this rich man to help that poor man—and perhaps with more than money. It is especially the duty of Christians:

> Taking [the poor] to her arms with maternal affection, and knowing that they in a manner represent the person of Christ Himself, who accounts as done unto Him any benefit conferred upon the lowliest among the poor, [the Church] holds them in great account, [and] brings them aid to the utmost of her power.

The Church reminds them, meanwhile, with a clear-eyed realism and genuine solicitude for their welfare, "of the words by which Jesus pronounced the poor to be *blessed*," not to fool them into being content with injustice, but to encourage them neither to envy the rich nor to despise their own lot.

Ringing throughout the works of Leo are the call for a fair deal for workers, and the assertion of the primary rights of those small incarnate groups without which we can hardly be called men, no matter how rich we are. First among these is the family, that stubborn old institution marked for destruction by the new "societies":

We have the family; the "society" of a man's house—a society limited indeed in numbers, but no less a true "society," anterior to every kind of State or nation, invested with rights and duties of its own, totally independent of the civil community. (*Rerum Novarum,* May 15, 1891)

But even those groups are not simply ends in themselves. It is the most practical and genuinely economic thing in the world to recognize that man is not simply a practical and economic animal. Therefore even to understand and enjoy the perishable things of the earth, man must raise his head high toward the things that do not perish:

The things of earth cannot be understood or valued aright without taking into consideration the life to come, the life that will know no death. Exclude the idea of futurity, and forthwith the very notion of what is good and right would perish; nay,

God Is Not Quite Dead

He prayeth best, who loveth best
All things both great and small;
For the dear God who loveth us,
He made and loveth all.

Samuel Taylor Coleridge, *The Rime of the Ancient Mariner* (614–17)

In Coleridge, the Romantic love of nature is inseparable from piety: we love these things because God made them and loves them. His is not a nature religion, but old-fashioned and humble Christianity, rightly applied to our treatment of nature. It is a universe away from the inhumanity of politically correct environmentalism—saving seals and slaying children.

the whole scheme of the universe would become a dark and unfathomable mystery.

And with that most politically incorrect lesson, an embarrassing teaching about the nature of man, we end our purview of the century. Everywhere in the West we find man, uprooted from the families and communities that connect him to the past, homogenized into the "masses" of large cities. And we find the self-appointed intellectuals offering him a new futurity. Herbert Spencer and Thomas Huxley and John Stuart Mill hold forth the shimmering ideal of "science," ushering in a time when we will all be comfortable materially and satisfied with knowing, if not God, then how carbon molecules make up plastic polymers, or something equally exalting. Marx and his comrades offer the dictatorship of the proletariat—meaning, it turns out, a dictatorship *over* the proletariat, with everybody who is not a dictator a prole. Oscar Wilde and his fellows laugh at pretensions old and new, and enjoy a refined debauchery. America heralds herself as everyone else's future, brash and innocent.

The glorious future would come soon enough, with gunshots in Sarajevo and Moscow.

Chapter Nine

THE TWENTIETH CENTURY: A CENTURY OF BLOOD

How to write just a chapter on the glories and disgraces of the last tumultuous century? I might discuss the sad historical irony of good men portrayed as villains, and bad men, or at least morally compromised or unscrupulous men, hailed as heroes, whose portraits were fit to grace coins and stamps. The twentieth century had plenty of such, because it was a century of propaganda, of the visual image, of the art of rhetoric so debased (or perfected, the cynic would say) that people came to assume that all political discourse must be based upon lies. And then they ceased to care about the lies.

Take Herbert Hoover, for example. Unlike his predecessor, the quirky Calvin Coolidge, who parlayed deadpan silence into political fame, Hoover had no political skills, no presence. He was simply a mining engineer, a businessman who had developed industries in pre-Communist China, the husband of one of the first women to graduate from Stanford with a doctorate in geology, and the savior of postwar Europe, since it was he who had overseen distribution of food to all parts of the war-ravaged continent. Had he never become president, he would have died a hero. But the depression came, Hoover fought it feebly with liberal half-measures, was despised by men who had lost their jobs and their lives' savings, and was swept aside by Franklin Roosevelt, who ran on a platform of deficit cutting, and who then grew the federal government, in size and in reach,

Guess What?

- Socialism did not die; it only changed its dress.

- Hacks, frauds, and bad writers flourished in the twentieth century.

- A few people still believed in the dignity of man, the sanctity of human life, and the benefits of virtue and liberty. By the end of the century they were scorned as "conservative."

vastly beyond anything that previous Americans could ever have imagined, or tolerated. At the turn of the century, William McKinley, declined to campaign personally for his re-election, as he believed it was beneath the dignity of a sitting president. By the end of the century, image would be all in all, and, if William J. Clinton is any evidence, nothing was beneath the dignity of a sitting president.

Hacks, charlatans, hucksters, empty suits. We had the angry Rachel Carson, dying of cancer, cooking up statistics to show that pesticides were the cause, that pesticides would destroy all the birds on the planet. She succeeded so well that DDT was banned all over the world, condemning much of malarial Africa to poverty and underdevelopment.[1] Or Margaret Sanger, hater of blacks, hater of Catholics, admirer of Hitler, portraying herself as scientific, hiding her crusade against Christianity behind the rhetoric of care for children.[2] Or John Dewey, benevolent and learned, working to sever American education from its roots in the classics, to clear the way for a more "democratic" curriculum, designed to produce citizens in the new world—citizens who would be docile to their new governors.[3] Conservatives produced their share too: we could have done without the bigoted radio personality Father Coughlin, and although there were communists in the State Department in the 1950s, and although they were passing military information to the Soviets, America could have used a better man than the self-promoting Joe McCarthy to ferret them out.

These sorts of distorted and distorting men and women might have lived in earlier centuries, but their debasing ideas never could have gained currency had Western culture not been dragged into the pragmatic pit by the hubristic promises of the Enlightenment and the Romantics.

It was a century (really, a century and a half) of technological wonders. It's not easy to decide which invention changed life the most. The airplane? The radio? The telephone? Penicillin? Probably the microchip; possibly the automobile, which suddenly acquainted people familiar with cities far away, and estranged them from their own neighborhoods. The television wiped out local entertainment, not to mention local church clubs and fraternal organizations. It did so with very little compensation by way of great or even halfway decent art (*The Twilight Zone*, Rod Serling's series of morality plays with overtones of Greek tragedy and the New Testament, was one exception). My dark horse candidate would be the refrigerator. It was Clarence Birdseye and his frozen vegetables, ease and not drudgery, that set women looking out of the home for things to do.

Inventions came so quickly that people began to assume that the near future would look nothing like the past, whose wisdom might as well be discarded. "History is bunk," said Henry Ford. But the future, that was a different matter. Long before anybody coined the ugly term "political correctness," it was politically correct to believe that in the future everybody was going to be healthier and richer and happier, and that our beloved institutions would have to adapt to it, or die. Even the reader who considers himself inoculated against PC brainwashing might be surprised to notice that this notion of progress is not self-evident, nor has it always been held as dogma. The Athenian in the days of Pericles or the Englishman in the days of Chaucer would have laughed at the idea that the future would inevitably be better than the present.

But by the twentieth century, the idea of "progress" is unassailable. A *Life* magazine article from 1965 gives us a typical example of the silliness: we are told that by the year 2000, we'd all be flying private planes and we'd have increased our intelligence by 50 percent.[4] It was all nonsense; the flood of new, bulky, body-moving and matter-changing inventions was about to come to a halt.

One of the features of an ideology based on false premises is that it contradicts itself. Thus, a very different strand of "political correctness" predicted the horrors of the world to come, sometimes (understandably) because of the depredations of government, or the spread of stupidity

(George Orwell's *1984*, Ray Bradbury's *Fahrenheit 451*). More often, the world was going to come to misery because of a fearful explosion in population or a worldwide nuclear disaster or uncontrolled pollution (*Soylent Green*, *Logan's Run*, *The Omega Man*, *Silent Spring*, *Cat's Cradle*).

What all the rosier futurists had in common was a detachment from history, and an obliviousness to the nature of man, which is not, after all, infinitely malleable. But it was assumed, without much thought, that because modern man had motorcars and medieval man had horses or his two feet, modern man must be superior, and medieval man might be ignored.

The churches got in on the act. Liberals came to preach a Jesus not much different from Buddha, a man like us in all things including ignorance and maybe sin. The true gospel lay not in Jesus' miracles nor in his claim to be the son of God, and certainly not in his redemptive death on the Cross and his resurrection. Those latter were deemed merely mythical, a bald lie told by the diabolically cunning apostles or a bald lie believed by the rustically credulous apostles or an instance of mass hysteria undergone by the stark raving apostles. The call went forth not to repent, but to work hard for liberal political programs, ostensibly to feed and house and clothe the poor, for the Kingdom of God is of this world.

Even the plodding Roman Catholic Church, like a rustic who discovers moving pictures while everyone else has moved on to the computer, held its Second Vatican Council to herald a new day in the church's engagement with the world. The documents of that council taught no new doctrine, and are notably conservative in many ways. They affirm Latin as the language of the Church, they call for the revival of ancient chant, they insist upon a separation of roles for laymen and clergy, and they defend the sanctity of human life from conception to death.[5] But a document is a document, and a spirit is a spirit, and in a battle between the two, one should bet on the spirit every time. The "Spirit of Vatican II," summoned from no one knows where, marched forth in triumph and leveled centuries of Catholic tradition in the name of embracing the future, when all along, in the midst of the council fathers, something was happening that would empty thousands of Catholic schools and hospitals and convents and seminaries, their buildings sold or torn down. That something, which I'll be discussing soon, was the Sexual Revolution.

Walter Mitty, rugged individual

Certainly one of the energizing myths of the twentieth century has been that of the limitless possibilities opened up for the ambitious, creative individual. "Be all that you can be," sang a notorious commercial for the United States Army, using the lures of college scholarships and high-paying careers to bring in recruits. In one breathtaking slogan it contradicted the essence of an army, which can only fight if its men are not for themselves but for the platoon, and for one another.

Here we need to distinguish between one form of individualism and another: between what I'll call the individualism of competence and the individualism of desire. The former individualism has come under suspicion, based as it is upon the traditions of family, civic duty, and hard and often unrewarding work. This kind of individualist is oriented towards the community in a powerful but easily overlooked way. He announces to his neighbors, "You may depend on me. I'm in charge of my household. My children won't loiter about your streets, or break your windows, or burn your barns down. Should any of them do so, let me know, and I assure you we'll pay for it and it won't happen again. I can take care of my property. If you need a hand fixing your carburetor, I know a little about that, and I'm not bad at sawing,

A Book You're Not Supposed to Read

The Everlasting Man by G. K. Chesterton; Ft. Collins, CO: Ignatius Press, 1993.

Chesterton's an antidote to the scientism that would see in man nothing more than an interesting animal, and to the dull modernism that can no longer see how one Man changed the world utterly.

planing, turning, and joining, either. I never could get the feel of cement, though, and I may some time ask you to help me lay down a sidewalk. But rest easy: this house is in order."

Now this form of individualism—manly, tied to duty, more than able to fulfill the responsibilities of ordinary domestic and civic life—has been buffeted throughout the century. Let me list a few of the ways:

1. Ordinary men and women were considered incapable of educating their children. They must leave that to the experts, and, increasingly, the experts were not teachers of their choice. Compulsory schooling spread from Bismarck's Germany across the continent, in some places under the banner of "efficiency," but in America, due to the influence of the tradition-despising Dewey, under the banner of "democracy." (In the early days of our current century, naturally, a court in California ruled that parents may not educate their children without a state-issued teacher's certificate.)

2. The home was no longer sacrosanct. "A man's home is his castle," went the old saying, meaning that, in that one place, no matter how humble it was, a man was fortified with traditions and laws against outsiders, including the State. But universal suffrage built a road from the home to the capital of every nation in the West: and a road takes traffic two ways. That movement should be seen against the backdrop of the social sciences, with their offspring in social work and state welfare agencies. All at once, a stranger from a government office or from a charity with close ties to the government could hold a hammer over the head of a poor family. The result is, all in all, to demote first the father and then the mother, and introduce, regardless of good intentions, dependency and chaos into every city in the western world.

3. Traditions fell into disuse. In their various ways, such diverse thinkers as Edmund Burke, Alexis de Tocqueville, Friedrich von Hayek,[6] and others going all the way back to Sophocles, had argued for what Chesterton called "the democracy of the dead," the respect the living owe to their forebears, which they show not by following blindly all that their forebears have done, but by being inspired by their example, carrying on their work, and shunning any hasty departure from established wisdom. This reverence for tradition, as Hayek pointed out, allows a man to drink from the wisdom distilled from millions of past experiments. It is perfectly compatible with the individualism of competence.

But almost everywhere one turns, one sees twentieth century statesmen and intelligentsia and artists treating tradition with a sneer. There are plenty of heartening exceptions—T. S. Eliot, Tolkien, Sigrid Undset, Francois Mauriac, Edward Hopper, Russell Kirk. But in music we have the defiantly antimusical atonalism of Alban Berg—and what difference does it make if simple people can't stand it? We have incompetence in painting and sculpture masking itself as anti-representationalism, meeting a cold reception from the people (with some brilliant exceptions: Joan Miro, Paul Klee). We have the Bauhaus architecture of Le Corbusier, with his up-to-date dismissal of all that had passed for warm, human places to live and work in. A "machine" for human dwelling, that is what he said he strove to build. Newspapers, schools, "scientists" ranging out of botany and into social planning, self-styled philosophers and artists, united to cry down the old, the shopworn, the faded, and herald a new day of free love or psychic enhancement or redefined families or whatever the commercials of the day happened to hawk.

4. Machines, and the cheap materials made available by plastics and other products of industrial chemistry, turned the artisan into the rare worker for the rich, rather than a common fellow in every neighborhood.

5. The grand selling of college degrees, deflated in intellectual value, demoted the mere working man, and set him up as easy prey.

6. Religion, which once bound the individual to his community, defining his relationship to the people among whom he worked and played, recast itself as therapy. It was degraded to a personal choice, one among many, and therefore sought, if at all, as a hobby that might give solace to Mrs. Smith, even as Mrs. Jones preferred psychotherapy or Mrs. Brown preferred the massage parlor.

Marx's Fruit

In terms of having his teachings implemented, Marx, perhaps, saw far more success than any other political writer in history. His impact was, to say the least, dramatic:

> On body count alone, *The Communist Manifesto* could win the award for the most malicious book ever written. Now that we have more accurate calculations of corpses—perhaps upwards of 100,000,000—even the tenured Marxists are a bit squeamish about tooting the *Manifesto* as a horn of plenty.

> **Benjamin Wiker**, *10 Books That Screwed Up the World*

Between Stalin, Mao, Pol Pot, and the lesser imitators, Marx's followers freed quite a few people of their mortal chains in the twentieth century.

These developments accompanied a trumpeting of a debased autonomy, that of a consumer choosing among boisterously promoted goods, few of which he needed. In many cases their principal "value" lay in a reflected glory, wherein the rich had always foolishly invested, but wherein even a working man might now invest. The narcissism of this sort of individualism can be seen in a slogan which abortion proponents in the United States slid into: the "right to choose." Such a right, with the object of the infinitive "to choose" left marvelously indeterminate, would have been incomprehensible even to the liberal mind of previous generations.

The trouble with worshipping economic choice as an end, according to an agrarian conservative like Wendell Berry, is that it leaves the small farmer and the local craftsman and the corner grocer little opportunity to be an independent businessman and to choose some things that are genuinely good: a house in decent repair, well-read children, a few days of leisure in the month, and a nice suit for Sundays.[7] The aim of liberty is the good, and not the satisfaction of the arbitrary will; and the good is an objective good. But now the aim of liberty is liberty, nothing beyond. It is to choose for the sake of choosing, regardless of what one chooses. Choice—not family, not faith, not community, not one's nature as a human being, certainly neither nation nor God—is the expression of an individual's very being. If I wear a ring in my nose like a sow, you had better not smirk at it, because that is my choice.

Now it should be easy to see that the latter form of individualism undermines the former. It's radically at odds with it, since its presupposition is that there are no objectively good things to seek, only things that are called "good" because they are sought by many, or, most important, by me.

So here is the most politically incorrect thing I can say about the twentieth century: The history of the last 100 to 150 years is the sorry tale of the growth of the State, and of the State's toadies in education, mass media, and mass entertainment, encouraging the community-dissolving individualism of desire (in the West; in the East people did not even get that), at the expense of the individualism of competence. It is a war of the individual now seen as a random atom of sovereign choice, united with the almighty State, against their common enemies in the middle: the family, the community, national heritage, and the liberty they depended upon and fostered.

The empire strikes back

It had been one of the great victories of the Jewish and Christian traditions, this dissociation of God from the State. "Render therefore unto Caesar that which is Caesar's," said Jesus, granting the realm of "Caesar" a range of independence, but always subordinate to the things of God. "Put not your trust in princes," said the Psalmist, and the prophecies of Jeremiah should have made that wisdom plain enough. If your trust rests in a city or a temple or a king, you're a fool, and you will be hauled away in captivity to Babylon.

With religion emasculated, the State could resume its old place as chief god on the totem and the benevolent oppressor of mankind. It could do so most safely if it yielded some bread and circuses to the narcissistic individual, as the West learned, and the communist East did not. But the Empire has struck back. Recall what man, no longer protected by the overarching law of God, has wrought:

+ In Russia, the earthy and simple faith of the peasants and the common people was brutally repressed, to make room for Marxism. It was a man-made monstrosity, its goal a "dictatorship of the proletariat," a dreamland wherein the distinction between ruler and ruled would vanish, and all would be united in a paradise: not the comprehensive will of God, who makes individual saints stand out sharply like sabers, but the shapeless and uniform will of the people. It turns out that, in the meantime, the "will of the people" was simply the will of their overlords, just as the will of Rome in the days of the empire was the will of the emperor.

* In China, Mao-Tse Tung, impatient with the sluggish industrialization of his country, slaughtered millions in a movement aptly and ghoulishly called the Cultural Revolution. The most venerable Chinese tradition of natural law—Confucianism—was condemned as retrograde. Village, clan, family, temple, all had to yield to the new power coming from the Western intelligentsia.

* Lenin and Stalin murdered their own citizens. Said Lenin with a diabolical carelessness, "You have to break some eggs to make an omelet."[8] Well, twenty million eggs got broken in Stalin's forced collectivization of the Ukraine and the famine that followed. But then, why did the intelligentsia in the West ignore it, or, in the filthy case of Pulitzer Prize winner Walter Duranty, cover it up?[9] What had they got against Ukrainian peasants? The same thing they had against all peasants, all "backward" communities, all village churches, all self-governing schools. They understood that under the old regime, a professor of sociology might aspire to be a lovable oddball in his neighborhood. Under the new regime, that man would be running the show. In the old world of sin and strife and repentance and grace, the Professor of Sociology had to crack his arthritic knees in prayer like his neighbor the plumber. In the new world, whose only sins are political, admitting of no repentance except reeducation, the Professor dons the alb of the priest, with the nightstick of the policeman. Class envy may explain very little enough in this life of ours. But the appeal of

Marxism to the intellectual elites, that it certainly *does* explain.

✦ Hitler and Mussolini denounced Christianity as effeminate (and Judaism, in the case of Hitler, as envy-poisoned), and tried to replace the traditional religion of their countries with worship of the State, the bloody-minded Hitler using the Jews as his sacrificial lambs. The Italians were to recapture the glory of the old Empire, apparently by seizing Ethiopia, and Germans sang, with no sense of hyperbole, *Deutschland über Alles!* In Germany, as in the Soviet Union, the economy, the schools, and local government were all to be controlled by a single party, the national party.

✦ These titanically wicked men so tower over their comrades in devilry that we forget how many others there were, and the hatreds that united them. The Ottoman Turks, their imperial dreams fading, slaughtered a million Armenian shepherds and farmers.[10] The Viet Cong backhoed over a French-Indochinese Catholic culture that dated back to the Renaissance. A litter of toadies to the Soviets savaged Eastern Europe.

✦ Franklin Roosevelt—not a wicked man—broke with American traditions, not simply by discarding the wisdom (and humility) of Washington, who refused to seek a third term in the presidency. Had Roosevelt succeeded in all he attempted, the Supreme Court would be an appendage to the legislature, and the American federal government would be the undisputed master of every arena of national life. In this regard he tried to carry out the daydreams of Woodrow Wilson, who disliked the road blocks built in to the American government and preferred the parliamentary system of Europe.[11] He preferred, in other words, the unitary state.

✦ Human sexuality was to be managed by self-appointed experts. Margaret Sanger, bigot extraordinaire, hater of "lesser" breeds, despiser of simple family women, preached birth prevention, calling it "birth control."[12] She sold it to the rich—in those days, Republican women's groups were fond of planning the non-parenthood of poor Democrats—as a means of controlling the poor, which in America meant immigrant Catholics, blacks, Indians, and other undesirables. Sanger had plenty of eugenic "science" to back up her racism. She sold it to the poor as an opportunity for "choice," meaning the freedom from being burdened with yet another child. Alfred Kinsey and his associates committed thousands of acts of pederasty while conducting "scientific" experiments on babies and children, jiggered his statistics, belittled the idea of a sexual norm, brought his prurience into every living room in the nation via the magazines, and

Ignorance Has Consequences

The man of culture finds the whole past relevant; the bourgeois and the barbarian find relevant only what has some pressing connection with their appetites. Those who remember alone have a sense of relatedness, but whoever has a sense of relatedness is in at least the first grade of philosophy.

From **Richard Weaver**, *Ideas Have Consequences*

The modern man forgets the past, and finds himself at the mercy of technocrats, propagandists, and snake-oil salesmen. The postmodern man is no longer aware that he has any past to forget. To remember and honor the hard-won achievements of our civilization is to have a fair chance of freedom; to forget them or despise them is to have no chance at all.

yet sold himself as an old-fashioned Indiana husband and father.[13]

+ Freud, far more intelligent and learned than his descendants and his detractors, has been even more influential dead and discredited than alive. No one now chatters about the *id* and the *ego*, yet psychology and sociology have accepted, as plain fact, that religion is a product of a certain kind of psyche, and probably not a healthy one. No one sends a troubled teenager to a priest, or to a wise man who leads a life of profound and regular prayer. The teenager is sent to a psychologist, who increasingly is not much more than a pharmacologist. Sin has dropped out of that "scientific" discourse.

+ The more popular destroyers of community life and traditional faith tempted the people with the drug of license. The Great Depression and World War II interrupted a sexual revolution that had begun long before the 1960s. What with the automobile, the slow takeover of family businesses by large corporations, the increased demand for "higher" education, the pill, the replacement of local sports and entertainment with the mass product peddled over the radio and the television, not to mention the school's insatiable fascination with matters that are not the school's business, it is no surprise that sexual activity eluded the oversight of family, community, or church.

The health of the State, the poverty of the soul

If we examine them in the light of our distinction between two different kinds of individualisms, and in the light of who profits and who loses by them, we can see that every important political and social development of the twentieth century enriched and empowered the State and the narcissist at the expense of the community and the free, competent, dutiful individuals that were its pillars.

Take, for example, the federal income tax. At a stroke it made everyone beholden to the empire for tax "breaks," and the empire learned that the canniest use of the tax system was not to collect money fairly to pay for roads and railways, but to influence behavior—to bring the subjects to heel. The enormously enriched Empire also saw, in the West, that it could entangle more people by shrewdly calculated "gifts" than by threats. One American court decision, typical of the century, placed every college in the country under the imperial eye: no matter for the local culture, for the college's traditions, for the free decisions of trustees or faculty or students. So long as a single student received one dollar, not of federal money but of federally backed student "loans," that college must abide by sheaves of federal regulations. It was as if the student were a mere bagman, delivering the money over from the Empire to the subsidiary school's treasury.[14]

Or take freedom of speech. We know what kinds of speech the American Founders were most careful to protect: the kinds that had been most curtailed in European nations, namely, religious speech and political speech. We also know, from the laws they and their contemporaries passed, that they did not regard obscenity or even profanity as worth protecting. Certainly they took no care to ensure that people could draw or paint whatever they liked and sell it on the streets. They had the common sense view that speech was speech. But by the end of the twentieth century, it was precisely political and religious speech that came under scrutiny. Who benefits from such speech, if proclaimed boldly and vigorously, in the public square? The local community does. It cannot exist without it. There is no way the people of Altoona or Ironwood can condemn violations of what they consider central to their common welfare, unless they can speak their minds and their passions without fear of reprisal. But political correctness (and the sickly sweet tyranny of a nanny state, a *tyrannanny*, wherein you can be punished not for an action but for the wrong feeling) curbed that speech. Nor could the community unite to celebrate its submission to the divine law and its gratitude for divine favor. The sometimes tricky negotiations that could unite Protestant with Catholic, and Christian with Jew, and believer with unbeliever, were snatched from the people most concerned, by a small club of over-schooled judges. But if the people of Ironwood are not competent to determine what kind of prayer should be said in the locker room before a football game, to unite the players without unduly hurting the feelings of any tackle or linebacker, then the people of Ironwood are not competent to determine anything at all. Then Ironwood is a fiction, or a specter.

One more example: pornography. A few cases in America, over the decades, settled the matter. A picture of a naked body is not speech; it does not function as words do; it makes no proposition that can be analyzed rationally; it asserts no truth. It "expresses" something: mainly, it expresses one's desire to paint or shoot a picture of a naked person and make money from it. Here again the principle of a free community should come into play. If you are Hugh Hefner and you want to persuade the people of Hollidaysburg to let the drug stores carry your wares, then by all means go to them and argue that having *Playboys* in the hands of idle teenage boys would conduce to the common good, would be just

A Book You're Not Supposed to Read

The Conservative Mind: From Burke to Eliot by Russell Kirk; Washington, D.C.: Regnery Publishing, 2001.

> [John] Adams himself had been a farm boy, a teacher, a lawyer, a legislator, an ambassador; he knew men and things; talk concerning a "state of nature" or "natural equality" or universal benevolence exasperated both his common sense and his New England morality. (76)

A book that may change your mind—and your life. To read Kirk is to climb to the top of a high hill to survey the logic and experiences and passions of great political and ecclesiastical thinkers, statesmen who struggled with the eternal questions—many of whom have been unconscionably ignored: Brownson, Disraeli, Calhoun, J. F. Stephen, Paul Elmer More, and many others. It is a university education, in a few hundred pages.

and right, would help the trolleys run on time, would concentrate the boys' minds on their studies, or would make for excellent streamers for the Memorial Day parade. Persuade them. If you can't persuade them, go somewhere else. But the courts swept that wholesome debate aside. All at once we have that small club of judges determining what does or does not violate some vague restrictions which they have arbitrarily established, while pretending to defer to vague "community standards." It did not occur to the majority that such "standards" are themselves often the products of energetic and passionate debate, of commendation and condemnation and compromise.

Art from the people; Art against the people

By the middle of the century, as I've suggested, "modern" had come to denote all things "scientific," up-to-date, intelligent, and bold, as opposed, it was thought, to the sickly sentimentalism of such popular artists as Norman Rockwell, or such writers as Dickens. High art turned away from what a common person might at least apprehend. An unlettered old woman might kneel before Michelangelo's *Pietà* and be moved to tears, without knowing a bit about sculpture or the Renaissance; but artists had no use for such people. The result was some very fine and unusual art, and a great lot of trash. That's because, for all their vaunted boldness, for all their drearily homogeneous originality, the artists traded the solid judgments of history and tradition for the caprices of the academy and the self-styled intellectuals. For every T. S. Eliot—an innovator steeped in tradition[15]—you had thirty or forty "famous" poets who were strictly unreadable, spared the necessity of writing grammatical sentences that could at least tell you whether a lizard was bleeding, even if you did not know what that portentous action meant or why you should care.

It became more and more difficult for people to recall when one could make a name for oneself across the country by writing verses that were quite good, and obviously beautiful, and expressive of something dear to the hearts and minds of his countrymen. There would be no more John Greenleaf Whittiers, no more Longfellows.

Robert Frost is arguably the most underrated writer in English in the last two hundred years. He was dismissed by the politically correct academy on precisely the same grounds that make him good. He was dismissed because people actually read his poems; he may have been the last genuine poet of the American people. Certainly it did not help that he wrote with a clarity that belied a profound meditation upon good and evil, human loves and hate, the beauty and terror of nature, our longing for permanence and our resignation to change and death. Consider the last two lines of "The Oven-Bird," a poem about a small ground sparrow, one of the few songsters in the dead summer. It could be a comment— Frost never bludgeons us with his Great Ideas—about the thinness of the modern world:

> The question that he frames in all but words
> Is what to make of a diminished thing. (13–14)

Eliot could hardly do better:

> This is the way the world ends
> This is the way the world ends
> This is the way the world ends
> Not with a bang but a whimper. ("The Hollow Men," 95–98)

The dead hand of academe lay upon the throat. Novels and poems and plays of the late century smelled of the faculty lounge. "Serious" novels were still read by people who thought themselves better educated than their fellows, but there could be nothing like a Dickens writing novels that ranked among the best in any language, serially, for a popular weekly magazine. Meanwhile, almost all of what people did read was unrelievedly banal: romance novels put out by formula, suspense novels with clipped or infantile sentences, and weird fantasy novels trying desperately to echo J. R. R. Tolkien, that kindly man of the Middle Ages who heard the songs of Valhalla above the drone of trams and trains. Never have books been so cheap; never has it been so easy to obtain a first-rate education in the classics of ancient and modern literature; never have so many readers walked the earth; and never has so much paper been stolen from more practical and hygienic uses.

Still, the finest writers of the century cry out for a return to the local, the earthy, the solid realities of male and female, the community-building role of tradition. Flannery O'Connor's "You Can't Be Any Poorer Than Dead" is a scathing satire against the clumsy do-gooding of liberal social work, powerless against the hard realities of sin and guilt. Sigrid Undset seems to cast the entire century aside as she sets her epic novels in the Scandinavia of the Middle Ages, dramatizing, in *Kristin Lavransdatter* and *The Master of Hestviken,* the slow awakening of a human soul from barbarism and selfishness to humility and life; yet she saw, as the Nazis swelled in might on the other side of the Baltic, into just what barbarism Europe was slouching.

Graham Greene, a hater of American bravado and no conservative, did what few dabblers in Marxism dared. He actually went to the miserable Communist nations and watched the oppression. In *The Power and the Glory,* set in socialist Mexico, he shows that the might of love, which is the humility of the despised and beaten Christ, triumphs over the deadly materialism of the modern socialist state.

Malcolm Muggeridge visited the Ukraine after the *New York Times'* liar Duranty did, wrote about what he saw, and was consigned to intellectual Siberia by the elites in England. That began his long sojourn from atheism to faith. Many years later, in his old age, he would write the biography of a small Albanian nun whom the world at once admired for her charity and despised for her supposed ignorance: Mother Theresa.[16]

So the novel fell on rough times, but for a while the film took its place, serving some of the old functions of popular art. In its early days, and in its golden age from 1935 to 1955, film directors, writers and actors could tap a rich popular tradition of ritual celebrations (consider the Fourth of July oration, wherein a local grandee might play Daniel Webster), local theater, vaudeville, and the small opera house. For the most part, the men and women who made and acted in these movies did not come from the academy, and did want to make money. More than that, they came from the people about whom they wrote. They too had struggled through war and depression. They had carried a bayonet alongside their countrymen, baled hay, chopped wood, fought in alleys, played baseball, sang hymns on Sunday, got drunk on Saturday, and crouched by the radio to hear news from the Pacific.

A Movie You're Not Supposed to Watch

On the Waterfront, directed by Elia Kazan, starring Marlon Brando

Their work often enough showed the hypocrisy of people who called themselves religious, as for instance the sour church council in John Ford's *How Green Was My Valley*; but then, the honest preacher was the hero in that film. The faith and patriotism of such directors as Ford, Frank Capra, Alfred Hitchcock, Elia Kazan, and William Wyler were not blemishes upon their genius. Sometimes they indulged in sentimentality; most popular art does. But without the subtle pressure of a religious faith that believes that man and woman marry until death, there is no drama in Ford's *Rio Grande*, and without the oddly pre-modern conviction that holiness and duty outweigh all utilitarian calculations, the wrongly accused priest in Hitchcock's *I Confess* would shrug and give up the murderer. We would not have the near-tragic self-sacrifice of George Bailey in Capra's *It's a Wonderful Life*, ending with a celebration of the babe born in a manger. Nor, in Kazan's *On the Waterfront*, Marlon Brando's staggering walk along a dingy Via Dolorosa, his priest and his beloved watching each step of agony, as he defeats, with Christlike humility, the wickedness of the union machine. Without the wellsprings of popular piety, patriotism, and tradition to assist the director, actor, and audience in the subtle examinations of what it means to be human and how we can build a community in a world rife with our own wickedness, there could be no *Friendly Persuasion*, or *High Noon*, or *In the Heat of the Night*. Even when the directors were not filming Biblical or national epic, the strains of old hymns were not too distant for them to hear.

Science without knowledge

But there were anthems in the twentieth century that threatened to drown out those hymns. One such is still with us, though tattered and tarnished. It could be heard from all kinds of choristers. Kinsey sang it, when he told the world that, according to his scientific research, 10 percent of the male population was homosexual.[17] Margaret Mead, more honest than Kinsey (which is not saying much), sang it when the teenagers of Samoa hoodwinked her, and she reported, scientifically, that free love reigned in the South Pacific, and all the youth were happy.[18] The Marxists sang it to the strains of a military march, when they "proved," with scientific accuracy, that the world was inevitably going to evolve into the great and final Communist State, when the State itself would wither away, and every tear should be wiped from the eyes of man. You hear it in a particularly silly form in a bad movie called *The Day the Earth Stood Still*: we were going to be "saved" from our sins not by God but by a superior race of aliens come down to help us and bring us peace and prosperity. (The State, social workers, aliens, what's the difference?) You hear it in *Inherit the Wind*, the dishonest but artful play about the Scopes "monkey trial," when a schoolteacher in Tennessee had been arrested for teaching evolution. In the play, the atheist and bigot Clarence Darrow is portrayed as the true respecter of Holy Writ, and the populist liberal William Jennings Bryan is portrayed as a blathering fool. The song is the Ode to Science, and it is the fight song of political correctness, regardless of how unscientific and foolish those prejudices are.

A Book You're Not Supposed to Read

The Abolition of Man C. S. Lewis; New York: HarperCollins, 1974.

You will hear from your PC teachers that to make judgments about what is beautiful and ugly, or good and evil, is to shut your mind or to offend those who feel otherwise. Lewis shows instead that when we teach young children that these terms have no meaning in themselves, we rob their young minds of something essential to their humanity. We pretend to be overcoming nature when we destroy the notion that there is a natural law for us to obey and natural ideals of beauty for us to aspire to. But all we do is to *abolish man*. We make what Lewis calls "men without chests," people who can no longer feel the power of a deed nobly done. His verdict against modern education might as well be a verdict against the welfare state, or against religion turned into therapy for weaklings:

> We make men without chests and expect of them virtue and enterprise. We laugh at honor and are shocked to find traitors in our midst. We castrate and bid the geldings to be fruitful. (26)

Earlier ages had understood "science" as "knowledge," and had distinguished natural science or the knowledge of nature from other forms of science. In the twentieth century, natural science claimed victory over all others: it alone constituted genuine knowledge. To be sure, natural science is a useful thing. It has revealed to us the glories of quasars and the bending of light and the elongation of objects as they approach the speed of light. If you are interested in the arrangement and composition and decomposition and movement of matter over time, natural science is your ticket. The trouble is that natural science, limited by its method and subject, cannot tell you about the human heart. It cannot tell you about the good and the beautiful. It cannot tell you about justice, temperance, prudence, and fortitude. It can sometimes reduce its subjects to mathematical expression, but it cannot even prove the validity of mathematics. More than that, as the greatest mathematician of the century, Kurt Gödel, showed, mathematics itself is necessarily "incomplete." Every mathematics of more than elementary simplicity will embrace non-axiomatic statements which are true, but which cannot be proved to be true. Gödel thought that his work went a long way toward demonstrating the necessary existence of God.[19]

But we were all to be saved from ourselves by science, and when science helped us destroy tens of thousands of people in a minute, and dump so much toxic waste into our streams that Lake Erie nearly died, and the Cuyahoga River actually caught fire,[20] some people turned against science with a ferocity as irrational as was the initial blind faith in it. So the century presents us with a strange irony. It begins with the popularizers of science, like H. G. Wells, predicting a world of free love and governments managed by the intellectual elites.[21] Or it begins with every field of knowledge trying desperately to be as precise and mathematical as physics: even philosophy, with men such as A. J. Ayer, is cramped and reduced to the analysis of language.[22] But when the cracks in this modern faith begin to show—in the German concentration camps, or in the slums of "scientific" urban planning, such as at the ugly Pruitt-Igoe development in Saint Louis[23]—then "postmodern" man announces the death of reason. Students are taught that there is no absolute truth; feminists will go so far as to assert that mathematical logic is a masculine tool of oppression.

The Pill's bitter effects

Political correctness, in its essence, is about transforming a radical notion into dogma. An idea one day is radical, but liberal tolerance forbids us to shun it. As the Clarence Darrow character says in *Inherit the Wind*, we all have "the right to be wrong."[24] But before long it's a dogma that only a bigot or a fool would question. The most insidious successes of political correctness are those that even we self-styled conservatives don't realize we've bought into. One such near-total victory by the forces of political correctness might fairly be reckoned as the critical push that has sent our civilization reeling.

As often happens, the pivot in a civilization's decline is reached with hardly anyone noticing. In 1930, at the Lambeth Conference, the Anglican Church managed to combine three of the destructive trends of the early century: a foolish trust in technological innovation as always and inevitably good, and in the predictions of technocrats as always and inevitably true; a foolish rejection not only of traditional morality but of nineteen centuries of church teaching; and a foolish acceptance of the primacy of individual desire. The council members voted to approve artificial contraception, now so widely accepted that the reader must smile at my belief that the event was so important. Pope Pius XI quickly responded with *Casti Conubii*, a treatise on the natural law and its implications for marriage and sexual morality; Aldous Huxley, an atheist, responded with *Brave New World*, a satirical prophecy of a world of cloned men, a eugenically engineered society whose people are drugged up with plenty of food, easy sex, and the mind-blearing soma.

The Depression and the second World War delayed the onset, but Lambeth, and then the invention of the Pill, made the full sexual revolution possible. And it is that revolution, not the television, perhaps not even the computer, that most cleanly severed Western civilization from its past. In 1940, Frances Perkins, the first female cabinet member in the

Centrally Planned Non-Parenthood

The "pro-choice" movement in America today makes more sense when considered in its intellectual context. We should be thankful for the forthrightness of Margaret Sanger, founder of Planned Parenthood:

> When we realize that each feeble-minded person is a potential source of endless progeny of defect, we prefer the policy of immediate sterilization, of making sure that parenthood is absolutely prohibited to the feeble-minded.
>
> **Margaret Sanger**, *The Pivot of Civilization*

Pro-choice: and the choice is in the hands of the elites.

United States, was dismayed to learn that welfare payments to unwed mothers might be having the perverse effect of preventing marriage, and thus perpetuating moral and material poverty.[25] By 2000, the suggestion that one should be married before one has a child would be decried as bigoted, and one third of all American children would be born out of wedlock.

In 1946, Pope Pius XII called for women's suffrage in all Catholic countries, and urged the women of Italy, to whom he directed many addresses full of praise and encouragement, to vote to protect the family against hypermasculine ideologies such as fascism.[26] By 2000, in almost every nation of the West, millions of "liberated" women will have abandoned the family as the locus of their chief concern. In America, single and divorced women will ally with homosexual men to push for the normalization of any kind of "family" arrangement imaginable, regardless of the welfare of children, so long as the adults involved consent. None of this could have happened without both the Industrial Revolution—which took from women much of the economic value of their work at home— and the Pill.

If you don't like the Pill, it must be because you want women enslaved to the messy drudgery of child-rearing, or because you are a meddling Puritan who wants to suppress the natural sexuality of our youth, or simply because you are backwards. But watch a rap video or browse a magazine rack at a convenience store, and ask how women are more respected today than before the Pill. Look at statistics about teen pregnancy or venereal disease (not to mention teenage girls' and college girls' depression) and ask if sexual liberation has been liberating.

It's hard to see where the West can go from here, without repentance and return to the wellsprings of its being. As I write, not one nation in Europe is replacing its population. The birth rate in supposedly family-friendly Italy is 1.2 women per child. Among the French of Quebec it is 0.7. Such rates cannot be sustained for more than one generation without the nation lapsing into swift and irreversible decline, because not enough children will be born to produce the wealth necessary for the pensions and benefits that the aged have voted for themselves and will hardly want to defer or discontinue. Then the few that are born will have to be more heavily taxed to make up the shortfall. But that will compel all women to work for wages, which will cause the birth rate to drop further—if it is possible to drop further than Quebec's. But why should the individual care? Says Burke, "People will not look forward to a posterity, who never look backward to their ancestors" (*Reflections on the Revolution in France*). The individualism of desire demands that people "fulfill" themselves in the only time available for them, now. Even those who are prudent plan for themselves and their careers. Some soldiers sacrifice for their country, but, comparatively speaking, they are the blessed few. So we have prudent hedonists and imprudent hedonists, but out of hedonists even Epicurus could only fashion a community by means of austere moderation and careful retreat from the world.

History can restore us

Is there no hope? Throughout the surging and dying fads of the century, the bloodshed, the degradation, the pride and folly, there were still some who believed in the natural law, in man's freedom to live among his fellows in accord with it, and in the capacity of reason to help us discern the good from the bad, the beautiful from the ugly, and the true from the false. They did not fear natural science, but they did not fall before its idol, either. They were not afraid to go to war, but they gave their hearts to peace. They saw through the shallowness of the false gods: the State, the Party, das Volk, sex, "freedom of choice," science, an airplane in every garage and two wives in every bed. These were true liberals, because they believed passionately in liberty, though some of them, the more conservative, doubted the State's capacity to secure such freedom. As the century closed, they began to seek one another out, to begin, slowly, to form communities anew, wherein words like virtue would resume their honored place.

Who were these people? There were many; I have space to mention only a few. There were Chesterton and Belloc, capitalists in this radical sense: they wanted everyone to possess capital, not just the few, and certainly not just the State. The State would cut a girl's red hair because it had lice; Chesterton would start a revolution to give the girl's father a chance at a better job so that her mother could enjoy leisure—not idleness but complete responsibility for her time—and clean her daughter's hair properly.[27] Their call against the inhumanity of socialism and the crass ugliness of the consumer state would be heard by the American agrarians, by maternalist women in Sweden[28] and America in the mid-century, and by the trend-bucking economist E. F. Schumacher.[29] Some of these people were sentimentally attached to a way of life long past: as Evelyn Waugh lamented the passing of the virtues of the English aristocracy in *Brideshead Revisited*, and the emergence of a culture of democratic banality.

Some stood up for man in all his glory as the creature *capax Dei*, capable of conceiving of God and of becoming like God. Such was the theologian Romano Guardini, who saw with dismay the age of the "mass man,"[30] or the philosopher Joseph Pieper, who retained his belief that "wisdom" meant more than the possession of linguistic codes or scientific data, and who argued, historically and anthropologically, that a community that does not worship is no community at all.[31] Some, rejecting the animalism at the base of the individualism of desire, sang of the holiness of the human body, male and female, and the divine creativity intrinsic to the act of married love. Such was the great Pope John Paul II, almost universally misunderstood.[32] The brave priest who helped, with the simple electrician Lech Walesa and an affable actor from rural Illinois, to bring down Poland's communist dictatorship and then the Soviet Union, stood uncompromisingly against the slaughter of infants in the womb, against the rearrangement of family relations to suit the capricious tastes of adults, and against all attacks on the dignity of woman—attacks increasingly coming from feminists, some of whom hated a feminine woman even more than they hated a masculine man.

Does Western Civilization possess the resources for renewal? It possesses a greater wealth of them than any previous falling civilization could count on. We might listen to Aeschylus again and be warned that natural law must be the foundation of a democratic state. We might turn to Virgil and recall that the role of the true father, one of self-sacrifice in leadership, is indispensable. We might turn to the Rule of Benedict and recover a healthy appreciation for the dignity of hard labor, and the richness of silence. We might turn to Dante and attempt to see all love as the expression of the Love that truly is. We might turn to Shakespeare and learn anything about man there is to learn. We might turn to the sage and serious Doctor Johnson and imitate the solid common sense of a man who could not be moved by the wispy intellectual fad, but could be moved by penetrating argument, or by a beggar on the streets of London. We might return to Dickens and remember that if we lose the child, we lose everything. We might turn to the dour Jeremiah of the twentieth century, Alexander Solzhenitsyn, and learn that if the West's victory over communism means a victory for license and banality and a real servitude for the human soul, then we are the losers, too.

We might drink from all these fountains, but it will all be in vain if we do not keep our culture grounded in the one foundation without which Western civilization is inconceivable, and must fall. It may not be so in India or China, not yet, but for us, it is the Messiah—to come, or having come—or it is Nothing. Reason may tell us to refrain from harming our neighbors; it is only God who can command us to love our neighbors as ourselves. Reason may suggest that the Good is ever to be sought, regardless of the pain it might cause us, regardless even of death. But only the

One who loves can give us the strength to seek it, because it is He. Reason may falter in justifying itself, but the One who made the world in measure, weight, and number, guarantees also that reason is good and worthy of honor. And He promises more.

For Western civilization cannot be closed upon itself without dying. It longs for the "day of the Lord," and the New Jerusalem descending from heaven like a bride. If the people of the West begin to believe that matter is all there is, they shall cease to be people of the West; they shall part company with their heritage. If Europe continues to pursue the path of secular liberalism, and America follows a few steps behind, it will find the road leads not to an unprecedented age of reason, but to one or another all-too-familiar age: another age of Lenin and Stalin, or another age of Mohammed.

But in the end I believe the West will not commit suicide in this way. For the history of man will bear no such lid to be forced upon it. Whether Western civilization will revive in Europe, or in America, or rather in Nigeria and India and Korea and the Philippines, I do not know, and, were it not for my feelings of patriotism, I would not care. But it will

Dewey Decimates Tradition

Education has accordingly not only to safeguard an individual against the besetting erroneous tendencies of his own mind—its rashness, presumption, and preference of what chimes with self-interest to objective evidence—but also to undermine and destroy the accumulated and self-perpetuating prejudices of long ages.

John Dewey, *How We Think*

That there are such prejudices no one will deny. What conservatives deny is the wisdom of having an arm of the government wipe them out by replacing them with prejudices favored by the educational elites.

revive. There is hope for it, if only because it is the sole civilization founded upon hope, because it is founded, finally, upon the word of the One who keeps His promises.

NOTES

Chapter One

Ancient Greece: Love of Wisdom and Beauty

1. *Presocratic Fragments*, 80B1. The quote was widely known, for centuries; see Sextus Empiricus, *Against the Mathematicians*, 7.60.

2. Cf. Thucydides, *The Peloponnesian War*, 5.86–116.

3. See the story of Pandora in *Works and Days,* lines 24–82.

4. Cf. Herodotus, *The Persian Wars,* 1.60.

5. Plato, *Republic,* 8.555b–562a.

6. See *The Sand-Reckoner,* in *The Works of Archimedes,* ed. T. L. Heath (Cambridge, UK: Cambridge University Press, 1897). The account of the scientist's role in the defense of Syracuse, and his death, may be found in Plutarch's *Lives,* in the "Life of Marcellus."

7. Cf. Diogenes Laertius, *On the Lives and Opinions of Eminent Philosophers,* 9.44.

8. See Norman O. Brown's introduction to *Hesiod: Theogony* (Indianapolis: Bobbs-Merrill, 1953); Gilbert Murray, *Five Stages of Greek Religion* (New York: Doubleday, 1951).

9. Aeschylus relates the myth, which he uses to celebrate the establishment of a democratic Athens, in his *Oresteia* trilogy: *Agamemnon, The Libation Bearers,* and *The Eumenides.*

10. See for instance E. Norman Gardiner, *Athletics in the Ancient World* (Mineola, NY: Dover, 2002; first published by Oxford University Press, 1930), 55–58. How important this education was is made clear by Gardiner's pithy remark: "To be ashamed to be seen naked was to the Greek a

mark of a barbarian" (57). At age sixteen, a boy might be admitted to train at the men's clubs, the *gymnasia*. A charming summary of the whole "curriculum" can be found in *The Education of the Greek People and its Influence upon Civilization,* by Thomas Davidson (New York: Appleton, 1897).

11. See Herodotus, *The Persian Wars,* 7.228.

12. Aristotle, *Politics,* 1.1253a.

13. Plato, *Republic,* 1.338c.

14. Cf. Diogenes Laertius, 1.27.

15. Cf. Diogenes Laertius, 2.3.

16. Anaximander's thought survives in fragments, quoted by other authors. An excellent analysis of his contributions can be found in G. S. Kirk et al, *The Presocratic Philosophers,* 2nd edition (Cambridge, UK: Cambridge University Press, 1983), 100–142.

17. Cf. Aristotle, *Politics,* 1.1259a.

18. Cf. Diogenes Laertius, 8.1–50.

19. The account is first found in John Philoponus, a sixth-century commentator on Aristotle's *De Anima* (*De Intellectu,* Book XV, 29).

20. For Plato's doctrine of the forms, and the soul's natural longing to know universal truth, see, for example, *Phaedo,* 67ff.; *Meno,* 81ff.; *Phaedrus,* 244–56; *Republic* 6.505–7.520.

21. *Republic,* 4.435–48.

22. Aristotle, *Physics,* 2.194b–195a; also *Metaphysics,* 12.6–10. "The act of contemplation is what is most pleasant and best. If, then, God is always in that good state in which we sometimes are, this compels our wonder; and if in a better this compels it yet more. And God is in a better state." (6.72b)

23. See Aristotle, *Nicomachean Ethics,* especially Book X, 1176a–1179b.

24. Aristotle, *Politics,* Book I, 1259b, 1260b; Book II, 1260b–1262b.

Chapter Two

Rome: An Empire of Tradition and Patriarchy

1. Torquatus figures prominently in Book VII of Livy's History of Rome. The story was as well known as legends of Washington used to be in America; cf. Sallust, *The Conspiracy of Catiline,* 52. William Smith, in *The Dictionary of Greek and Roman Antiquities* (1870), gives the full account, with citations in ancient authors (1162–63).

2. The story, possibly merely legendary, is found in Livy, *History of Rome,* 2.4–5.

3. *History of Rome,* 1.23.

4. Cornelia was the most learned woman of her day, and arguably the noblest matron Rome ever produced; see Plutarch, *Lives* ("Tiberius Gracchus," "Gaius Gracchus"). For the story of Cloelia, see Livy, *History of Rome,* 2.13.

5. Livy, *History of Rome,* 3.26–30.

6. *Aeneid,* 2.717–24.

7. It was in 494 BC; see Livy, *History of Rome,* 2.23–32.

8. See Polybius, *The Rise of the Roman Empire,* 3.83–85; Livy, *History of Rome,* 22.4–7.

9. For Fabius' career, see Plutarch's *Lives;* for Scipio's victory at Zama, see Livy, *History of Rome,* 30.32–35.

10. *Aeneid,* 8.671–713.

11. Livy, *History of Rome,* 2.32.

12. The complete story is laid out in Smith, *Dictionary of Greek and Roman Antiquities* (1870), 737. It was perhaps Rome's most beloved heroic legend; see Cicero, *On Duties* 3.99–115.

13. See Polybius, 3.37.

14. Chesterton, Nietzsche, Gibbon

15. The decline in the Spartan population was dramatic and well-noted by many ancient writers. Cicero gives a most politically incorrect reason for it: "Spartan girls care more for wrestling, bathing in the River Eurotas, the sun, dust, and martial exercise than they do for the barbarous bearing of offspring" (*Tusculan Disputations,* 2.36).

Chapter Three

Israel: How God Changed the World

1. The following is a summary of the Babylonian epic, *Enuma Elish.*

2. See Plutarch, *Isis and Osiris,* 356, 358b.

3. Augustine, *City of God,* 15.5.

4. The institution of the Eleusinian mysteries is recounted in the Homeric *Hymn to Demeter.* They lasted for almost two millennia, until Emperor Theodosius shut down their sanctuaries in 392.

5. The initiation rites of the Dionysian cult are nicely preserved in the frescoes of the so-called Villa of the Mysteries, in Pompeii. The induction of the protagonist into the mysteries of Isis and Osiris is the climax of Apuleius' comic novel, *The Golden Ass.*

6. Thammuz was the Phoenician Adonis, whose death the goddess of love mourned (cf. Ezek. 8:14). His female devotees in Syria would celebrate his feast days by repairing to the temple of the Astarte (Venus) at Gebal, for orgies.

7. In love with a married woman, that is; see Horace, *Satires* 1.2; Cato hated the whorehouses (Livy, *History of Rome* 34.4), but Lucretius would use the advice to help a young man guard against love (*On the Nature of Things,* 4.1062). Cicero defends the civic usefulness of whorehouses (*Pro Coelio,* 20).

8. Cicero was so distraught, he left his wife behind and retreated to his villa in Astura, south of Rome, where he wrote a book called the *Consolatio,* most of which is now lost.

Chapter Four

The Early Church: Charity and Tolerance Are Born

1. From *The Greek Anthology*, ed. Peter Jay (Hammondsworth: Penguin, 1981).

2. Catullus 63 is the most famous poetic treatment of the Great Mother cult; Attis, the speaker, castrates himself in a frenzy of devotion. Catullus' concluding prayer is rich: he begs Cybele to drive *other* men into madness. See also Lucretius, *On the Nature of Things,* 2.599–643; Ovid, *Fasti,* 4.183.

3. Athenagoras defends Christians against the common charge, in his *Embassy for the Christians,* 31–36, addressed to Marcus Aurelius in 177.

4. See his discussion of that letter in *Selected Letters of Pliny the Younger* (Boston: D. C. Heath, 1937).

5. Augustine, *City of God,* 14.28.

6. See Justin Martyr, *First Apology,* 15–17, 27, 29, 67; *Second Apology,* 2.

7. See Julian's letter to Arsacius, ca. 360 AD; in Edward J. Chinnock, *A Few Notes on Julian and a Translation of His Public Letters* (London: David Nutt, 1901) 75–78.

8. Jerome, *Letters,* 22.30.

9. That is one of the brilliant insights of Etienne Gilson; see, for instance, his work *Christianity and Philosophy* (New York: Sheed and Ward, 1939).

10. See Paulinus of Milan, ca. 412, *The Life of Saint Ambrose,* 24.

11. The delightful story of Daniel may be found in *Three Byzantine Saints: Contemporary Biographies of St. Daniel the Stylite, St. Theodore of Sykeon and St. John the Almsgiver*, trans. Elizabeth Dawes, and introductions and notes by Norman H. Baynes, (London: Blackwell Publishing, 1948).

12. Bede, 4.24. The translation of Caedmon's hymn is mine.

13. Alcuin wrote that rhetorical question in a letter to Bishop Higbald of the monastery at Lindisfarne, in 797.

14. The Circumcellionists, and perhaps some of the more zealous Donatists, sought martyrdom. The Manichees preached the evil of the body. The Docetists believed that Jesus did not genuinely come in the flesh. Marcion in Ephesus taught that the God of the Old Testament was evil. The Arians believed that Jesus was the highest of all creatures, but still a creature. A quick introduction to such beliefs may be found in Chas S. Clifton, *Encyclopedia of Heresies and Heretics* (Santa Barbara, CA: ABC–CLIO, 1992).

15. See the final chapter of *The Abolition of Man* (New York: Macmillan, 1955).

16. So Bede recounts in his *Ecclesiastical History of the English People*, 2.1.

17. See the Koran, 5:64, and the discussion of Allah's unfettered will, in Robert Spencer, *The Politically Incorrect Guide™ to Islam* (Washington, DC: Regnery, 2005).

Chapter Five

The High Middle Ages: The Bright Ages

1. The well-attested phenomenon is called the Medieval Climate Optimum. See, for example, "The Science Won't Stay Settled!", in *World Concerns*, 2.1 (June 9, 1998).

2. The poems may be found, in the original language, in Maxwell S. Luria and Richard L. Hoffman, *Middle English Lyrics* (New York: W. W. Norton, 1974). The translations are mine.

3. See, for instance, *The Divine Names*, 697b–700c.

4. The complete texts of Suger's accounts *On His Administration* and *On the Dedication of the Church of Saint-Denis* may be found in Erwin Panofsky, *Abbot Suger on the Abbey Church of Saint-Denis and Its Treasures* (Princeton: Princeton University Press, 1946); see pp. 47–49 for the dedication upon the doors, in a slightly different translation.

5. See *The Stones of Venice,* 2.6, "The Nature of the Gothic" (1851).

6. See V. A. Kolve, *The Play Called Corpus Christi* (Stanford, CA: Stanford University Press), 1966.

7. See "The Deliverance of Souls" in *The Wakefield Mystery Plays,* ed. Martial Rose (New York: W. W. Norton, 1961).

8. For example, Bernard Spivack, *Shakespeare and the Allegory of Evil* (New York: Columbia University Press, 1958), traces the influence upon Shakespeare's villains of the "Vice" figure in medieval drama.

9. From *Saint Louis' Advice to His Son*, in *Medieval Civilization*, trans. and eds. Dana Munro and George Clarke Sellery (New York: The Century Company, 1910), paragraphs 18 and 21.

10. Actually, the witch trials begin in earnest only in the late 1400s. Dante expressed the most common attitude towards witches, at least among learned men of the high Middle Ages, that they were mainly bunko artists. He placed them in Hell among the fraudulent; see *Inferno* 20.

11. See for instance the phallic procession in Aristophanes, *The Acharnians,* 241ff.

12. See chapter 2, "The World Francis Found," in Chesterton, *Saint Francis of Assisi* (New York: George H. Doran, 1924).

13. See Father Cuthbert, *The Life of Saint Francis of Assisi* (London: Longmans, Green, and Co.: 1927), 194–95; the story is told originally in *The Little Flowers of Saint Francis,* ch. 21 (see *Francis of Assisi: The Prophet* [New York: New City Press, 2001]).

14. See Villon's "Ballade of the Ladies of Bygone Time," in *The Testament, in Poems of Francois Villon*, tr. Norman Cameron (London: Harcourt, Brace, and World, 1951).

15. From Sermon 7 *On the Song of Songs;* see G. R. Evans, *Bernard of Clairvaux: Selected Works* (Mahwah, N. J.: Paulist Press, 1987).

16. From Frederick Goldin, *Lyrics of the Troubadours and Trouveres* (Gloucester, MA: Peter Smith, 1983), 26–33.

17. See part 11 of Beroul, *The Romance of Tristan,* tr. Alan S. Fedrick (London: Penguin, 1970).

18. See Chretien, *The Knight of the Cart,* in *Arthurian Romances* (London: Penguin, 1991).

19. That is "Rule" 26 of the ironical *De Amore* of Andrew the Chaplain (Andreas Capellanus).

20. See *The Twelve Patriarchs,* in *Richard of Saint Victor,* ed. and trans. Grover Zinn (Mahwah, N. J.: Paulist Press, 1979).

21. That is the meaning of the title of Bonaventure's greatest work, the *Itinerarium Mentis in Deum.*

22. See *The Book of Secrets of Albertus Magnus,* ed. Michael R. Best and Frank H. Brightman (London: Oxford University Press, 1974).

23. In *Summa Theologica* 1. q. 88, Thomas makes it quite clear that man cannot know immaterial things directly, but only by reasoning from those things he can sense, as from effect to cause.

24. On whether telling an untruth can be justified, see *Summa Theologica* 2.2 q. 110; on equity, see 2.2 q. 120.

25. *Summa Theologica* 1 q. 2, art. 2.

26. See G. K. Chesterton, *Saint Thomas Aquinas: "The Dumb Ox"* (New York: Image Books, 1956), 74–78.

27. See: https://netfiles.uiuc.edu/rwb/www/15c/medieval-lecture.jpg.

28. See *The Land of Cockaygne* in *Early Middle English Verse and Prose,* 2nd ed., ed. J. A. W. Bennett and G. V. Smithers (Oxford: Clarendon Press, 1968), 136–44.

29. See his *Micrologus,* ca.1026.

30. See *The Oxford Book of Medieval Latin Verse,* ed. F. J. E. Raby (Oxford: Clarendon Press, 1959), no. 183, lines 45–48. The translation is mine.

Chapter Six

The Renaissance: It's Not What You Think

1. According to Georges Duby, these popular reforms "helped create a space in which communal gatherings could take place," encouraging the growth of villages "in the shadow of the church, in the zone of immunity where violence was prohibited under peace regulations." See *A History of*

Private Life, II: Revelations of the Medieval World (Cambridge: Harvard University Press, 1988), 27.

2. Thomas Aquinas, *Summa Theologica* 1.109, 114; 2.1.80.

3. The work is by Jacobus Sprenger and Heinrich Kramer (1486); see the translation by Montague Summers (London: Folio Society, 1968).

4. See Thomas S. Kuhn, *The Copernican Revolution* (Cambridge: Harvard University Press, 1957), 217–19.

5. The meditations are Donne's *Devotions Upon Emergent Occasions* (1624); Izaak Walton tells of his shroud portrait at the end of his *Life of Dr. John Donne* (1640); see Alexander M. Witherspoon and Frank J. Warnke, *Seventeenth Century Prose and Poetry* (New York: Harcourt, Brace, Jovanovich, 1963), 269.

6. See Eugenio Garin, *Prosatori Latini del Quattrocento* (Milan: Ricciardi, 1952), 829–31; translation mine.

7. See William Ellery Leonard and Stanley Barney Smith, eds., *T. Lvcreti Cari De Rervm Natvra Libri Sex* (Madison, Wis.: University of Wisconsin Press, 1942), 108–110.

8. See David M. Whitford, "The Papal Antichrist : Martin Luther and the Underappreciated Influence of Lorenzo Valla," in *Renaissance Quarterly* 61.1 (Spring, 2008), 26–52. Valla's *Dialogue on Free Will* (1439) set the stage both for Renaissance skepticism regarding man's freedom and the Protestant assertion that unredeemed man's will was wholly bound by sin.

9. See *The Divine Weeks,* tr. Josuah Sylvester; ed. Susan Snyder (New York: Oxford University Press, 1979).

10. For the yawn with which the Church greeted the heliocentrism of Nicholas of Cusa, see Kuhn, *The Copernican Revolution*, 197, 233–35.

11. See Kuhn, *The Copernican Revolution,* 188, 193.

12. The famous dictum is *"Pluralitas non est ponenda sine necessitate,"* meaning, roughly, that the rule of parsimony is to be used in explaining phenomena.

13. In Book One of *The Advancement of Learning* (1605), Bacon accuses the Aristotelians of having spun out "laborious webs of learning" on "vermiculate questions." He does not so much argue against them as ridicule.

14. The anecdote is well known, but it may be an invention. There was a meeting in 1802 between Laplace and Napoleon, nor was the tyrant entirely pleased by the "mechanics" of the heavens. That at least is the

account given by the astronomer William Herschel, who was present. See Constance Lubbock, *The Herschel Chronicle* (1933), 310.

15. Richard M. Weaver, *Ideas Have Consequences* (Chicago and London: Chicago University Press, 1948), 3.

16. The Portuguese missionary was Francisco d'Alvarez. The 1533 Basel edition of Robert the Monk's account of the First Crusade, *Bellum Christianum principum*, includes letters from one David, the chief of the Nestorian Christians in Ethiopia, appealing to his comrades in the faith to unite with him against the Muslims.

17. See "On Cannibals," in *Montaigne: Selected Essays,* tr. William Hazlitt, ed. Richard Bates (New York: Modern Library, 1949), 74–89.

18. Lawrence Washington bought Sulgrave Manor in 1539.

19. Note the expression of potent desire in Saint John of the Cross's best known poem, "En un noche oscura":

> On a night of darkness,
>
> kindled with the flames of longing in love,
>
> oh blessed chance!
>
> I left, and no one knew,
>
> for all my house was stilled in sleep. (translation mine)

For John's poetry in Spanish and English, and for an excellent discussion of the Carmelites, see Gerald Brennan, *St. John of the Cross: His Life and Poetry* (Cambridge, UK: Cambridge University Press, 1973).

Chapter Seven

The Enlightenment: Liberty and Tyranny

1. Kant, *What Is Enlightenment?* From *Kant,* ed. Gabriele Rabel (Oxford: Clarendon Press, 1963), 140.

2. Burke, *Reflections on the Revolution in France* (London: J. M. Dent, 1910), 84; Burke was writing in 1790.

3. See Luther's 1545 Preface to his *Complete Latin Writings,* from *Luther's Works,* vol. 34, ed. and trans. Lewis W. Spitz (Philadelphia: Muhlenberg Press, 1960), 327–38.

4. The slogan attributed to the Dominican friar Johann Tetzel epitomized the sale of indulgences: "As soon as the coin in the coffer rings, the soul from purgatory springs." That prompted a reply from numbers 27 and 28

of Luther's famous Ninety-Five Theses (1517).

5. I'm not being fair to Pelagius (c.350–c.418), the monk for whom the heresy is named. He believed that Augustine's doctrine that we must rely wholly upon God's grace provided people with an excuse for moral laxity. He, as much as anyone, would despise what has come to be called Pelagianism—the belief that we are all naturally good and can merit salvation by our own middling efforts: "If it should be thought to be nature's fault that some have been unrighteous, I shall use the evidence of the scriptures, which everywhere lay upon sinners the heavy weight of the charge of having used their own will and do not excuse them for having acted only under the constraint of nature" (Letter to Demetrias, 7).

6. From the Council of Trent (1547): "When the Apostle says that man is justified by faith and freely, these words are to be understood in that sense in which the uninterrupted unanimity of the Catholic Church has held and expressed them, namely, that we are therefore said to be justified by faith, because faith is the beginning of human salvation, the foundation and root of all justification, without which it is impossible to please God and to come to the fellowship of His sons; and we are therefore said to be justified gratuitously, because none of those things that precede justification, whether faith or works, merit the grace of justification" (Session 6; Decree Concerning Justification, ch. 8).

7. Calvin, see *Commentary on Saint John*, 6:41–45; *Institutes of the Christian Religion*, 3.21, on efficacy of grace; 3.19, on the fact that even the saintly Christian merits nothing by his works.

8. Thomas Middleton wrote a rakish satire against them, *The Family of Love* (1608). The Familists were followers of one Hendrik Niclaes, a Dutch merchant. He urged all men and women, from all nations and faiths, to join him in discarding dogma and living in peace. Christopher Hill gives the Adamites and other sexual radicals a great leftist cheer in *The World Turned Upside Down: Radical Ideas During the English Revolution* (London: Penguin, 1975).

9. Hobbes, *Leviathan*, 1.13.

10. "When Brutus inspired the Romans with a boundless love of liberty," wrote Bossuet, thinking not of the saintliness of kings but of God's providential order, "it did not occur to him that he was planting the seeds of that unbridled license through which the very tyranny he wished to destroy

was one day to be restored in a harsher form than under the Tarquins" (*Discourse on Universal History*, 3.8; trans. Elborg Forster [Chicago: Chicago University Press, 1976]), 375.

11. Lucretius, *On the Nature of Things,* 1.418–48, 2.62–141.

12. From "Mock On, Mock On, Voltaire, Rousseau", 9–12 (ca. 1810).

13. Cragg, *The Church and the Age of Reason, 1648–1789* (Hammondsworth: Penguin, 1960), 12.

14. See Norman L. Torrey, ed., *Les Philosophes* (New York: Capricorn Books, 1960), 185.

15. Not until 1828 did Roman Catholics in England enjoy full voting rights; by then, toleration would be championed not by the crown but by the many and various sects of dissenters from the established Church of England.

16. The businessmen of Manchester were the economic and social liberals of the day, the egalitarians, who understood equality only as leveling. See chapter four, "Romantics and Utilitarians," in Russell Kirk, *The Conservative Mind: From Burke to Santayana* (Washington, DC: Regnery, 1986), 99–129.

17. The story of Father Ricci (1552–1616) is told by Jonathan D. Spence, in *The Memory Palace of Matteo Ricci* (London: Penguin, 1985).

18. See Bernal Diaz, *The Conquest of New Spain,* trans. J. M. Cohen (Hammondsworth: Penguin, 1963).

19. Burke accepted Franklin's views on the unfairness of British taxation of America; see Carl Van Doren, *Benjamin Franklin* (New York: Viking, 1938), 331–35.

20. John Witherspoon, for instance, was a Presbyterian minister; the bold John Hancock was a deeply devout man who implored his fellow members of the First Continental Congress to turn remorsefully to God for forgiveness in their troubled times. The presidency, and the accident of its being occupied by Christians more or less veering away from Trinitarianism, has tended to overshadow who the rest of the men were and what they believed.

21. Jefferson called it "The Life and Morals of Jesus of Nazareth," and "offered it as proof that he whom the priests and Pharisees called an infidel was 'a true Christian' in the only sense that mattered" (Merrill D. Peterson, in *The Portable Jefferson* [New York: Penguin, 1977], xxxviii.)

22. Adams to Jefferson, in their very old age, January 22, 1825: "The Europeans are all deeply tainted with prejudices both Ecclesiastical, and Temporal which they can never get rid of; they are all infected with Episcopal and Presbyterian Creeds, and confessions of faith, They all believe that great principle, which has produced this boundless Universe. Newtons Universe, and Hershells universe, came down to this little Ball, to be spit-upon by Jews; and untill this awful blasphemy is got rid of, there never will be any liberal science in the world." From *The Adams-Jefferson Letters*, ed. Lester J. Capon, vol. 2 (Chapel Hill, NC: University of North Carolina Press, 1959).

23. See Locke, *Second Treatise on Government,* ch. 6, "Of Paternal Power."

24. See *The Federalist*, no. 55.

25. In 1787, Adams in fact writes a *Defence of the Constitutions of Government of the United States of America* against the radical French democrat Turgot, who criticized it for its system of checks and balances, blending monarchy, aristocracy, and democracy.

26. The infamous Peter Singer, co-editor with Paola Cavalieri of *The Great Ape Project: Equality Beyond Humanity* (London: Fourth Estate, 1993).

27. It is the academic liberal, not the conservative, who nowadays writes with glee about the racism of the Enlightenment, tainting everyone from Locke (who profited indirectly by the slave trade), Voltaire, the American Founders, Kant, Hegel, and many others. It is interesting that for two hundred years, the more *conservative* societies of Catholic Spain and Italy will suffer the same rationalist judgment of inferiority; cf. the appreciative but almost insufferable condescension of the great Hawthorne towards Italy in *The Marble Faun.*

28. Aristotle, *Nicomachean Ethics,* 1.3.1095a.

29. See D. E. Smith, *History of Mathematics* (New York: Dover, 1958), 382.

30. Hume, *An Enquiry Concerning Human Understanding,* section 4, "Sceptical Doubts Concerning the Operations of the Understanding."

31. See Kant, *Foundations of the Metaphysics of Morals,* trans. Lewis White Beck (Indianapolis: Bobbs Merrill, 1959), 37.

32. Boswell, *The Life of Samuel Johnson* (New York: Modern Library,

1952), 807.

33. Opposing the American argument for independence, Johnson wrote, "How is it that we hear the loudest yelps for liberty among the drivers of negroes" (*Life of Samuel Johnson*, 747–48). Boswell continues, giving us Johnson's empassioned argument against what Boswell called a "humanely regulated" British slave trade (748–50).

Chapter Eight

The Nineteenth Century: Man Is a God; Man Is a Beast

1. See the mild feminism of Chapter 12, "Concerning the Arrangement of Life."

2. Wister, *The Virginian: A Horseman of the Plains* (1902). Wister dedicated it to Theodore Roosevelt, who would also have appreciated its elegiac regrets for a past heroic age.

3. Byron died on April 19, 1824, of a fever he caught while preparing for an attack on the Turkish-held fortress of Lepanto.

4. "Though often possessing well-developed body and arms, the Papuan has very small legs; thus reminding us of the man-like apes, in which there is no great contrast in size between the hind and fore limbs." Spencer, in *First Principles of a New System of Philosophy* (1862), ch. 15, par. 121.

5. See, for example, the darling of the 1960s, Herbert Marcuse, *Eros and Civilization: A Philosophical Inquiry into Freud* (Boston: Beacon Press, 1966).

6. For instance, the free-love community begun by John Humphrey Noyes in 1848, in Oneida, New York.

7. That is a paraphrase of the rhetorical cry that ends Marx's and Engel's *Communist Manifesto*.

8. That is the elegiac thrust of Freud's *Civilization and Its Discontents* (1929).

9. For the notion of "touchstones," see *Essays in Criticism, Second Series*, "The Study of Poetry" (1880); for "sweetness and light," see the Preface to *Culture and Anarchy* (1869).

10. "This has to be said: by ceasing to take part in the official worship of God as it now is . . . thou hast one guilt the less, and that a great one: thou dost not take part in treating God as a fool." From *This Has to Be Said; So*

Be It Now Said (1855). See Kierkegaard, *Attack Upon 'Christendom'*, tr. Walter Lowrie (Boston: Beacon Press, 1960), 60.

11. For Newman, the conscience is more than a policeman; it urges us on to the knowledge of God: "It is not wonderful that the notices, which He indirectly gives us through our conscience, of His own nature are such as to make us understand that He is like Himself and nothing else" (*An Essay in Aid of a Grammar of Assent*, 1.5). It does not allow us to do as we please; it encourages us to do as God pleases.

12. Witness Adams on the breadth of the Middle Ages, as compared against his own utilitarian time: "A Church which embraced, with equal sympathy, and within a hundred years, the Virgin, Saint Bernard, William of Champeaux and the School of Saint Victor . . . , Saint Thomas Aquinas, and Saint Bonaventure, was more liberal than any modern State can afford to be . . . Such elasticity long ago vanished from human thought." From *Mont-Saint-Michel and Chartres* (New York: Mentor, 1961), ch. 16, 351.

13. In *The Outline of Sanity* (New York: Dodd, Mead, and Co., 1927), Chesterton called himself a capitalist, for the simple reason that he wanted everybody to enjoy capital. He distrusted both the capitalists who were constantly pleading that they could not pay higher wages because they were on the brink of bankruptcy, and the socialists whose answer to the inequality is a controlled state that everybody detests equally.

14. See Ruskin, *Unto This Last* (1860).

15. See, for example, *The Wedding Sermon,* in *Mystical Poems of Nuptial Love,* ed. Terence L. Connolly, S. J. (Boston: Bruce Humphries, 1938).

16. Dostoyevsky, *The Idiot* (1869), part 4, ch. 7.

17. Dickens is a merciless critic of the Church in *A Child's History of England;* his prejudices would remain with him to the end, in his incomplete novel of suppressed desire, *Edwin Drood,* set in a place called "Cloisterham."

18. *The Brothers Karamazov,* 1.2.7.

19. Ibid., 1.1.2.

20. Ibid., 2.5.4.

21. Ibid., 2.4.7.

Chapter Nine

The Twentieth Century: A Century of Blood

1. See Tom Bethell's account of Carson's statistics-cooking, in *The Politically Incorrect Guide to Science* (Washington, DC: Regnery, 2005).

2. See Anne Barbeau Gardiner's devastating critique of Sanger's blood-lust, in "Margaret Sanger's Multifaceted Defense of Abortion and Infanticide," in *Life and Learning XVI* (2006), 413–38.

3. Consider the bland self-satisfaction with which Dewey assumes that the school is a social controller, in place and time: "It is the business of the school environment to eliminate, so far as possible, the unworthy features of the existing environment from influence upon mental habitudes. It establishes a purified medium of action. Selection aims not only at simplifying but at weeding out what is undesirable. Every society gets encumbered with what is trivial, with dead wood from the past, and with what is positively perverse." From *Democracy and Education* (New York: Macmillan, 1916), 2.4, "The School as a Special Environment."

4. The September 10, 1965, edition of *Life* foretold "superbabies with improved minds and bodies, and even a kind of immortality."

5. Typical of the caution and moderation of most of the documents of Vatican II is the one that shook the Church most thoroughly, *Sacrosanctum Concilium*. So we read therein that Gregorian chant "should be given pride of place in liturgical services" (116). In D*ignitatis Humanae*, liberals say, the Church finally caught up with the idea of religious freedom. Actually, the Church was calling the world, especially the communist world, to return to sanity: "Every family . . . is a society with its own rights . . . The civil authority must therefore recognize the right of parents to choose with genuine freedom schools or other means of education" (1.5). See *Vatican Council II: The Conciliar and Post Conciliar Documents*, ed. Austin Flannery, O. P. (Northport, NY: Costello, 1975).

6. Friedrich von Hayek, *The Road to Serfdom* (Chicago: University of Chicago Press, 1944).

7. Wendell Berry, *Sex, Economy, Freedom and Community: Eight Essays* (New York: Pantheon Books, 1993).

8. The attribution of the saying to Lenin is ubiquitous. For its effects

upon a real political thinker and a genuine human being, Vaclav Havel, see Robert Pirro, "Vaclav Havel and the Political Uses of Tragedy," in *Political Theory* (April, 2002), 246.

9. See Sally J. Taylor, *Stalin's Apologist: Walter Duranty: The New York Times' Man in Moscow* (New York and Oxford: Oxford University Press, 1990).

10. See Michael J. Arlen, *Passage to Ararat* (New York: Farrar, Straus, and Giroux, 1975).

11. Wilson's preference for the parliamentary system can be seen, for example, in his essay *The English Constitution* (1890–1891). See *Woodrow Wilson: Essential Writings and Speeches of the Scholar-President,* ed. Mario R. DiNunzio (New York and London: New York University Press), 282–296.

12. For example: "We do not want word to go out that we want to exterminate the Negro population and the minister is the man who can straighten out that idea if it ever occurs to any of their more rebellious members." (Margaret Sanger to Clarence Gamble, October 19, 1939, quoted in Linda Gordon, *Woman's Body, Woman's Right: Birth Control in America*, 2nd edition (New York: Penguin Books, 1990), 332–33.

13. For Kinsey as a combination of folk-hero and liberator, see the biography written by his old colleague, Wardell B. Pomeroy, *Dr. Kinsey and the Institute for Sex Research* (New York: Harper and Row, 1972).

14. The case was *Grove City College v. Bell*, 465 US (55), 1984.

15. See Eliot, *Notes Toward the Definition of a Culture* (New York: Harcourt, Brace, 1949).

16. Muggeridge, *Something Beautiful for God: Mother Teresa of Calcutta* (Garden City, N.Y.: Image Books, 1977).

17. The great exposé of Kinsey is Judith A. Reisman's *Kinsey, Sex, and Fraud: The Indoctrination of a People* (Lafayette, LA: Lochinvar-Huntington House, 1990).

18. Margaret Mead, *Coming of Age in Samoa* (New York: W. Morrow and Co., 1928).

19. For a brief account of Goedel's religious views, see John W. Dawson, Jr., *Logical Dilemmas: The Life and Work of Kurt Goedel* (Wellesley, MA: AK Peters, 1997), 210–12. Goedel believed that the principles of his

Incompleteness Theorem could be used to formalize the famous Ontological Argument of Saint Anselm, proving the existence of God.

20. The river had actually been plagued by fires since 1936. The notorious fire on June 22, 1969 may not even have been the worst.

21. Chesterton has some fun at the expense of the utopian visions of his friend Wells; see *Heretics* (Thirsk: House of Stratus, 2001), ch. 5, 26–35.

22. A. J. Ayer, *Language, Truth, and Logic* (New York: Dover, 1952).

23. The Pruitt-Igoe complex was heralded as a leap forward in urban renewal. Construction began in 1951; demolition began on March 16, 1972.

24. See Jerome Lawrence and Robert E. Lee, *Inherit the Wind* (New York: Bantam, 1955), 114

25. Dave Kopel and Michael Tanner, "Welfare Reform: Next Steps for Colorado," Independence Institute, January 14, 1997.

26. See, for example, the "Allocution of Pope Pius XII to the Congress of the International Union of Catholic Women's Leagues," Rome, Italy, September 11, 1947.

27. See his essay, "The Home of a Man," in *What's Wrong With the World* (1910).

28. See the work of Allan Carlson of the Howard Center, "The De-Institutionalization of Marriage: The Case of Sweden," in *The Family in America,* vol. 20 (2–3), February–March, 2006.

29. E. F. Schumacher, *Small Is Beautiful: Economics as if People Mattered* (New York: Harper Colophon Books, 1975).

30. Romano Guardini, *The End of the Modern World: A Search for Orientation,* tr. Joseph Theman and Herbert Burke; ed. Frederick Wilhelmsen (New York: Sheed and Ward, 1956).

31. Joseph Pieper, *Leisure: The Basis of Culture,* tr. Alexander Dru (New York: Pantheon, 1952).

32. See John Paul II, *The Theology of the Body according to John Paul II: Human Love in the Divine Plan* (Boston: Pauline Books, 1997).

INDEX

A

Abdala the Saracen, 172

The Abolition of Man (Lewis), 302

abortion, 11, 68, 289

Abraham, 79, 106, 233, 253, 263; God of, 67–70, 70–74; Isaac, sacrifice of and, 71–72

Academici (Cicero), 99

Achilles, 14, 20–21, 31

Adamists, 206–7

Adams, Henry, 127

Adams, John, 31, 224–25, 228, 263, 296

Adams, John Quincy, 127

Adams, Samuel, 224

Aeneas, 44–45

Aeneid (Virgil), 47, 51, 55, 57

Aeschylus, 12, 18, 239, 308

Agamemnon, 12

agnosticism, 98

Alaric, 65–66

Albert the Great, Saint, 154

Alcibiades, 30

Alcuin, 124

Alexander the Great, 13, 75, 84

Alexander VI, Pope, 191

Alien and Sedition Acts, 224

alienation, 4, 5, 80, 200

Ambrose, Saint, 120, 187

American Revolution, 2–3, 14

Ames, Fisher, 230

Amoretti (Spenser), 170

Anaximander, 27, 28, 29

Anaximenes, 26

Anchises, 44–45

ancient Greece. as American model, 228–30; art in, 8, 9, 261; democracy and, 4, 7, 8, 15–16, 22–25, 31–33, 37, 229; drama and, 9, 184; fall of, 2–4, 4–7, 17–18; family and, 5, 24–25, 36; fertility cults and, 10–13; freedom and, 36; government and, 8, 9, 12–13, 13–17; homosexuality in, 6; love and, 26, 91; materialism and, 27, 34; medicine and, 21; moral relativism and, 1, 19–25; natural law and, 17–19, 22–25; patriarchy and, 53; patriotism and, 25; philosophy and, 1, 8, 9–10, 15, 26; piety and, 6–7, 18; *polis* and, 12, 13–17, 23; religion and, 10–13; science and, 8, 25–29; slavery and, 6, 8, 128; sports and, 3, 21; State and, 33–38, 45; superior culture of, 1, 7–10; tradition and, 12, 14, 17–19, 24; women and, 8, 25, 42

Antigone (Sophocles), 22–25

Antoninus Pius, 110

Anubis, 51

Apollo, 11, 12

Apollonius of Perga, 232

Apology for Poetry (Sidney), 176–77

Appias Claudius, 46

Aquinas, Thomas, Saint, 109, 112, 148, 155–58, 160–62, 169, 183, 234

Arcadia (Sidney), 186

Archesilaus, 99

Archimedes, 9

An Argument Against the Abolishing of Christianity (Swift), 205

Arianism, 126–27, 194

Aristarchus, 194

Aristippus, 98

Aristophanes, 19

Aristotle, xii, 17, 84, 98, 114, 183, 188–89; causes and, 33–35; family and, 36; good and, 30; Middle Ages and, 154–55, 156–57; morality and, 33; reason and, 231–32

Arnold, Matthew, 259–63, 273

art. ancient Greece and, 8, 9, 261; Israel and, 69; man, perfection of and, 244; Middle Ages and, 164; modern, 151; nineteenth century and, 260–63; Renaissance and, 9, 147, 167, 171,

art. ancient Greece and, (continued) 182–85; Rome and, 41–42; twentieth century and, 297–301
ascetism, 46–47
atheism, xii, 124, 209
Athena, 8, 12
Athens, Greece. *See* ancient Greece
Athletics in the Ancient World (Gardiner), 21
Atwood, Margaret, 261
Augustine, Saint, xii, 59, 104, 109, 110, 113, 114, 116, 120, 134, 186, 250, 259
Augustus, 44, 51, 52, 55, 56, 59–61, 65
Autobiography (Mill), 255
Averroes, 155, 161
Avicenna, 161
Ayer, A. J., 303

B
Babylonians, 9
Bacon, Francis, 196, 197
Barber, Francis, 241
Barnaby Rudge (Dickens), 265
Bartholomew, Saint, 182–83
Bede, Venerable, 123
Beethoven, Ludwig von, 151
Belloc, Hilaire, 127, 306
Benedict, Saint, 121, 135
Beowulf, 123, 124
Berg, Alban, 287
Bernard of Clairvaux, Saint, 151, 160
Bernini, Gian Lorenzo, 188
Beroul, 152
Berry, Duc de, 148
Berry, Wendell, 289
Beyond Good and Evil (Nietzsche), 247
Bible, 61, 90, 114, 194, 206
Bill of Rights, 39
birth control, 41, 293, 294, 303–6
Bishop Blougram's Apology (Browning), 268
Blake, William, 210, 271
Bleak House (Dickens), 266, 268–71
Boccaccio, 148
Boethius, 114
Bonaventure, Saint, 112, 154
Boniface, 95, 129
The Book of the Courtier (Castiglione), 188
Boswell, James, 239, 240
Botticelli, 179–80
Bracciolini, Poggio, 184
Bradbury, Ray, 284
Bradford, William, 219, 220, 221, 222
Brando, Marlon, 300
Brave New World (Huxley), 304
Brewster, William, 219
Brideshead Revisited (Waugh), 93, 306
The Brothers Karamazov (Dostoyevsky), 266, 271–72

Browning, Robert, 265, 267–68, 273–74
Brownson, Orestes, 296
Brutus, 42
Bryan, William Jennings, 301
Buddhism, 7, 86, 284
Burke, Edmund, xii, 43, 203, 215–16, 223, 236–38, 268, 287, 306
Byron, Lord, 254–56

C
Cabot, John, 218
Caedmon, 123–24
Calhoun, John C., 296
Calvin, John, 182, 185, 194, 206
Camillus, 47
Camoens, Luis Vaz de, 199
Candide (Voltaire), 213
The Canterbury Tales (Chaucer), 136–37, 148, 163, 164–65, 193
Canticle of Brother Sun (Francis of Assisi), 148
Canzoniere (Petrarch), 93
capitalism, 163
Capra, Frank, 300
Caravaggio, 93, 200
Carcopino, Jerome, 41, 57
Carson, Rachel, 282
Casti Conubii (Pius XI), 304
Castiglione, Baldassare, 188
Catholic Church. Enlightenment and, 213–14; Luther, Martin and, 205; piety and, 214; social teaching of, 250; superstition and, 241; twentieth century and, 284–85
Cato, 42, 91
Cat's Cradle, 284
Celestial Mechanics (Laplace), 196
charity, 97, 114, 128–29
Charles I, King, 44
Charles II, King, 222
Charles V, Emperor, 207
Chaucer, Geoffrey, 114, 136–37, 148, 163, 164–65, 193
Chesterton, G. K., 61, 147, 263, 285, 287, 306
"Children? Not if you love the planet" (Steyn), 81
China, 217, 281, 291
Chretien de Troyes, 152–53
The Christian Doctrine (Milton), 194
Christianity. charity and, 97, 128–29; civic responsibility and, 118–20; culture, elevation of by, 115–24; drama and, 142–44; equality and, 106–8; heresies, correction of and, 97, 124–28; love and, 93–94; manual labor and, 120–21, 135; medieval, 35; mercy and, 104; nature and, 250; pagan cruelties and, 116–18; pagan philosophy and, 108–15, 186; patriotism and, 111; Renaissance and,

167; Rome and, 57, 61; slavery and, 117–18, 121; State and, 108–15, 118; tolerance and, 97, 104–5, 106–8; West, saving of and, 101–6; women and, 115–16, 119. *See also* religion

A Christmas Carol (Dickens), 251

Church. *See* Christianity

Cicero, 42, 89, 91, 99, 183, 205, 261

Cincinnatus, 42, 55

City of God (Augustine), 104

civic responsibility, 118–20

Civil War, U. S., 44

Clagett, Marshall, 112

Clement of Alexandria, 110, 117

Cleon, 30

"Cleon" (Browning), 273–74

Cleopatra, 51

Clinton, Hillary Rodham, 81

Clinton, William J., 282

Cloelia, 42

The Clouds (Aristophanes), 19

Coleridge, Samuel Taylor, 255, 278

Colet, John, 185–86

Columbus, Christopher, 187, 218

communism, 220–22, 282

The Communist Manifesto (Marx and Engels), 245, 275

Confessions (Augustine), 116, 259

Confucianism, 291

A Connecticut Yankee in King Arthur's Court (Twain), 252

conservatism. Burke, Edmund and, 208; of Founding Fathers, 223–28; of Rome, 53, 56; twentieth-century, 281

The Conservative Mind: From Burke to Eliot (Kirk), 296

The Consolation of Philosophy (Boethius), 114

Constantine, 61, 66

Constitution, U. S., 230

Coolidge, Calvin, 281

Cooper, James Fenimore, 252

Copernicus, 170, 195

Cornelia, 42

Council of Trent (1545-1563), 205, 206

Cragg, Gerald, 213

creation, 68, 79, 99–100, 109, 212

Creation of Adam (Michelangelo), 175, 189

Creon, 23–25

Crito (Plato), 16

Croesus, 31

Crombie, A. J., 144

Cronus, 11, 12, 22

Crusades, 61, 162, 197

Cultural Revolution, 291

culture. ancient Greece, 7–10; barbarian, 122–24; Christianity and, 115–24; equality of, 7–8; global

warming and, 131, 134–35; Middle Ages and, 131–32

D

Daily Life in Ancient Rome (Carcopino), 41, 57

Daniel the Stylite, Saint, 121

Dante, 9, 93, 96, 114, 131, 140, 148–49, 153, 160, 165, 169, 183

Darius, 8, 25

Darrow, Clarence, 301, 303–6

Darwin, Charles, 109, 247, 251, 257

David (Donatello), 171

David (Michelangelo), 182

Da Vinci, Leonardo, 171, 176, 184, 189, 199

Dawkins, Richard, 109

Dawson, Christopher, 147

The Day the Earth Stood Still, 301

DDT, 282

Dead Christ (Mantegna), 185

Decalogue, 89

Declaration of Independence, 223

Deism, 194, 211; Founding Fathers and, 224–26

democracy. ancient Greece and, 4, 7, 8, 15–16, 22–25, 31–33, 37, 229; Enlightenment and, 215; freedom and, 4, 229–30; modern, 36; moral relativism and, 5; public education and, 7–8; radical, 22–25; Rome and, 50–55; tyranny and, 37, 215

Democracy in America (Tocqueville), 217, 229

Democritus, 34, 210

Denis, Saint. *See* Dionysus, Saint

Derrida, Jacques, 260

The Descent of Man (Darwin), 247

De Spectaculis (Tertullian), 116

The Devils (Dostoyevsky), 266

Dewey, John, 282, 286, 309

Dialogue against the Luciferians (Jerome), 126

Dialogue Concerning the Two Chief World Systems (Galileo), 174

Dickens, Charles, 251, 265–71, 297, 298

The Didache, 68

Diet of Worms, 204

Diocletian, 64, 120

Diogenes, 38

Dionysus, 9

Dionysus, Saint, 100–101, 138

A Discourse on the Origin of Inequality (Rousseau), 221

Discourses (Epictetus), 98

Disraeli, Benjamin, 296

The Divine Comedy (Dante), 96, 150, 164

The Divine Weeks (Du Bartas), 187

divorce, 105–6, 116

Doctor Faustus (Marlowe), 177, 253

Donatello, 171, 184

Don Juan (Byron), 255, 256

Donne, John, 171, 194

Dorians, 10

Dostoyevsky, Fyodor, 245, 265, 266, 267, 271–72

Drake, Francis, 218

drama, 9; ancient Greece and, 184; Christianity and, 142–44; Middle Ages and, 142–44, 164

Dryden, John, 92

Du Bartas, Guillaume de Salluste, 187

The Duchess of Malfi (Webster), 171

Duranty, Walter, 291, 299

Durkheim, Emile, 257

E

Early Church. *See* Christianity

Ecclesiastical History of the English People (Bede), 123

Edict of Milan (318), 61

education. individualism and, 286; man, perfection of and, 244; Middle Ages and, 160, 162–63; twentieth century and, 286

Edwards, Jonathan, 224

effeminacy, 6, 7, 47, 101, 263, 292

Einstein, Albert, 174

Eleanor of Aquitaine, 153

Eliot, T. S., xii, 287, 297, 298

Empedocles on Etna (Arnold), 261

The End of the Affair (Greene), 93

The End of the Modern World (Guardini), 76

Engels, Friedrich, 245, 275

English Civil War, 207

Enlightenment. Burke, Edmund and, 236–38; Catholic Church and, 213–14; Deism and, 194; democracy and, 215; God and, 211–12; heritage of, 203–4; Johnson, Samuel and, 239–41; Kant, Immanuel and, 234–36; materialism and, 209–10, 213, 233–34; misrepresentations of, xi; natural law and, 212; patriotism and, 215; Pilgrim Fathers and, 216–23; progress and, 203; racialism and, 146; reason and, 231–38; religion and, 207–8, 213–14; Renaissance and, 204; Rousseau, Jean-Jacques and, 238–39, 240; salvation and, 204–5; science and, 203, 231; State and, 203, 208–9, 214; tradition and, 203; twentieth century and, 212; tyranny and, 207–12; United States and, 203; Western civilization and, 203–41; will of man and, 204–7

environmentalism, 88, 278

Epictetus, 86, 98

Epicurus, 98

"An Epistle of Karshish" (Russell), 275

equality. Christianity and, 106–8; of culture, 7–8; family and, 39

Erasmus, 185

Eros, 31

Eros and Culture (Marcuse), 271

Eteocles, 19, 22

eternal law, 23

ethnography, 9

Euclid, 28, 188

Euripides, 18

Euthyphro (Plato), 18

The Everlasting Man (Chesterton), 285

evil. ancient Greece and, 26; ignorance and, 211; nineteenth century and, 266; as social construction, 19; State and, 211

evolution, 88

F

Fabius, 50

The Fable of the Bees (Mandeville), 210

The Faerie Queene (Spenser), 199

Fahrenheit 451 (Bradbury), 284

faith. Middle Ages and, 151; philosophy and, 84, 167; reason and, 112; salvation and, 204

family. ancient Greece and, 5, 24–25, 36, 37; city and, 40–41; equality and, 39; feminism and, 41; nineteenth century and, 244, 277–78; Rome and, 39, 39–44, 44–50; State and, 45, 255; Western civilization and, xi

Faustus, 169, 177, 247–48, 253

Fawkes, Guy, 214

federalism, 13, 237

feminism, 39, 88, 160; family and, 41; marriage and, 89; matriarchy and, 221; in Middle Ages, 136; nineteenth century and, 244

fertility cults, 10–13, 70–71, 72–74

Fibonacci, 158–59

Ficino, Marsilio, 170

Fielding, Henry, 93

Five Stages of Greek Religion (Murray), 38

Ford, Henry, 283

Ford, John, 300

Founding Fathers. ancient Greece and, 228–30; checks and balances and, 43; conservatism of, 223–28; Deism and, 224–26; freedom of speech and, 295; happiness and, 228; Rome and, 51, 55, 228, 230–31; secularism and, 226–27; State and, 227

France, 44

Francis of Assisi, Saint, 94, 109, 147–48, 154, 236

Franco, Francisco, 44

Franklin, Benjamin, 224, 225

freedom. ancient Greece and, 36; democracy and, 4, 229–30; Middle Ages and, 135; of religion, 213–14, 222–23; of speech, 295–97; State and, 216, 306; of will, 204–7
French *philosophes*, 211
French Revolution, 208
French Revolution, 214, 224, 227
Freud, Sigmund, 257, 259, 294
Friendly Persuasion, 301
Frost, Robert, 14, 160, 298
Furies, 12

G
Gaia, 10–11
Galileo, 170, 174, 179
Gallic Wars, 53–54
Gardiner, E. Norman, 21
Genealogy of Morals (Nietzsche), 263
geography, 9
geometry, 9
George III, King, 223
Georgics (Virgil), 56
Gibbon, Edward, 61, 261
Gilson, Etienne, 104
Giotto, 148
Gladstone, William, 263
global warming, 131, 134–35
Glorious Revolution (1688), 214
Gnosticism, 85, 116, 126, 154
God. of Abraham, 67–70, 70–74, 74–78; as Being, 79, 84, 257; creation and, 79, 99–100, 109, 212; Enlightenment and, 211–12; existence of, 302; humility and, 80–85; Israel and revelation of, 69–70, 70–74; justice of, 68; as King of Kings, 74–78; knowledge of, 155, 157–58; love and, 91, 127, 128–29; man, dignity of and, 92; man as image of, 80, 176; nature and, 72–74, 78, 252; peace of, 95–96, 168; philosophy and, 114; as political, 74–78; salvation and, 85–88; science and, 78–80; sovereignty of, 233; State and, 290; as watchmaker, 211–12
Gödel, Kurt, 302
Goethe, Johann Wolfgang von, 247–48, 253
Goldberg, Stephen, 53
Gore, Al, 134
Gothic cathedrals, 138–42
government, xii; ancient Greece and, 8, 9, 13–17; Rome and, 43; self-, 12–13, 14–17
grace, 204–6
Great Awakening of 1739-1742, 224
Great Depression, 281, 294, 304
The Great Heresies (Belloc), 127
Greece. *See* ancient Greece
Greek Isles Effect, 13–17

Greek Science in Antiquity (Clagett), 112
The Greeks (Kitto), 18
Greene, Graham, 93, 299
Gregory I, Pope, 120
Gregory X, Pope, 151
Guardini, Romano, 76, 306
Guinevere, 152–53
Gutenberg, Johann, 193

H
Hamilton, Alexander, 229
Hamlet (Shakespeare), 181
The Handmaid's Tale (Atwood), 261
Hannibal, 49, 50, 55, 58, 84
Hanson, Victor Davis, 32
happiness, 33–35, 228, 246
Hawkins, John, 218
Hawthorne, Nathaniel, 251–52
Hayek, Friedrich von, 287
Heath, John, 32
Hecate, 11
Hector, 20–21
Hefner, Hugh, 296
Helen of Troy, 31
Hellenica (Xenophon), 4
Helvetius, 210, 211, 213, 225
Henry, Patrick, 224
Henry VII, King, 218
Henry VIII, King, 198–99
Henry VI (Shakespeare), 177
Heraclitus, 188
heresy, 85; Arianism, 126–27, 194; Christianity and, 97, 124–28; Gnosticism, 85, 116, 126, 154; Islam, 127
Hermes, 78
Herodotus, 9, 25, 184
Hesiod, 8, 10
Hexameron (Ambrose), 187
High Middle Ages. *See* Middle Ages
High Noon, 301
Hippocrates, 11
Hippocratic Oath, 11
Hippolytus, 19
The History of Medieval Europe (Thorndike), 141, 155, 159
Hitchcock, Alfred, 300
Hitler, Adolf, 68, 247, 258, 292
Hobbes, Thomas, 168, 208–9, 222, 225, 226, 240, 260, 276
"The Hollow Men" (Eliot), 298
Homer, 9, 15, 17, 57, 183, 184, 197
homosexuality, 6, 60, 275, 305
Honorius, 65, 104
Hooker, Richard, 227
Hoover, Herbert, 281
Hopper, Edward, 287
Horace, 56, 62
How Green Was My Valley (Ford), 300
How We Think (Dewey), 309
humanism, 182, 185

Humanist Manifesto, 185
Hume, David, 234
Huxley, Aldous, 304
Huxley, Thomas, 279
Hymne of Love (Spenser), 175

I

I, Claudius, 61
I Confess (Hitchcock), 300
The Idea of a University (Newman), 263
Ideas Have Consequences (Weaver), 211, 293
Ignatius of Antioch, Saint, 101
Ignatius of Loyola, Saint, 122, 200
Iliad (Homer), 9, 14, 20–21, 184
immigration, 59
Indians, 219–20
individualism. education and, 286; religion and, 288; Renaissance and, 200; State and, 289–90; twentieth century and, 285–90
Industrial Revolution, 138, 256
The Inevitability of Patriarchy (Goldberg), 53
Inferno (Dante), 169
Inherit the Wind, 301, 303
Interior Castle (Teresa of Avila), 201
In the Heat of the Night, 301
Isaac, 71–72, 233, 253, 263
Isaiah, 82–83, 87, 101, 102
Islam, 127, 132–34, 141, 168
Isolde, 152
Israel. art and, 69; democracy and, 69; God, revelation of and, 69–70, 70–74; God of Abraham and, 74–78; history, view of and, 88; humility and, 80–85; importance of, 68–71; Jesus and, 88–94; nature and, 72–74; salvation and, 85–88; women in, 42
The Italian Renaissance (Plumb), 167
It's a Wonderful Life, 300
Iulus, 44
"I Wandered Lonely as a Cloud" (Wordsworth), 249

J

Jacob, 233, 253
James I, King, 169–70, 214
James II, King, 214
James VI, King, 169
Jefferson, Thomas, 223, 224, 225, 226, 227–28
Jerome, Saint, 112, 113, 126
Jerusalem, xii, 59
Jerusalem Delivered (Tasso), 200
Jesus, xii; baptism of, 104; crucifixion of, 95–96; heresies and, 126–27; as homeless, 81; Incarnation of, 154; Israel and, 88–94; law and, 103; light and, 138; love and, 89–94, 95–96, 117; miracles of, 226; salva-

tion and, 85; slavery and, 117; Western civilization and, 67, 88–94
Jews. *See* Israel
Joan of Arc, 86
John, Saint, 113, 153
John of Leyden, 206
John of the Cross, Saint, 200–201
John Paul II, Pope, 306
Johnson, Samuel, 239–41, 246, 308
Joplin, Scott, 245
Julian the Apostate, 111, 219
Julius Caesar, 49
Julius II, Pope, 185
justice, 20; ancient Greece and, 23, 24, 31; of God, 68; suffrage and, 7
Justinian, 114
Justin Martyr, Saint, 110, 111
Juvenal, 61–62, 99, 250

K

Kant, Immanuel, 28–29, 203, 229, 234–36
Kazan, Elia, 300
Keats, John, 250, 251
Kennedy, Anthony, 4
Kepler, Johannes, 170–71
Kerry, John, 68
Kierkegaard, Soren, 263
King Lear (Shakespeare), 169, 180, 193, 194
Kinsey, Alfred, 293, 301
Kirk, Russell, 287, 296
Kitto, H. D. F., 18
Klee, Paul, 287
Koran, 155

L

labor, 120–21, 135
"The Lake Isle of Innisfree" (Yeats), 251
Lambeth Conference (1930), 303–4
La Mettrie, Julien Offray de, 212, 225, 239
Lancelot, 152–53
Laplace, Pierre-Simon, 196
Last Judgment (Michelangelo), 182
The Last of the Mohicans (Cooper), 252
Last Supper (Da Vinci), 189, 199
La Vite Nuova (Dante), 93
law. ancient Greece and, 4–7, 11–12; eternal, 23; Jesus and, 103; natural, 17–19, 22–25, 89, 212, 227
The Lay of the Last Minstrel (Scott), 266
Leaves of Grass (Whitman), 253
Le Corbusier, 287
Left, 74, 104–5
Leibniz, Gottfried Wilhelm, 213, 224
Lenin, Vladimir, 291, 309
Leonidas, 29–30
Leo XIII, Pope, 133, 250, 265, 267, 268, 275–79
Leviathan, 208, 209. *See also* State

Leviathan (Hobbes), 240
Lewis, C. S., 127–28, 302
Libertas Praestantissimum (Leo XIII), 276
Life and Morals of Jesus of Nazareth (Jefferson), 226
Life magazine, 284
Life of Pericles (Plutarch), 29
Lister, Joseph, 245
literature. medieval, 136–37; nineteenth-century, 248–51, 248–52; Renaissance, 147; twentieth-century, 297–301
Lives of the Painters (Vasari), 199
Livy, 183, 184, 185, 186
Locke, John, 226–27
Logan's Run, 284
Longfellow, Henry Wadsworth, 298
Louis IX, Saint, 145, 162
Louis XIV, King, 168, 209
love. *agape* and, 93; ancient Greece and, 26, 91; Augustine, Saint and, 114; charity and, 97, 114, 128–29; Christianity and, 93–94; *eros* and, 91, 93; free, 250, 257; God and, 91, 127, 128–29; Jesus and, 89–94, 95–96, 117; lust and, 114; Middle Ages and, 131, 147–53; paganism and, 91–93; Plato and, 91, 92; poetry of, 170; Rome and, 91
Lucius Junius Brutus, 40
Lucretius, 91, 184, 187, 209–10, 211–12, 226–27
Luke, Saint, 103
The Lusiads (Camoens), 199
Luther, Martin, 169, 185, 191, 198, 204–6

M
Macbeth (Shakespeare), 169, 176, 180–81, 193
Machiavelli, Niccolò, 177, 178, 185, 186, 191, 235
McCarthy, Joseph, 282
McKinley, William, 282
Madison, James, 228, 229, 237
Madonna, 14
man. causes of, 33–35; dignity of, 92, 106, 172–73, 281; end of, 33–38, 213; fall of, 178, 226, 253; glory of, 172–83; as image of God, 80, 176; as machine, 212, 215; nature of, 172–83, 206; perfection of, 34–35, 244, 245, 253; Renaissance and glory of, 171; as social construction, 254; State and end of, 33–38; will of, 177, 185, 204–7
Manasseh, 83–84
Mandeville, Bernard, 210
A Man for All Seasons, 196
Manicheans, 162

Mantegna, Andrea, 185
manual labor, 120–21, 135
The Man Who Shot Liberty Valance, 94
Mao Tse-tung, 288, 291
Marc Antony, 51
Marcellinus, 104
Marcus Aurelius, 61, 111
Marcuse, Herbert, 271
Marius, 56
Marlowe, Christopher, 177, 253
marriage, 41, 89, 105–6, 119, 304
The Marriage of Heaven and Hell (Blake), 271
martyrdom, 101
Marx, Karl, 20, 133, 243, 245, 257–58, 275, 288
Marxism, 88, 96, 209, 258, 275, 290–91
Mary Magdalene (Caravaggio), 93
materialism, xii, 98; ancient Greece and, 27, 34; Enlightenment and, 209–10, 213, 233–34; Plato and, 99
mathematics, 9, 28–29, 302
Matthew, Saint, 63–64
Mauriac, Francois, 287
Mead, Margaret, 301
Measure for Measure (Shakespeare), 190–92
media, xii
medicine. *See* science
Medieval and Early Modern Science (Crombie), 144
Melville, Herman, 245, 252
Memorabilia (Xenophon), 3
The Merchant of Venice (Shakespeare), 192–93
"The Merchant's Tale" (Chaucer), 148
mercy, 104
metaphysics, 153–59, 234
Metaphysics (Aristotle), 36
Methodism, 214
Michelangelo, 175, 176, 182–83, 186, 188, 189, 193, 297
Middle Ages. Aquinas, Thomas, Saint and, 155–58, 160–62; Aristotle and, 154–55, 156–57; art and, 164; Christianity in, 35; culture and, 131–32; as dark, 131, 144–46, 155, 159; drama and, 142–44, 164; education and, 160, 162–63; global warming and, 131, 134–35; Gothic cathedrals and, 138–42; Islam and, 132–34; literature of, 136–37; love and, 131, 147–53; metaphysics and, 153–59; myths about, 144–46, 153–59; nature and, 147–53; paganism and, 183; reason and, 156; Renaissance and, 167, 168; salvation and, 247; science and, 131; witches and, 169; women and, 146
Mill, John Stuart, 255, 279
"The Miller's Tale" (Chaucer), 137, 148

Milton, John, 175–76, 178, 188, 194–95, 239
Miro, Joan, 287
Moby-Dick (Melville), 252
"Mock On, Mock On, Voltaire, Rousseau" (Blake), 210
modernity. Renaissance and, 167, 168; tradition and, 18
Mohammed, 105, 107, 134, 141, 309
Montaigne, Michel de, 198
morality. Aristotle and, 33; nineteenth century and, 244; Western civilization and, xi
moral relativism, 182; ancient Greece and, 1, 19–25; democracy and, 5
More, Henry, 170
More, Paul Elmer, 296
More, Thomas, 171, 179, 185
Morris, William, 252
Mosee, 76
Moses, xii, 73–74, 79, 81–82, 89, 105, 106, 113, 173
Mother Earth, 10
Mozart, Wolfgang Amadeus, 244
Mucius, 48–49
Muggeridge, Malcolm, 299
multiculturalism, xi, 47
Murray, Gilbert, 38
music, 14, 163
Mussolini, Benito, 292
"My Last Duchess" (Browning), 267
mysticism, 126, 154, 170

N
Napoleon, 37, 196, 238
natural law. ancient Greece and, 17–19, 22–25; Enlightenment and, 212; Jesus and, 89; Locke, John and, 227; marriage and, 304; piety and, 18
natural science. *See* science
nature. ancient Greece and, 147; Christianity and, 250; cult of the child and, 247–48; God and, 72–74, 78, 252; Middle Ages and, 147–53; paganism and, 147; Romantic worship of, 243, 246–52
Nazism, Nazis, 30, 157, 209, 261, 299
Nebuchadnezzar, 84
Nero, 59, 61
The New Life (Dante), 148–49
Newman, John Henry, 263
News from Nowhere (Morris), 252
Newton, Isaac, 159, 174, 210, 232, 233
New York Times, 299
Nicholas Nickleby (Dickens), 266
Nicomachean Ethics (Aristotle), 188
Nietzsche, Friedrich, 61, 247, 263–65, 273
1984 (Orwell), 284
nineteenth century. Arnold, Matthew and, 259–63; art and, 260–63; cult of

the child and, 247–48; evil and, 266; family and, 244, 277–78; feminism and, 244; man, perfection of and, 244, 245, 253; man, worship of and, 253–57; morality and, 244; nature, worship of and, 246–52; Nietzsche, Friedrich and, 263–65; poetry of, 248–51; progress and, 243; science and, 243, 244–45; United States in, 243; women and, 243, 244, 254. *See also* Romanticism, Romantics
nominalism, 195–96, 209

O
Ockham, William of, 194–95
O'Connor, Flannery, 299
Ode. Intimations of Immortality (Wordsworth), 249
Ode to a Nightingale (Keats), 251
Odysseus, 19, 21–22, 44, 57
Odyssey (Homer), 9, 17, 21–22, 57, 184
Oedipus, 1–2, 4–5, 22, 30, 95
Oedipus at Colonus (Sophocles), 1–2, 4–6, 9–10, 17, 22, 30
Old Testament, 79
Oliver Twist (Dickens), 36, 266
The Omega Man, 284
On Christian Doctrine (Augustine), 186
On the Life of Moses (Philo Judaeus), 84
On the Nature of Things (Lucretius), 91, 184, 211–12
On the Waterfront, 300
Orange County Register, 81
Oration on the Dignity of Man (Pico della Mirandola), 172, 178
Orczy, Baroness Emmuska, 224
Orestes, 12
Origin of the Species (Darwin), 251
Orwell, George, 284
Otto the Great, 131, 133
Ouranus, 10–11, 12
"The Oven-Bird" (Frost), 298
Ovid, 183

P
Paedogogus (Clement of Alexandria), 117
paganism, 10–13, 70–71, 72–74; God of Abraham and, 74–78; love and, 91–93; Middle Ages and, 183; nature and, 147; Renaissance and, 171, 183–89; salvation and, 85–88; State and, 108–15
Paine, Thomas, 224, 225, 266
Paracelsis, 185
Paradise Lost (Milton), 175, 178, 188
Paradiso (Dante), 140, 148, 160, 165
Pascal, Blaise, 73, 232–33, 246–47
Pasteur, Louis, 244–45
paterfamilias, 40, 116, 121–22

patriarchy, 22; ancient Greece and, 53; Rome and, 39, 39–44, 44–50, 53
patriotism. ancient Greece and, 25; Christianity and, 111; Enlightenment and, 215; Rome and, 47–49, 52
Paul, Saint, 58, 93, 103–4, 107, 119, 120, 122, 129, 135, 153, 204
Paul III, Pope, 191
peace. of God, 95–96, 168; Islam and, 141
Peace of Augsburg (1555), 207
Pearl, 148, 164
pederasty, 8, 293
Pelagianism, 205, 206
Penn, William, 222
Pensées (Pascal), 73, 232, 247
perfection of man, 30–31, 34–35, 244
Pericles, 2–3, 6, 22, 29, 89
Perkins, Frances, 304–5
Persians, 4, 7, 30
Persian War, 9
The Persian Wars (Herodotus), 25
pesticides, 282
Peter, Saint, 120
Petrarch, 93, 184
Petronius, 61
Phaedra, 19
Phaedrus (Plato), 37
Philip of Macedon, 97, 229
Philoctetes, 18–19
Philo Judaeus, 84
philosophy. ancient Greece and, 8, 9–10, 15, 26; birth of, 1, 15; faith and, 84, 167; God, understanding of and, 114; modern, 28; natural, 194; Renaissance and, 167, 194
Pico della Mirandola, Giovanni, 172–73, 175, 178–79, 182
Pieper, Joseph, 306
Pietà (Michelangelo), 297
piety. ancient Greece and, 6–7, 18; Catholic Church and, 214; natural law and, 18; Rome and, 44, 52
Pilgrim Fathers, 207; Enlightenment and, 216–23
Pill. *See* birth control
Pisistratus, 8
Pius II, Pope, 185
Pius III, Pope, 191
Pius XI, Pope, 304
Pius XII, Pope, 305
The Pivot of Civilization (Sanger), 304
Planned Parenthood, 304
Planned Parenthood v. Casey, 4
Plato, xii, 9, 14, 18, 84, 98, 114, 183, 188–89, 194, 211, 212; Academy of, 28, 98–99, 114; democracy and, 8, 31–33, 37; family and, 37, 45; good and, 30; justice and, 20, 31; love and, 91, 92; materialism and, 99; mathematics and, 28–29

Pliny the Younger, 108
Plumb, J. H., 167
Plutarch, 29, 64, 73
poetry. *See* literature
polis, 12, 13–17, 23
political correctness. destruction of, xi, xii; patriotism and, 47; twentieth century and, 295–96; Western civilization and, xi
political science, 9
Pol Pot, 288
Polybius, 52, 56, 60, 184
Polynices, 22
pornography, 296–97
"Porphyria's Lover" (Browning), 267
Porsena, 48–49
Portia, 42
Poteat, Hubert, 109
The Power and the Glory (Greene), 299
The Prelude (Wordsworth), 254
Priam, King of Troy, 20–21
The Prince (Machiavelli), 177, 178
printing press, 193–94, 206
progress, xi, 4; Enlightenment and, 203; nineteenth century and, 243; science of, 215; twentieth century and, 283
Prohibition, 259
Prometheus, 19
Prometheus Unbound (Shelley), 253
Protagoras, 5, 6, 20
Protestant Reformation, 121, 194, 216
Ptolemy, 194
public education. democracy and, 7–8; diversity and, 15; effeminacy and, 20; God and, 182; Middle Ages and, xi
Punic Wars, 46, 49–50, 53, 56, 57
Puritan revolt of 1642, 194, 209
Puritans, 146, 170, 201, 217, 222
Pythagoras, 27–28, 114, 231

Q
Quakers, 206
The Quest for the Holy Grail, 152, 164
Quintus Fabius Maximus, 50
Quod apostolici muneris (Leo XIII), 277

R
racialism, 146
racism, 231, 293
Raleigh, Walter, 218
Ramses II, Pharaoh, 73–74
Raphael, 171, 188–89, 193
Rasselas (Johnson), 241, 246
reason, 22; Aristotle and, 231–32; Enlightenment and, 231–38; eternal law and, 23; faith and, 112; feelings and, 238–39; limits of, 233; Middle Ages and, 156; passions and, 11

The Reason of Government (Milton), 194

Reflections on the Revolution in France (Burke), 43, 208, 237–38, 268, 306

Reign of Terror, 224, 238

relativism, xii, 182

religion. ancient Greece and, 10–13; Enlightenment and, 207–8, 213–14; freedom of, 213–14, 222–23; individualism and, 288; mystery, 85, 92; Renaissance and, 167, 168; Rome and, 57; science and, 194; twentieth century and, 288. *See also* Christianity

Religion and the Rise of Western Culture (Dawson), 147

Rembrandt, 200

Renaissance. art and, 9, 147, 167, 171, 182–83, 184–85; authority, collapse of and, 171, 193–201; Christianity and, 167; community and, 200–201; Enlightenment and, 204; humanism and, 182, 185; individualism and, 200; man, fall of and, 253; man, glory of and, 171, 172–83; Middle Ages and, 167, 168; misrepresentations of, xi; modernity and, 167, 168; myths about, 168–71; nominalism and, 195–96; paganism, resurgent and, 171, 183–89; philosophy and, 167, 194; religion and, 167, 168; science and, 158, 170–71, 174, 194–97; secularism and, 167, 168; witches and, 170

Republic (Plato), 14, 20, 31, 37, 45, 92, 211, 212

Rerum Novarum (Leo XIII), 250, 278

Revolutionary War, 2–3, 14

Rhea, 11

Ricci, Matteo, 217–18

Richard III (Shakespeare), 193

Richard of Saint Victor, 154

The Rime of the Ancient Mariner (Coleridge), 278

The Ring and the Book (Browning), 267, 274

Robespierre, 238

Robinson, John, 217

Rockwell, Norman, 297

Romanticism, 187

Romanticism, Romantics. Browning, Robert and, 265, 267–68; cult of the child and, 247–48; Dickens, Charles and, 265, 267; Dostoyevsky, Fyodor ad, 267; Dostoyevsky, Fyodor and, 265, 271–72; Leo XIII, Pope and, 265, 267, 268, 275–79; man, worship of and, 243, 253–57; nature, worship of by, 243, 246–52; women and, 254. *See also* nineteenth century

Rome. as American model, 228, 230–31; anti-democratic features of, 39; art and, 41–42; ascetism and, 46–47; Christianity and, 57, 61; citizenship in, 58–59; civic responsibility and, 118–19; conservatism of, 53, 56; democracy and, 50–55; fall of, 61–66; family and, 39, 39–44, 44–50; homosexuality and, 60; love and, 91; manual labor and, 135; patriarchy and, 39, 39–44, 44–50, 53; patriotism and, 47–49, 52; peace through strength and, 55–60; piety and, 44, 52; religion and, 57; Senate of, 41, 43, 45, 50–55, 56; slavery and, 39, 62–63, 64; State and, 42–44, 45, 108–11; taxation and, 39, 62, 63–64; tradition and, 50–55; women and, 42, 115–16

Romulus Augustulus, 66

Roosevelt, Franklin D., 281–82, 292

Rousseau, Jean-Jacques, 221, 238–39, 240

Rugby Chapel (Arnold), 261

Ruskin, John, 141, 259, 265

Russell, Bertrand, 274–75

Russia, 290

S

Sacred and Profane Love (Titian), 93

Saint Teresa in Ecstasy (Bernini), 188

Sallust, 184

salvation, 76; Enlightenment and, 204–5; faith and, 204; God and, 85–88; grace and, 204–6; Jesus and, 85; Middle Ages and, 247; paganism and, 85–88; time and, 86–88; by works, 204–5

Sánger, Margaret, 282, 293, 304

Satyricon (Petronius), 61

Savonarola, Girolamo, 179

The Scarlet Letter (Hawthorne), 251–52

The Scarlet Pimpernel (Orczy), 224

School of Athens (Raphael), 171, 188–89

Schumacher, E. F., 306

science. ancient Greece and, 8, 25–29; Enlightenment and, 203, 231; eugenic, 293; God and, 78–80; Middle Ages and, 131; natural, 131, 158; nineteenth century and, 243, 244–45; Old Testament God and, 67, 76; of progress, 215; religion and, 194; Renaissance and, 158, 170–71, 174, 194–97

scientism, 285

Scipio, 50

Scopes "monkey trial", 301

Scott, Sir Walter, 266

Scotus, John, 172

Index

Second Treatise of Government (Locke), 227

Second Vatican Council, 284–85

secularism. Founding Fathers and, 226–27; Renaissance and, 167, 168

Seneca, 183, 186

sentimentalism, 239, 240, 297

Septuagint, 79

Sexual Revolution, 285, 294, 304

Shakespeare, William, xii, 9, 93, 114, 144, 169, 176, 177, 180–81, 187, 190–93, 194, 236

Shelley, Percy Bysshe, 253

Short Treatise on God, Man, and His Well Being (Spinoza), 212

Sidney, Phillip, 93, 176–77, 186–87

Silent Spring, 284

Sir Gawain and the Green Knight, 148, 164, 193

slavery. ancient Greece and, 6, 8, 128; Christianity and, 117–18, 121; Jesus and, 117; Rome and, 39, 62–63, 64

social atomism, 203

socialism, 47, 281

Socrates, 8, 16, 19, 28, 30, 31, 98–99, 229

Solzhenitsyn, Alexander, 308

Song of Myself (Whitman), 251

Sophists, 19

Sophocles, 1, 2, 4–5, 7, 9–10, 12, 18, 22–25, 31, 38, 236, 287

The Sound of Music, 157

Southey, Robert, 255

Soviet Union, 74, 258

Soylent Green, 284

Spanish Inquisition, 168–69

Sparta, 2–3, 5, 7, 8, 15, 16

Spencer, Herbert, 257, 279

Spenser, Edmund, 93, 170, 175, 176, 199

Spinoza, Baruch, 212, 213, 217, 224

Spiritual Exercises (Ignatius of Loyola), 122, 200

sports, 3, 21

Stalin, Joseph, 147, 235, 288, 291, 309

Standish, Myles, 219, 220

State, 4; ancient Greece and, 45; Christianity and, 108–15, 118; Enlightenment and, 203, 208–9, 214; family and, 45, 255; Founding Fathers and, 227; freedom and, 216, 306; God and, 290; good and evil and, 211; individualism and, 289–90; man, end of and, 33–38, 213; paganism and, 108–15; Rome and, 42–44, 45, 108–11; twentieth century and, 294–97; worship of, xii

Stephen, J. F., 296

Steyn, Mark, 81

Stoicism, 55, 86–87, 113, 114, 117, 228

The Stones of Venice (Ruskin), 259

Stowe, Harriet Beecher, 261

Suetonius, 62

suffrage. justice and, 7; women and, 115, 244, 258–59, 305

Sulla, 56

Summa Contra Gentiles (Aquinas), 160

Summa Theologiae (Aquinas), 155

Summa Theologica (Aquinas), 169

Supreme Court, U. S., 4, 292

Swift, Jonathan, 205

Symposium (Plato), 37, 91

T

Tacitus, 99, 184

Tarquin the Proud, 30, 42, 48

Tasso, Torquato, 200

taxation. Rome and, 39, 62, 63–64; twentieth century and, 295

The Tempest (Shakespeare), 181–82

10 Books That Screwed Up the World (Wiker), 288

Ten Commandments, 68, 76, 89, 274

Teresa of Avila, Saint, 201

Terminus, 56

Tertullian, 111, 116, 124

Thales of Miletus, 26

Themistocles, 29

Theodosius, 65

Theogony (Hesiod), 10

Theresa, Mother, 299

Theseus, 5, 12, 19, 20, 30, 40

Thirty Years' War, 168, 207, 208

Thoreau, Henry David, 251

Thorndike, Lynn, 141, 155, 159

Thrasymachus, 20

Thucydides, 20, 184, 185

Tiberius, 42, 62

Tintoretto, 200

Titans, 11

Titian, 93

To Autumn (Keats), 250

Tocqueville, Alexis de, 31, 217, 229, 287

tolerance, 5, 59; Christianity and, 97, 104–5, 106–8; Left and, 104–5

Tolkien, J. R. R., 287, 299

Tom Jones (Fielding), 93

Torah, 69, 172

tradition. ancient Greece and, 12, 14, 17–19, 24; Enlightenment and, 203, 236–37; modernity and, 18; Rome and, 50–55; twentieth century and, 287; Western civilization and, xi

Trajan, Emperor, 108

Tres Riches Heures (Duc de Berry), 148

Tristan, 152

Trojan War, 19

Twain, Mark, 245, 252

The Twelve Caesars (Suetonius), 62

twentieth century. art and, 297–301; birth control and, 303–6; Catholic

twentieth century. art and, (continued)
Church and, 284–85; communism and, 282; education and, 286; Enlightenment and, 212; history and, 306–10; human sexuality and, 293–94; individualism and, 285–90; literature in, 297–301; nineteenth-century science and, 243; political correctness and, 295–96; progress and, 283; religion and, 288; science and, 301–3; Sexual Revolution and, 194, 285, 304; socialism and, 281; State and, 294–97; taxation and, 295; technological advances in, 282–83; tradition and, 287; women and, 283

tyranny. democracy and, 37, 215; Enlightenment and, 207–12; Marxism and, 209

U

Uncle Tom's Cabin (Stowe), 261
Undset, Sigrid, 287, 299
Unitarianism, 127, 226
United States. ancient Greece as model for, 228–30; Enlightenment and, 203; immigration in, 59; in nineteenth century, 243; Pilgrim Fathers and Enlightenment and, 216–23; Rome as model for, 228, 230–31
Urban II, Pope, 162
utilitarianism, 42, 47
Utopia, 33, 47
Utopia (More), 185

V

Valla, Lorenzo, 185
Vasari, Giorgio, 199
Vatican II, 284–85
Vietnam War, 50
Virgil, 44, 47, 51, 54–55, 56, 57, 183, 236, 261, 308
Virginia, University of, 226
Vitruvius, 184
Voltaire, 109, 213
voting rights. *See* suffrage
Vulgate, 194

W

Walesa, Lech, 306
War Between the States, 44
Washington, George, 2–3, 55, 243, 292
Waugh, Evelyn, 93, 306
Wayne, John, 94
Weaver, Richard, 196–97, 211, 293
Webster, Daniel, 300
Webster, John, 171
Wells, H. G., 303

Wesley, John, 224
Western civilization. ancient Greece and, xii, 1–38; Christianity and, xi, 97–129; Enlightenment and, 203–41; family and, xi; Israel and, 67–96; Jerusalem and, xii; Jesus and, 67, 88–94; Middle Ages and, 131–65; morality and, xi; nineteenth century and, 243–79; political correctness and, xi; Renaissance and, 167–201; renewal of, 308–10; Rome and, xii, 39–66; tradition and, xi; twentieth century and, 281–310
"What is Enlightenment?" (Kant), 203
Whitman, Walt, 251, 253
Whittier, John Greenleaf, 298
Who Killed Homer? The Demise of Classical Education and the Recovery of Greek Wisdom (Hanson and Heath), 32
"The Wife's of Bath's Prologue" (Chaucer), 136
Wiker, Benjamin, 288
Wilde, Oscar, 279
William of Aquitaine, 151
William of Orange, 214
Wilson, Woodrow, 292
The Winter's Tale (Shakespeare), 187, 193
witches, 146, 169, 170
Witherspoon, John, 224
Wollstonecraft, Mary, 243
women. ancient Greece and, 8, 25, 42; Christianity and, 115–16, 119; in Israel, 42; Middle Ages and, 146; nineteenth century and, 243, 244, 254; Rome and, 42, 115–16; suffrage and, 115, 244, 258–59, 305; twentieth century and, 283
Wordsworth, William, 249, 254
World War II, 294, 304
Wyler, William, 300

X

Xenophon, 3, 4
Xerxes, King of Persia, 31

Y

Yeats, William Butler, 251
"You Can't Be Any Poorer Than Dead" (O'Connor), 299

Z

Zeus, 8, 10–13, 19, 22, 92, 97